ECONOMIC DIMENSIONS OF PUBLIC SCHOOL FINANCE:
Concepts and Cases

ADMINISTRATION IN EDUCATION

BENT AND MCCANN Administration of Secondary Schools
FIELDS The Community College Movement
HACK AND WOODARD Economic Dimensions of Public School Finance:
Concepts and Cases
JONES, SALISBURY, AND SPENCER Secondary School Administration
LUCIO AND MCNEIL Supervision: A Synthesis of Thought and Action
MORT, REUSSER, AND POLLEY Public School Finance
ROE School Business Management
STOOPS AND JOHNSON Elementary School Administration
STREVELL AND BURKE Administration of the School Building Program
SUMPTION AND ENGSTROM School-Community Relations: A New Approach

McGRAW-HILL SERIES IN EDUCATION

THE LATE HAROLD BENJAMIN, Consulting Editor-in-Chief

ARNO A. BELLACK Teachers College, Columbia University
Consulting Editor, Supervision, Curriculum, and Methods in Education
THE LATE HAROLD BENJAMIN Emeritus Professor of Education
George Peabody College for Teachers
Consulting Editor, Foundations in Education
PHILIP M. CLARK Ohio State University
Consulting Editor, Psychology and Human Development in Education
WALTER F. JOHNSON Michigan State University
Consulting Editor, Guidance, Counseling, and Student Personnel in Education

Economic Dimensions of Public School Finance: Concepts and Cases

Walter G. Hack

Professor of Education
Ohio State University

Francis O. Woodard

Professor of Economics
Wichita State University

McGraw-Hill Book Company
New York   St. Louis   San Francisco   Düsseldorf
London   Mexico   Panama   Sydney   Toronto

Economic Dimensions of Public School Finance: Concepts and Cases

Library of Congress Catalog Card Number 76-114447

25388

1 2 3 4 5 6 7 8 9 0   MAMM   7 9 8 7 6 5 4 3 2 1

This book was set in Cairo Light by Monotype Composition Company, Inc., and printed on permanent paper and bound by The Maple Press Company. The designer was Marsha Cohen; the drawings were done by John Cordes, J. & R. Technical Services, Inc. The editors were Nat LaMar and Ellen Simon. Peter D. Guilmette supervised production.

Although the cases presented in this book are designed to place the economic concepts in a reality setting, the situations are hypothetical and any similarity to actual incidents and persons is entirely coincidental.

TO OUR WIVES
BARBARA AND MAXINE

Preface

Two of the many hard facts in our American life are (1) there are severe problems in financing the public schools and (2) these problems have been a part of our society for a long time and will continue to be a part of it. In the immediate future most persons who are reputed to have expertise in public school financing suggest that these problems will indeed become more severe. Expanding educational demands and the increasingly crucial role the American public school is being called upon to play will require a larger share of the nation's scarce economic resources.

However, the straight-line projection of educational needs, costs, and severity of problems caused by these conditions does not necessarily follow. Our increasingly sophisticated society has provided new ways to view the problems. In recent years new conceptual tools as well as electronic capabilities have been developed to enable more responsive and comprehensive decision making.

The expansive and expanding educational programs and the concomitant massive spending can now be considered as an investment in providing a wholesome and stable growth in the gross national product which in turn provides for such public investments.

The ways in which public agencies, such as the American public school systems, are held accountable have changed and will continue to change. Cost-benefit analysis, once thought to be impossible in the schools, can begin to provide more rationality in allocating economic resources in both the public-private sector concept and the functions within the public sector concept.

The increased drive for rationality in these allocated decisions in turn necessitates the utilization of economic concepts in those decisions pertaining to public education. Our conceptual and technological capabilities enable us to upgrade the rationality of these decisions, for the critical times will not permit us to do otherwise.

Since this work of the authors is not a conventional textbook, a rationale for its somewhat unique approach is presented in the Introduction. In this same segment the purposes of the book are spelled out as well as brief descriptions of the two major components—the concepts and the cases. The authors also describe their own perceptions of appropriate uses of the book. The Introduction is completed by setting the concept, which in one sense extends the authors' ideas of appropriate employment of economic concepts, to cases in the study of problems in financing public education.

The body of the book has four major components. Part 1. "The Economic Setting of Public School Finance," includes concepts relating to scarcity, markets, income determination, and full employment. Twelve cases accompany the four concept statements.

Part 2, "The Role of Government and the Character of Public Finance," is built around concepts concerning influences on government's role, economic dimensions of public finance, education as a public or private activity, and education as a governmental function.

"Differentiation of Functions among Levels of Government" is the title of Part 3. The following basic question is explored by the concepts included in this component of the book. How does the economy dictate the functions of government in general and of educational government in particular? The concepts described in this section relate to powers and functions of local, state, and federal levels of government.

The fourth part of the book is entitled "The Tools of Government." In essence this section deals with the means used to achieve the educational objectives of government and to execute the responsibility of governments. The seven concepts presented include public finance theory in terms of shifting and incidence as well as distributive aspects; transfer payments from state and federal levels; local, state, and federal tax systems; and debt and borrowing.

Because this book was developmental and because it literally grew out of the authors' experience, many individuals and groups contributed to it by providing a stimulating environment for the writers. Jack Culbertson, Director of the University Council for Educational Administration, initiated several seminars in which the writers were able to articulate their concerns and interests and gain insights from others who were interested in the multidisciplinary approach programs for educational administrators. Professor Meno Lovenstein participated extensively in one of the interdisciplinary seminars and contributed greatly to the body of knowledge through his monograph *Economics and the Educational Administration*. The individual graduate students who participated in the seminars made a major contribution to the book through their candid and insightful criticisms as well as their encouragement.

Especial thanks must be expressed to Professor Helen Cameron and Professor Frederick Stocker of The Ohio State University for their general interest in the preparation of school administrators and their specific commitment to and participation in the interdisciplinary seminars. Their contributions constituted behavioral evidence of the viability of the multidisciplinary mode of teaching.

Walter G. Hack
Francis O. Woodard

Contents

Introduction

Public school finance as an area of study is generally conceded to be concerned with marshalling the fiscal resources necessary to provide the kind of education desired in a given community. The process of financing schools is decisional in nature and cognitive in a value orientation. More specifically, it deals with making decisions regarding the amount and kind of resources to be allocated to public education and how these resources are going to be obtained. When put into operational terms, one can see that there are some questions inherent in this activity, and thus some guidelines are needed in order to answer them.

Since the discipline of economics deals with man's efforts to satisfy his wants through utilizing limited or scarce resources, it becomes apparent as one considers the nature of these questions, that the needed guidelines are economic in nature. Thus, it is not only profitable but absolutely necessary to turn to the discipline of economics for guidelines in making decisions pertaining to public school finance. It is the authors' thesis that basic economic principles permeate all key decisions in public school finance.

The authors acknowledge the fact that the discipline of economics alone does not solely hold the key to the resolution of all problems of public school finance. Many other disciplines and fields of study contribute to the allocation of resources problem. However, the application of economic concepts, principles, and theories is imperative in this process.

Specific Purposes of the Book

To be a contribution, a book must do something better or do something in addition to those things already appearing in the literature of the field. The present volume has been designed to do both. Public school finance as an area of study in the training of school administrators is of relatively recent origin. As was true in most of the areas of study in this type of preparation program, the early textbooks tended toward the "recipe book." Students were admonished to follow the practices of "good" administrators, to follow certain "efficient" procedures, and to gauge their educational progress by the use of means, medians, and modes. All these approaches are easily recognized in the early writing in public school finance.

Only recently have writers in this field recognized the economic bases for the study of public school finance. But, by and large, these considerations have been limited to the recognition of the existence of the economic base and to the identification of basic economic concepts with only a bit of interpretation as to how this applies to financing the public schools.

Probably a far more serious limitation to this approach has been the fact that these considerations of the economic bases for school finance have been limited to a chapter or two tucked in near the beginning of the volume. Few, if any, economic concepts are referred to in succeeding chapters of the text. Once the content has been introduced, the reader is on his own to apply it to the rest of the material.

In more recent years progress has been made to provide firm economic foundations for the study of public school finance. However, in so doing, the students in these courses, usually without extensive course work in economics, fall into difficulties in applying the economic concepts to actual problems encountered in the area of school finance.

In view of this, the authors of the present volume have developed a book to present the most relevant economic concepts applicable to each of the primary problems encountered in public school finance. The methodology incorporates the case method in which the concept is aptly demonstrated in a hypothetical situation where the student is obliged to make his own decisions.

The two major dimensions mentioned above, i.e., selection of economic concepts and the use of the case method of instruction, are deserving of some expansion.

selection of economic concepts

The authors recognized that it was not feasible to identify and describe all the economic concepts which have a bearing on problems of resources allocation for the public schools. Consequently, a choice or selection of concepts had to be made. It was decided that the criterion for concept selection would be that of applicability to the primary and generally recognized problems of public school finance. That is, the authors included basic economic concepts which are useful in resolving the crucial, highly visible problems of public school finance.

Further, it has been the intention of the authors to present the problems of public school finance, and hence the applicable economic concepts, in a sequence which would enable the student to build a developmental concept of school finance. This, it is hoped, will not only make unnecessary the repetition of describing a concept applied in the new situation, but will also add a heuristic or self-teaching dimension to the student's experience.

the use of the case method

The case method of teaching has become well established in professional schools among American universities. It has been particularly conspicuous in its performance in those professional schools where instruction involves the application of principles from one or more disciplines to problems of individuals or social groups, e.g., schools of law, medicine, business administration, public administration, and the like.

Case method instruction in the training of school administrators has expanded gradually since it was introduced in this area during the 1940s. Considerable impetus was given to the method with the publication of a collection of cases in educational administration by Cyril Sargent and Eugene Belisle titled *Educational Administration: Cases and Concepts.*[1] In 1960, Jack A. Culbertson, Paul B. Jacobson, and Theodore L. Reller authored *Administrative Relationships: A Casebook*[2] which incorporated an interdisciplinary dimension in problem resolution.

The University Council for Educational Administration, an organization of approximately fifty-seven universities, has stimulated much activity in both the interdisciplinary study of school administration and the development of cases for instruction. The authors have actively participated in both these types of council activities and owe UCEA a considerable debt of gratitude for the impetus it provided in the development of the present book.

The case method of instruction is peculiarly suited to a course in public school finance. As pointed out above, it has proven its worth in graduate level instruction in other professional schools. With its content being primarily derived from the discipline of economics, a course in public school finance must have a vehicle to move it into the field for application to the problems of the school administrator. The case method is ideally suited to do this as it subsumes the concept in a reality setting. At the same time, it places the student in a position

[1] Cyril Sargent and Eugene Belisle, *Educational Administration: Cases and Concepts*, Houghton Mifflin Company, Boston, 1950.
[2] Jack Culbertson, Paul Jacobson, and Theodore Reller, *Administrative Relationships: A Casebook*, Prentice-Hall, Inc., Englewood Cliffs, N.J., 1960.

approaching reality as he must make a decision in light of the data supplied in the case. Consequently, the case method not only provides a demonstration of the concept but also enables the student to simulate the role of an active decision maker.

Other Features of This Book

The nature of this book mitigates against its use as a recipe book for the ready solution of problems in school finance. Readers who seek easy and directly applicable remedies to the fiscal woes of school districts will be disappointed. Two major factors are responsible for the impropriety of such a prescriptive approach to the resolution of school finance problems. First, the complexity and uniqueness of individual school districts illustrate vividly the fact that many, varied, and varying forces interact in this dimension of community activity. In this volume the authors are primarily concerned with assisting the student in exploring and comprehending appropriate and major features of the economic forces. So, any conclusion the student makes regarding the predictive power of economic theory and principles will have to be considered along with the many other forces operative in the given problem.

A second major factor responsible for the impropriety of prescriptive solutions of the problems of school finance lies in the nature of the economic concepts, theories, or principles themselves. In problem situations these systems of thought do not communicate a specific course of action to either the school administrator or the economist. Instead they suggest what must be considered in order to make a decision.

This volume gives substance to another contention held by the authors. In essence, it is held that the nature of public school administration, including the administration of a school system's fiscal affairs, requires the marshalling of many disciplines in order to adequately study it. The professional educator is the person best able to see the phenomenon in totality. But it requires the involvement of scholars in the social and behavioral sciences to assess and order the antecedent forces that interrelate to produce the unique environment in which the educational practitioner executes his responsibility.

The authors support the notion that this type of relationship is appropriate in all sectors of public school activity. Consequently, the authors urge that educators broaden their participation to include cooperative enterprises with scholars in the disciplines of psychology, sociology, political science, philosophy, and the like.

The present volume is evidence of such a partnership, involving a professor from the discipline of economics and one from the professional study of education, dedicated to the investigation of guidelines for the resolution of problems in one sector of a community's activity—public school finance.

Genesis of The Book: Purpose and Process of Development

In setting the context for *Economic Dimensions of Public School Finance: Concepts and Cases*, a description of its origin is an appropriate vehicle. From a casual meeting, two faculty members from different colleges in The Ohio State University discovered a broad area of common interest—the financing of public education. Each, from his own unique vantage point—Professor Woodard from the discipline of economics and Professor Hack from the professional study of educational administration—recognized in the other a valuable source to complement his own skills and to contribute to the exploration of a specific area of common interest, the financing of public schools.

Further exploration of interests and personal sources resulted in the decision to formalize the inquiry and to mount an interdisciplinary seminar involving the department of economics and the department of education. The initial seminar, "The Economics of Financing the Public Schools" was conducted during the Autumn Quarter, 1962. Graduate students from both economics and education participated in the seminar. A team-teaching approach was used with the responsibility for several aspects of each seminar session divided between the two professors. However, each session was jointly planned so as to assure maximum coordination and articulation. A typical session of the seminar would begin with Professor Woodard identifying and describing an economic concept followed by Professor Hack describing the application of the concept to a problem in school finance. Both professors would then guide student discussion of the applications of the concept for the analysis of the problem and implications for its resolution.

In the process of developing the content of the seminar, it was recognized that a considerable part of the instructional material had to be developed "from scratch." Thus it was quite natural after the completion of the initial seminar that the two collaborators begin to consider the worthwhileness of systematizing the material and publishing it in book form.

The economics-educational administration interdisciplinary seminars have been conducted each year at The Ohio State University since 1962. As instructional materials were developed, they were field-tested, evaluated, and modified as a result of student reaction to them. During this period the points of view of the authors have been altered since the instructional experience has broadened this perspective. As a result, *Economic Dimensions of Public School Finance: Concepts and Cases* represents a merger of a content and methodology which appears to be relevant in some of the major concerns of public education today.

ECONOMIC DIMENSIONS OF PUBLIC SCHOOL FINANCE:
Concepts and Cases

part 1

The Economic Setting of Public School Finance

concepts A–D

Scarcity and the Need to Choose

the problem

The educational program of any community involves economic goods such as buildings and books along with the services of teachers, bus drivers, and custodians. Public school finance is devoted to the obtaining of revenues which buy these educational goods and services. Since these are economic in nature and are not free goods, they are instead scarce. As such, educational goods and services can be obtained only by choosing to use a community's resources for this type of economic good rather than some other. Thus, a primary problem for a school administrator revolves around assisting communities in making decisions relative to how much should be allocated to education as opposed to other purposes.

the concept

One cold, hard fact which underlies the study of all economic problems is the reality of scarcity. All but a very few of the goods we consume are limited in quantity, and to increase the supply of any one of them requires a reduction in the availability of other goods. Even in the affluent society to which we in the United States have progressed, we cannot have all we want of everything. Such scarcity is caused by the existing limits in the quantity of our natural resources, our man-made capital goods, our labor force, and in the quality of our technology, that is, in our knowledge of how to blend the other elements of production so as to produce the greatest possible outflow of goods and services.

Scarcity implies choice, and choices we must make. At the personal level each of us must decide just what goods we want to acquire up to the limits of our money income. (Money is the means we use to translate the goods or services we *produce* into those goods and services we wish to *consume*.) At the public level, we must decide what portion of our total productive capacity shall be used for the creation of goods and services for common consumption and how this portion shall be divided among the various consumption possibilities. At both the private and the public levels we can increase our consumption beyond the limits of our current money income through the use of borrowing, but this results in a necessary reduction in consumption by others; it does not permit the production of goods beyond the limits placed by the four elements of production.

The capacity to produce can be increased, of course. We can discover more natural resources, build more capital goods, or increase our technology; but this requires a decision to forgo present consumption. Increases in our productive capacity tomorrow—and in the consumer goods we will have available at that time—require a choice today to invest a portion of our present output for that additional productive capacity. In this process today's consumption is necessarily reduced.

The basis upon which we logically make our choice between various types of consumption or between consumption or investment is utility, the satisfaction we receive from that consumption. If a color television set will yield us a greater utility than a summer vacation, we will logically choose the television set; if a new sewage disposal plant will yield a greater utility to the community than a new city hall or a corresponding amount of personal consumption on the part of the community's members, we will logically choose the sewage plant.

Our choice is also affected by the diminishing utility of increasing consumption. The first suit of clothes or the first television set or the first sewage disposal plant will possibly yield a high degree of utility, but the second suit or television set or sewage plant will yield a reduced utility, and succeeding units of these items will continue to yield a smaller and smaller amount of additional satisfaction.

The varying yield of utility from the myriad uses of our productive capacity, and the overall limits to that productive capacity, illustrates the great difficulty that many underdeveloped nations have in increasing their productive capacity. To increase their stock of capital goods, consumption must be reduced; but the utility yielded from today's consumption is so important—often it is a matter of life or death—that such reduction, or saving, cannot be attained.

To facilitate the choosing among various types of consumption, we adopt budgets. A budget is a system of rationing that will aid in the maximization of utility for individuals, businesses, and governmental units alike. A budget is a plan for consumption, and signifies our intentions for the allocation of our money income among the various opportunities for consumption, saving, and investment.

An official of a governmental unit has a special responsibility in the budgeting process. Since the spending decisions of governments are, at least to some extent, made without the concurrence of those who must reduce their private consumption in order that public consumption can be increased and since compliance with the plan for public consumption is compulsory (through our tax system), the government official must weigh carefully the utility of the private consumption which is lost against the utility of the public consumption which is gained. The utility of one public project compared with another must also be considered.

The utility or satisfaction yielded from certain goods or services is admittedly difficult to measure and certainly varies among individuals, but the need to consider this factor and to make the necessary subjective valuations of the utility involved for the various parties concerned is not reduced by this difficulty. The task of those charged with making the spending decisions is merely increased.

Case 1. Scarcity and Choices in Middledale

The terms "growth," "change," and "moving ahead" have been a constant part of the lexicon of the residents of Middledale. At the turn of the century it was a country crossroads community and several hours journey by horse and wagon to the heart of the state capital. Throughout the 1920s its location on a major east-west U.S. highway stimulated its growth, and Middledale became a way station to funnel people from the rural areas nearby into the capital city. At the same time it also developed commercial enterprises to serve the tourists of the day. Gasoline service stations sprang up as did restaurants, souvenir shops, and many tourist courts.

As the capital city spread its borders, Middledale became suburban in character. New residents built the houses and kept the lawns they could not have in the now crowded and cramped city. During the most recent decade the suburban character of Middledale has again changed. The urban area leapfrogged the little community that was once the outer fringe of the metropolitan complex. New and more up-to-date suburbs have been established beyond Middledale. The major U.S. highway is now quite obsolete as a key traffic artery, since this function has now been assumed by the high speed limited access interstate highway built parallel to it.

During much of its early history Middledale had the reputation for supporting very well its public schools. Citizens of the community always declared their interest in "good education." It is a matter of some pride that the voters have not defeated a tax levy for the schools in the last thirty years. The school tax rate, while once among the highest in like districts within the state, has been generally stable. During the past five years the rates have remained the same in Middledale while most surrounding communities have steadily increased theirs. Middledale now ranks about average in terms of local tax rates for like districts within the state.

The taxable wealth of the school district is largely derived from residential and small business property with only a little light industry on the tax duplicate. The homes themselves are relatively modest in appearance and cost. One distinguishing feature of the city is that 80 percent of the homes are owner occupied. This reflects a kind of community pride—"We are a city of homeowners." However, in recent years there has been considerable migration both into and from the community with resultant high rates of pupil turnover in the schools.

A closer look at the community reveals that Middledale is a city of first homeowners, that is, most of the residents have not previously owned property. In terms of sociological makeup, the city is "middle income" but does not consider itself "middle class." This condition is reflected in one particular point of view held by many of the Middledale residents. The community is perceived as a way station en route to the more plush suburban towns. As the executive trainees, the managers, and the technicians are promoted, they leave Middledale for these more affluent communities. Probably due to these conditions there appears to be an emergence of status consciousness of a considerable magnitude with emphasis on country club membership, Buicks, and seasonal weekends devoted to boating, skiing, or luaus. The few residents who have lived in Middledale for a generation or more observe that the new majority in the community probably live beyond their means, are aggressive and upward mobile, and are heavily betting on their ability to succeed in the future. Much of this motivation stems from the belief that one has to possess the outside trappings of wealth and success in order to attain these goals.

The school administration in Middledale is only generally perceptive of this unique aspect of the school district, but it is painfully aware of certain problems in the school system. The instructional program is essentially the same as it was years ago. Few changes have been made, and it has not moved ahead as fast as other schools in the area. General operating budgets and teachers' salaries are low when compared with those of neighboring school districts. As a result, the once "good educational program" now looks somewhat thin and shabby. The Superintendent and the board of education both recognize the necessity of increasing the local taxes to obtain enough revenue to make the needed improvements in the school program. Both parties also recognize the possibility of community resistance to any measure raising existing tax levels.

Questions for Discussion

1. What appears to be the basic problem in Middledale?

2. What factors must be considered in assessing the problem?

3. If a tax increase is put on the ballot, what values are apt to be in conflict?
   a. For the school administrator?
   b. For the resident voter?

4. What information must be conveyed to the voters if they are asked to vote for increased school taxes?

5. What alternative decisions might be made by the voters?

Case 2. *School Budget Decisions in Lawtonburg*

Some years ago Lawtonburg could have been considered typical of the county seat city found in most Midwestern agricultural states. However, in the past few years the city has prospered in ways atypical of its sister cities in this area.

Originally, the city was the retailing and transportation center for a rich agricultural region. As these enterprises prospered, agricultural and foodstuff-related industries sprang up, primarily as a consequence of the invention and manufacturing of a series of devices related to the processing of dairy and food products.

Within the last ten years Lawtonburg achieved a kind of wholesome balance in its local economy. Agriculture and the resultant agribusiness provided a stable base. A small plant of a medium-sized electrical appliance concern was established and was easily absorbed into the community.

More recently the national headquarters for an insurance company originally catering to farm families was located in the city. It was expanded by the company's establishing two satellite organizations, i.e., a mortgage company and an investment house dealing in mutual funds.

Fortuitous circumstances have continued to fall on Lawtonburg. The most recent event will, in all probability, result in a considerable local property tax "windfall." The electrical appliance factory attracted to the city five years ago transferred an entire, new operation to the Lawtonburg plant. This addition has more than doubled the square feet of the factory floor space, nearly doubled the square feet of warehousing space, and nearly trebled the value of the original installation of machinery and the like. Consequently, the community's total taxable wealth has increased from $63,000,000 to slightly less than $72,000,000.

As a further result there is high employment, general economic well-being in the community and an expected significant increase in the ability of citizens to pay property taxes to local governmental units.

The local school district's board of education, aware of the possibilities of expanding the Lawtonburg educational program, is in the process of budget planning for the immediate future. The board is faced with one or more decisions in this regard:

1. Should the availability of extra local tax monies be used to reduce the present school tax rate or expand the educational program?

2. If the educational program is to be expanded, what segments should be thus affected?

In considering these basic questions, it is felt that several factors must be considered. Thus, the questions are complex and not clear-cut. First, the board of education has for the past four years been bringing to the attention of the residents of the school district the necessity for and progress in upgrading the qualifications of the gradually expanding teaching staff. Lawtonburg, as nearly every other school district within the state, has had difficulty in hiring replacement as well as additional teachers with the desired professional training and experience. Members of the board see this as an unusually propitious time to implement these goals of upgrading staff through major salary schedule revisions and active teacher recruiting.

At the same time the board sees this local property tax windfall as an opportunity to resolve one of the problems which has plagued it for years—the minimal pupil transportation program. Traditionally, Lawtonburg has provided transportation to only those children who lived such distances from school that the state required the district provide such service. Almost without exception neighboring districts, under permissive legislation, transported at local school expense children living well within the mandatory limit. This was generally considered to be a convenience for the parents. Also, the district could provide such service at a cost which was less than that when parents themselves provided it.

In the Lawtonburg board's deliberations, another set of variables was introduced when the city council approved a resolution to put a $6,000,000 bond issue on the November ballot. The issue, to cover the renovation and expansion of the sewage disposal plant and system, is expected to add several mills on the local tax rate if approved. The board of education being fiscally independent from the city council is not necessarily limited by the latter's actions. The members of the board, however, recognize that the council's decision will affect the strategy which the board adopts and vice versa.

With all these variables introduced into the budget-making deliberations of the Lawtonburg Board of Education, the problem is further complicated by the fact there is no clear-cut consensus among the citizens in the community. No organized lobbies or pressure groups have made themselves or their views known. The chamber of commerce, highly active in promoting local industrial and commercial expansion, has taken no official position other than urging a decision which assures ". . . continued civic progress."

Questions for Discussion

1. What kind of questions about utility of the property tax windfall might the Lawtonburg Board of Education and the superintendent ask themselves?

2. What do you see as the most obvious choices available to the Lawtonburg Board of Education?

3. What are the criteria of utility which you suspect the board and the Superintendent will use as they formulate decisions regarding the property tax windfall?

4. What other related questions must be asked as any board of education develops a budget?

5. Are school budgets ever constructed without consideration of the economic concepts of scarcity and choices?

Case 3. Scarcity in Allocating State Resources to Education

Literally for generations the state legislature in its deliberations reflected the cultural dichotomy present in an Eastern coastal state. Points of view held by the state assemblymen readily identified them as representing "upstate" or "downstate" districts.

The upstate areas are urbanized, densely populated industrial areas. Nearly all major types of industry are represented—iron and steel, foundry and forging, petroleum refining, metal fabrication, electronics, and plastics and synthetics. With its ocean port facilities, worldwide commerce and shipping rank high also.

The downstate areas constitute a different type of diversification. Some areas reflect a highly productive agricultural economy. Truck gardening, dairying, and small grain farming predominate in one rural section. The other nonurban area, however, is far less productive. Subsistence farming and a little hardwood and pulpwood lumbering, along with the mining of low-grade coal, constitute the economic base of this semimountainous corner of the state.

In the past, the legislators of the two rural areas have tended to join together and vote as a bloc against the urban-oriented upstate legislators. Until very recently this rural combine constituted a formidable bloc which dominated the state legislature.

This pattern of domination was, however, upset recently with the federal government pressure for reapportionment within the several states. The "one man, one vote" concept, when applied to the state, shifted political power upstate so now there is a nearly even power balance.

Coincident with, if not resulting from, the reapportionment of state legislative districts, many bills reflecting basic changes in state policy have been introduced recently. Not the least among these is a modification of the state aid program to local school districts.

For nearly twenty years educators in the state had prided themselves on having one of the most forward-looking "state foundation programs" in the country. The program, adopted after a statewide study of school financing conducted by a national authority, incorporated at its adoption the best features known at that time. Heavy emphasis was given to the state-local partnership concept, i.e., the specification of a basic or foundation program supported by both the state and the local school district. The contribution from the local district was determined on the basis of relative wealth. If the foundation program could not be financed by the required minimum tax rate in a given local district, the state made up the balance. Every local school district was guaranteed the foundation program if it levied the required minimum tax.

In the intervening years since its adoption, this foundation program has been periodically updated and minor revisions have been enacted. However, the basic structure remains intact.

Currently two bills have been introduced into the state legislature. Even though both bills call for approximately the same appropriation, there is a marked difference between them. House Bill 977, sponsored by an upstate representative, proposes fundamental changes in the foundation program. If enacted, it will reduce the state assistance provided in the form of supportable aspects currently incorporated in the foundation program, e.g., special education, supervisory and administrative personnel, pupil personnel services, etc. Instead, additional monies will be channeled to local districts on the basis of per pupil expenditures, disregarding the specific programs. Thus a greater emphasis will be placed on distributing monies more uniformly to all districts. A relatively lesser emphasis will be placed on equalization which presently provides proportionately more assistance to poor districts than to the wealthy ones.

The rationale behind House Bill 977 as enunciated by the "upstaters" suggests that by and large these urban districts have programs that exceed the minimum specified in the states' foundation program, they have sufficient wealth to prevent them from obtaining substantial state support, and their local tax efforts exceed the state minimum rate. Consequently, it is argued that these districts should receive some financial incentive to maintain this high degree of local effort.

The rural bloc of downstate representatives have countered the urbanites' bill with their own proposal for state foundation program modification. House Bill 1042 proposed to upgrade the present state foundation program by expanding nearly all the elements within the program. Larger amounts of money would be allocated to teachers' salaries, administrative and supervisory services, special education units, and psychological and guidance services. Consequently the state would be contributing a greater proportion to the support of the local school districts under the same general pattern of distribution as incorporated in the existing plan.

The downstate school bloc predicates its proposal on the argument that this bill ". . . fully meets the principles and intent of the original school foundation bill . . ." enacted in 1956. This proposal does in fact give heavy emphasis to the equalization function of state educational financing. With the required local tax rate remaining the same and the amount of the state money increasing, the equalization function is extended. Consequently, it enables the small and less wealthy school district to expand its program considerably with little additional local effort.

Members of the legislature's education committees are well aware of the merits of each proposal. Each bill speaks to a fundamental problem; House Bill 1042 assists the poorer districts in providing an adequate educational program, whereas House Bill 977 stimulates the wealthier districts, which are able to provide basic programs, to use local initiative to upgrade these programs. It is obvious to the legislators that there are not sufficient state revenues to incorporate both features in a bill.

Questions for Discussion

1. How do the choices to be made by the state legislators regarding the foundation program to the local districts differ from those choices made by the individual as a consumer? How are they similar?

2. What are the differences in utility in the upstate proposal as compared with the downstate bill?

3. How do you believe these differences in utility can be measured by an individual legislator? How should they be measured by the individual legislator? How can and should they be measured by the legislative body as a whole?

4. What considerations should the individual legislator give in regard to the reduction of public consumption necessitated by either of the two bills?

Suggested Readings

Concept A—Scarcity and the Need to Choose

Benson, Charles: *Education Is Good Business,* Washington, D.C.: AASA, 1966.

Center for the Advanced Study of Educational Administration: *Perspectives on Educational Administration and the Behavioral Sciences,* Eugene, Oreg.: The Center, 1965.

Committee for Economic Development: *Raising Low Incomes Through Improved Education,* New York: The Committee, 1965.

Corbally, John E., Jr.: *School Finance,* Boston: Allyn and Bacon, 1962.

Galbraith, John K.: *The Affluent Society,* Boston: Houghton Mifflin, 1958.

Groves, Harold M.: *Education and Economic Growth,* Washington, D.C.: National Education Association, 1961.

Henderson, Herbert: *Supply and Demand,* Chicago: University of Chicago Press, 1921.

Lovenstein, Meno: *Economics and the Educational Administrator,* Columbus, Ohio: School-Community Development Study Monograph, College of Education, The Ohio State University, 1958.

McConnell, Campbell R.: *Economics,* 4th ed., New York: McGraw-Hill, 1969, chap. 5, 76–77.

Martin, Richard S., and Reuben G. Miller: *Economics*, Columbus, Ohio: Merrill, 1965.

National Committee for Support of Public Schools: *Changing Demands on Education and Their Fiscal Implications*, Washington, D.C.: The Committee, 1963.

National Education Association: *Does Better Education Cost More?*, Washington, D.C.: The Association, 1959.

National Education Association: *What Everyone Should Know about Financing Schools*, Washington, D.C.: The Association, 1960.

Samuelson, Paul A.: *Economics*, 7th ed., New York: McGraw-Hill, 1967, chap. 2, pp. 16–17, 21.

Markets and the Determination of Price

the problem

Since the goods and services necessary to initiate and sustain an education program are economic in nature, that is, they are scarce, choices must be made by a community as to the amount of economic resources which is to be allocated to the educational program as opposed to allocation for other purposes. Many factors enter into this choice. Thus, a concept is needed to order these factors so a rational decision may be made. The concept of markets and determination of price is useful in this context. The school administrator must consider the nature of the market for the educational services provided by the schools. He also must use the concept of price to determine the extent or intensity of the exchange value of the commodity as related to other goods.

the concept

The scarcity of economic goods and the need to choose those goods which we most desire require a system of allocation and a method of determining just how we will decide what will be produced with those scarce resources and productive tools at our disposal. Such a determination could be made in a number of ways. Some economies decide through political edict, others through custom; we in the United States arrive at a decision, for the most part, through a mechanism known as the market. Through the market those interested and able to buy goods and services inform the producers what goods are most desired, and there is a good chance that the producers will make those goods available in approximately the quantity desired by the purchasers.

Communication in the market is through price. If a particular good will yield a great deal of utility relative to the price which is being charged, people will tend to increase their purchases of that good. The increase in demand (if of sufficient magnitude) will cause the producers to raise the price of the good, thus increasing their profits. The increase in profits will induce these producers, or others, to increase the production of these particular goods so that more will be available at a price which is probably somewhat below the price which induced the increased production. The new price, however, will probably be somewhat above the price originally charged.

In contrast, if a good yields very little utility in relation to its price and in comparison to other goods, few people will buy it. This will induce the producer to reduce the price, which may cause him to suffer losses. If this is the case, production of this less-desired good will be reduced; such reduction will probably be accompanied by a lower price, so that the utility of the good, relative to its new price, will then be commensurate with the utility yielded by other available goods.

The price which prevails in the final analysis, even in our imperfect and often monopolistic markets, is determined by the interaction of the relative desires for the good by those who wish to purchase it and by the relative willingness to dispose of the good by the producer or merchant. In order to induce the prospective purchaser to buy increasing amounts of a good, it is usually necessary to offer it at continually decreasing prices. This is so either because each succeeding unit of a good which is obtained will yield decreasing amounts of utility or because at a lower price buyers will find that the good is more attractive relative to other goods.

On the other hand, to induce a producer to furnish increasing amounts of the good will eventually require a higher price. This is so because to produce the increasing amounts will increase the per unit costs of production. Increasing costs of production are the normal pattern of economic activity because of the *law of diminishing returns*. This economic law refers to the amount of additional output obtained when equal extra units of a varying input are successively added to fixed quantities of some other input. For example, if an acre of land is the fixed input and workers are the variable input, one worker on the acre of land will produce a given output. Two workers may be able to produce more than twice as much as one worker, and three workers might be able to produce in excess of 50 percent more than two workers. However, if workers are successively added to the acre of land, a point will be reached beyond which an additional worker will not produce as much as the worker who was added just before him, and eventually the addition of another worker will actually cause the total production to decline. This law of diminishing returns is a very real factor in our economic life and plays a very important role in determining the costs of producing additional units of a good.

The market is a very vital force in our economy. Not only is it here that prices are determined, but the information is obtained to permit producers to allocate the various scarce resources among the numerous production possibilities which are available. The freer and more perfect the market is, the better it performs in making these decisions. Regardless of the degree of perfection, however, it still plays an important part in this decision-making process.

Case 4. Markets and Prices for Individualized Instruction in Lake City

The Lake City School District is the largest school system in the state and is coterminous with the boundaries of the largest city. For many years it was recognized as the pacesetter for all systems in this primarily agriculture-oriented state. Prior to World War II it was the "big league" for teachers in the state. Many teachers from small outlying farm communities were attracted to it. Not only did Lake City offer the best salaries, but it also provided the best working conditions, e.g., most public support, best materials and equipment, most adequate service and supportive staff, most adequate physical plant, and the lowest pupil-teacher ratio of any of the eleven largest cities in the state. This latter feature was a source of considerable local pride and gave Lake City its hallmark as the school system with the individualized instruction approach.

Like most school systems in the nation during the period 1940–1945, the Lake City School District did not sustain its previous level of program quality. The curriculum became more or less frozen with the exception of the addition of some wartime emergency courses, e.g., upgraded machine shop courses to supply machinists for the booming war industries, increased physical education, and the like. Many Lake City teachers left the schools to join the armed forces or to be employed in war industries. For the first time in three decades, the school administrator encountered shortages in seeking qualified applicants to new and vacated positions. Administrators in the district recognized severe problems in both number and quality of incoming staff. However, the community as a whole had been well oriented to the idea of diversion of resources to the war effort and so accepted these educational sacrifices along with the material sacrifices of butter, gasoline, and nylons.

With the World War II prosperity continuing into the postwar years, the small suburban towns, which had sprung up on the city's periphery during the 1920s and 1930s, began to boom in the late 1940s. More and more of the executive class and monied people joined the migration to the suburbs. Families who placed considerable emphasis on education and were both willing and able to buy quality education were conspicuous among the emigrés moving out of the Lake City School District. The suburbs experienced a phenomenal growth in population and at the same time an increase in the demand for breadth and depth in the school program.

As the Lake City industries expanded in the 1940s, so did the work force. The 1950 census data indicated that the city's population had increased substantially despite the massive suburban movement. Workers attracted to the war industries in Lake City for the most part became permanent residents as the city readjusted to a diversified peacetime economy. Many of the industries set up during the national emergency made only slight production and sales changes and became permanent installations. Characteristic of these were a cluster of small and medium-sized companies which produce electronic controls now being supplied to the automotive, air conditioning, heating, and appliance industries.

Of late, school officials have become more cognizant of changes in the character of the population rather than the numbers involved. The massive expansion of the work force in Lake City, only slightly offset by the suburban movement, has resulted in a significant change of character of the city's population. A recent study has indicated that the percent of high-income families, adults with four or more years of college, and adults in managerial or professional occupations has been reduced.

The most obvious change in Lake City's educational climate was that of initial apathy, and now, more recently, hostility toward a relatively high local property tax levy necessary for the schools to support the "individualized instruction" approach. Appeals by the school personnel, the board of education, and even a "blue ribbon committee" of community leaders have gone unheeded. Taxpayers and school patrons, both as individuals and in groups, have demanded tax relief. When faced with the alternative program cutbacks necessitated by such relief, they have consistently chosen to increase the pupil-teacher ratio. Such moves, it is maintained, would increase both plant and staff utilization, would bring the pupil-teacher ratio up to a point which would not exceed the statewide average, and would still reduce school taxes.

Questions for Discussion

1. How has the status of the market for educational services changed in Lake City? How has the market for individualized instruction changed?

2. How did the community's concept of price for educational services change?

3. What are the major differences in concepts of market and price for goods and services in the private sector (such as food, automobiles, and homes) as compared with those in the public sector (educational services in general and particularly, low pupil-teacher ratios)? How are these differences demonstrated?

4. What is the significance of the following statement? In public education the producer is also the consumer.

5. What, if any, evidence points to a declining utility of individualized instruction methods in the city's public school classrooms?

Case 5.   *Budgeting for Salaries in Jamesville— an Example of the Market-price Relationship*

For as long as most "school men" in the area around Jamesville can remember, finances in that city's school system have always posed a severe problem to the school administrator. The present superintendent realizes that for at least the next two years the processes of budget development and administration are going to be critical tasks.

Fiscal controls in the state are such that local school taxes can be increased only with the approval of a majority of the electors voting on the proposition. The last such increase in the local school tax was approved only after it had been disapproved twice before. In a desperate move to ensure passage of the levy, the board of education assured the community that they saw no need for additional tax levies for three years.

Despite the availability of the extra monies to be brought in by the additional levy, the school district remains in financial trouble. The community, like the nation as a whole, has demanded an upgraded academic program. The community and pupil population are and have been very stable and in all probability will remain so in the immediate future. The pupil population has not varied more than 60 over or under the 2,500 mark in the past ten years. The taxable wealth of the school district has in the past five years shown a slow but steady decline as there has been little new construction and the original real property is depreciating in value.

The major financial problem is centered in the teachers' salary schedule. Currently, 60 percent of the total budget is allocated to administration and instruction (as opposed to 48 percent on a statewide basis), and prospects are that it will rise considerably in the near future. Two years ago, in order to stem the migration from the district of well-qualified and -experienced teachers, the board of education enacted a new teachers' salary schedule. The new schedule provided automatic annual increments for each year of teaching experience

Table 5.1. Selected Tax and Revenue Data, Jamesville School District, 1963–1968

Year	Local School Tax Rate (mills per dollar)	Local Tax Duplicate	Revenue Sources for Schools								Total Monies Available
			Local		State		Federal		Other		
			Amount	% of Total	Amount	% of Total	Amount	% of Total	Amount	%	
1963	20	$42,534,000	$850,680	75.9	$190,150	17.0	$75,000	6.7	$4,850	0.4	$1,120,680
1964	20	42,530,000	850,600	75.6	191,005	17.0	78,300	7.0	4,920	0.4	1,124,825
1965	20	42,532,000	850,640	76.0	191,116	17.1	73,115	6.5	5,106	0.5	1,119,977
1966	20	42,533,000	850,660	75.8	190,084	16.9	76,650	6.8	5,111	0.5	1,122,505
1967	20	42,530,000	850,600	75.6	189,650	16.8	79,150	7.0	6,320	0.6	1,125,702
1968	23	42,116,000	968,668	78.6	190,325	15.4	67,800	5.5	6,212	0.5	1,233,005

Table 5.2. Jamesville School District Expenditures, 1963–1968

Year	Administration and Instruction		School Plant		Transportation		Capital Outlay		Debt Service		Other		Total Expenses
	Amount	% of Total	Amount	% of Total	Amount	% of Total	Amount	% of Total	Amount	% of Total	Amount	% of Total	
1963	$640,826	57.3	$222,970	19.9	$3,283	0.3	$16,769	1.5	$ 98,562	8.8	$136,387	12.2	$1,118,797
1964	640,763	57.0	225,676	20.1	3,362	0.3	18,387	1.6	98,311	8.7	137,470	12.2	1,123,969
1965	642,371	57.4	225,898	20.2	3,389	0.3	21,331	1.9	96,160	8.6	130,111	11.6	1,119,260
1966	644,002	56.7	240,656	21.2	3,462	0.3	15,878	1.4	96,002	8.4	136,650	12.0	1,136,650
1967	700,211	61.1	201,311	17.6	3,834	0.3	16,826	1.5	95,880	8.4	130,071	11.3	1,146,897
1968	718,413	58.3	230,980	18.7	3,920	0.3	12,442	1.0	126,401	10.3	140,113	11.4	1,232,269

Table 5.3. Jamesville Teachers' Salary Schedule (effective July 1, 1968 through June 31, 1969)

Years Experience	Less Than 90 Semester Hours	90 Semester Hours or More	Bachelor's Degree	Bachelor's +20 Semester Hours	Master's Degree
0	$6,600	$6,700	$6,800	$6,900	$7,000
1	6,800	6,900	7,000	7,100	7,200
2	7,000	7,100	7,200	7,300	7,400
3	7,100	7,200	7,300	7,400	7,500
4	7,200	7,300	7,400	7,500	7,600
5	7,300	7,400	7,500	7,600	7,700
6	7,400	7,500	7,600	7,700	7,800
7	7,500	7,600	7,700	7,800	7,900
8	7,600	7,700	7,800	7,900	8,000
9	7,700	7,800	7,900	8,000	8,100
10	7,800	7,900	8,000	8,100	8,200

Table 5.4. Jamesville Teachers' Salary Schedule (effective July 1, 1969)

Years Experience	Less Than Bachelor's Degree	Bachelor's Degree	Master's Degree	Master's Degree +20 Semester Hours
0	$6,800	$7,000	$ 7,200	$ 7,400
1	6,900	7,100	7,300	7,500
2	7,000	7,200	7,400	7,600
3	7,100	7,300	7,500	7,700
4	7,200	7,400	7,600	7,800
5	7,500	8,000	8,400	8,800
6	7,600	8,200	8,600	9,000
7	7,700	8,400	8,800	9,200
8	7,800	8,600	9,000	9,400
9	7,900	8,800	9,200	9,600
10	8,300	9,600	10,200	10,800

plus substantial raises to teachers after the completion of five and ten years teaching experience. It also provided considerable financial recognition for teachers with advanced academic preparation. Consequently, many of the then young and/or beginning staff members, attracted by the salary schedule favorable to the "career teacher," have decided to remain with the school system. Since the adoption of the schedule, more and more teachers are being paid "at the top of the schedule," and prospects are that instructional costs will soon exceed 70 percent of the total school budget. The additional monies coming from the last increase in the levy temporarily wiped out the deficit incurred during the fiscal years 1966 and 1967.

The instructional budget will remain an acute problem since the state statutes prohibit any reduction of the salary schedule unless it is a uniform reduction in all categories. Such a reduction, affecting beginners and veteran teachers alike, would spell ruin for the professional staff morale, so this is no real alternative.

The budget situation is further complicated by the stability or actual increase in certain other relatively constant expenditures. The location of the school buildings and the school laws of the state obligate the district to continue a pupil transportation program for junior and senior high school youth since a majority of these pupils live beyond the mandatory transportation limit (1½ miles). This in turn dictates school cafeterias and lunchrooms in these two buildings.

The existing school plant is adequate for the student body in terms of size. All the present buildings were constructed between 1925 and 1940, so the costs of insurance and maintenance are not likely to be reduced.

The board of education and the superintendent now recognize the error in judgment made by increasing the salary schedule and then assuring no immediate increase in taxes. Although the error is attributed to a depreciating rather than appreciating tax base, the school administrator has been given the responsibility of providing the leadership in resolving the problem.

Questions for Discussion

1.   What was the most discernable change in the market for educational services in Jamesville in the past five years?

2.   What assistance might the school superintendent derive from the concept of markets and prices as he develops the educational budget for the school system for the next three years?

3.   What do you suspect happened to the community's concept of price for educational services? Did the price go up or down? What is the basis for your answer?

4.   What budgetary decisions would you make in resolving the problem? What effect would this action have on markets and prices for the several educational services included in the Jamesville school budget?

Case 6.   Diminishing Returns in State Subsidized Guidance Programs

The State Department of Education from a Great Plains state has been favorably disposed toward many features of the original National Defense Education Act since its enactment in 1958. The department has been supported in its position by a group of influential businessmen in the state who have been aware of the dramatic changes taking place in the state's economy. Traditionally agricultural, the state had been characterized by the small family farm or the larger but privately owned grain farm. More recently, however, the economic base has shifted toward larger corporate-owned farms, food processing plants, and small supportive agribusiness concerns.

These influential businessmen, perceptive of the changing economy, also recognized the problem of the state having many small rural high schools which provided little if any vocational or educational guidance. The consequences of this condition were readily apparent since these small secondary schools were graduating thousands of youth prepared only for the steadily diminishing numbers of on-the-farm jobs. At the same time relatively few youths had the preparation necessary to enter the rapidly increasing technological fields of agribusiness.

As a consequence, the vocational and educational guidance movement was welcomed. When it became a vital part of the National Defense Education Act of 1958, it was supported. By the time the Vocational Education Act of 1963 was enacted, the State Department of Education had incorporated substantial incentives for educational and vocational guidance into the state aid program for local school districts. Virtually every school district in the state has taken advantage of the heavy state and federal subsidy for this guidance program since very little "local money" was required in adding this dimension to the school program.

Despite the overwhelming success of providing educational and vocational guidance in the vast majority of school districts in the state, officials in the State Department of Education are concerned as to whether this highly supported program is as successful as it appeared to be originally. In the early years of the subsidized educational and vocational guidance program, the first group of participating school districts reported a relatively large proportion of youth changing their preparation programs from the crowded on-the-farm job to the more promising technological fields. However in succeeding years as more school districts have taken advantage of the guidance program, the proportion of youth shifting out of the traditional agricultural programs to the technological programs has steadily decreased. A recent research study conducted by the research division of the State Department of Education has found:

1. The early participating districts were those larger districts which had existing technologically oriented vocational education programs.

2. The most recent participating districts are generally the smaller school districts which have traditional vocational agriculture programs only.

3. The per pupil cost to the state for the subsidized educational and vocational guidance program has increased 62 percent from 1960 to the present. This is primarily due to the decreased guidance counselor–pupil ratio necessitated by the provision of a full-time guidance counselor in each secondary school regardless of size.

A major conclusion of the study was that which suggested the primary educational factor for "the apparent diminishing returns of the state subsidy in vocational and educational guidance are due to many of the smaller secondary schools having only meager technical and vocational programs for the youth in order to prepare themselves for the technologically oriented world of work today."

The major recommendation following the above conclusion was that which, because of limited State Department of Education finances, urged consideration of reducing state subsidies for guidance in those schools which did not have "a broadly based vocational education program including an 'adequate' balance of major vocational fields." These state monies so diverted from the guidance subsidy, should be used as an incentive for reorganization of school districts into larger units which offer the previously described "broadly based vocational education program."

Questions for Discussion

1. What evidence do you find in this case study that the law of diminishing returns was operative?

2. How was the utility of the state subsidized guidance program reduced?

3. How was the "price" of the guidance program reduced to reflect the reduction in utility?

4. In the research report of the State Department of Education, what other "good" appeared to have more utility and hence forced a lower price for the guidance program?

Suggested Readings

Concept B—Markets and the Determination of Price

Benson, Charles: *The Economics of Public Education*, Boston: Houghton Mifflin, 1961; 2d ed., 1968.

————: *Education Is Good Business*, Washington, D.C.: AASA, 1966.

Center for the Advanced Study of Educational Administration: *The Economic Returns to Education*, Eugene, Oreg.: The Center, 1965.

————: *Perspectives on Educational Administration and the Behavioral Sciences*, Eugene, Oreg.: The Center, 1965.

Clark, Harold F.: *Cost and Quality in Public Education*, Syracuse, N.Y.: Syracuse University Press, 1963.

Committee for Economic Development: *Raising Low Incomes Through Improved Education*, New York: The Committee, 1965.

Galbraith, John K.: *The Affluent Society*, Boston: Houghton Mifflin, 1958.

Groves, Harold M.: *Education and Economic Growth*, Washington, D.C.: National Education Association, 1961.

Hartley, Harry J.: *Educational Planning—Programming—Budgeting: A Systems Approach*, Englewood Cliffs, N.J.: Prentice-Hall, 1968.

Henderson, Hubert: *Supply and Demand*, Chicago: University of Chicago Press, 1921.

Hirsch, Werner Z., et al.: *Inventing Education for the Future*, San Francisco: Chandler, 1967.

James, H. Thomas, J. Alan Thomas, and Harold J. Dyck: *Wealth, Expenditures, and Decision-making for Education*, U.S. Department of Health, Education and Welfare, Office of Education, Cooperative Research Project No. 1241, an Extension of Cooperative Research Project No. 803, Stanford, Calif.: Stanford University, June, 1963.

Lovenstein, Meno: *Economics and the Educational Administrator*, Columbus, Ohio: School-Community Development Study Monograph, College of Education, The Ohio State University, 1958.

McConnell, Campbell R.: *Economics*, 4th ed., New York: McGraw-Hill, 1969, chap. 5, pp. 75–89.

Martin, Richard S., and Reuben G. Miller: *Economics*, Columbus, Ohio: Merrill, 1965.

National Committee for Support of Public Schools: *Changing Demands on Education and Their Fiscal Implications*, Washington, D.C.: The Committee, 1963.

Poole, Kenyon E.: *Public Finance and Economic Welfare*, New York: Rinehart, 1956.

Samuelson, Paul A.: *Economics*, 7th ed., New York: McGraw-Hill, 1967, chap. 4, pp. 57–68.

Income Determination

the problem

Financial support for education is derived from income as is true for any other long-term social enterprise. It is important not only to consider income in terms of adequacy for meeting educational objectives but also to consider the processes and factors responsible for income determination. Thus one must determine the amounts of income which are necessary and available. It is also necessary to consider the source of income and the processes whereby income is created.

Key concepts surround the relationships between income and education. Questions must be entertained in regard to how education and the support of it influence income, and the question of how income creation affects educational expenditures must also be asked. The concepts relating to the role of the school as a consumer of income must be examined, and conversely, the school as a producer of income must be explored.

the concept

Everyone approves of a high level of income. The higher the level of our income, the greater the amount of consumption goods we may buy and the more we may set aside for future needs. The source of income, however, is not quite so universally popular. Income is derived from expenditures, and no one will ever receive a dollar's worth of income without there being, for someone, a corresponding dollar's worth of expense. Over a given period of time the two are always in balance. Furthermore, it makes no difference to the recipient of the expended dollars who makes the expenditure; regardless of the source, the effect on income will be the same.

Who makes the expenditures which create income? Such expenditures can be attributed to any of four identifiable groups in our economy. By far the largest amount is spent by the consumers in this country who make outlays for the myriad items of consumption. Important outlays are also made by businesses for new producers' goods, that is, new plant and equipment. Such expenditures are called "investments." A third form of income is the difference between the expenditures made by residents of other countries in the United States and the expenditures made by residents of the United States in other countries. If more is spent here by foreigners than we spend elsewhere, this figure is positive and represents a net addition to income; otherwise, it represents a net subtraction. This source of income is called "net foreign investment." Finally, a large amount of our income originates as an expenditure by some unit of government.

When added together, the expenditures of these four segments of our economy are equal to the gross income of this country, or as it is usually called, the "gross national product." Expressed as an equation, it reads GNP (gross national product) $= C$ (consumption expenditures) $+ I_d$ (gross private domestic investment) $+ I_f$ (net foreign investment) $+ G$ (government expenditures). Furthermore, since net foreign investment is such a small figure (ideally it will just balance), it is usually combined with business expenditures. The equation then reads, GNP $= C + I + G$, and represents the gross income of our economy for a given period of time.

Since we are all interested in obtaining as high a level of income as possible, it follows that we must also be interested in achieving a correspondingly high level of expenditures. Otherwise the desired level of income will be unattainable. All factors which tend to reduce spending, then, should logically be reduced. The most important factor is saving. In disposing of the income which an individual has available for spending (called "disposable income"), that individual can choose to either spend or not spend it. If it is not spent it is saved; there is no other choice. Thus, if saving increases, spending and therefore the income for someone else will decrease. If saving decreases, that is, if each person chooses to spend a greater portion of his disposable income, expenditures, and subsequent income, will increase.

Another factor which will tend to reduce spending and future income is taxes. Taxes have the effect of making the disposable income smaller than would otherwise be the case, and thus it is likely that the amount of consumption spending will be thereby reduced.

Saving and taxes will mean a reduction in income unless there is a corresponding amount of spending from some other source than disposable income. The obvious offset for taxes is government spending (G), but to the extent that taxes exceed government spending there will be a net reduction in income. Of course, if G exceeds the amount of taxes collected there will be a net increase in income.

The obvious offset for saving is investment, that is, the expenditures for plant, equipment, and inventory made by business firms. A small amount of saving is used by the saver directly for an investment expenditure (almost always this will take the form of an outlay to build a new home), but in the great majority of cases the saving is by a consumer and the investment is by a business firm. Certainly there is no surety that investment will offset the amount of saving in the economy for a given period of time.

The steps necessary to increase income are thus apparent. The total amount of investment and government spending $(I + G)$ must exceed the total amount of saving and taxes. If these two totals are equal, income will remain constant; if the saving and taxes are greater, income will decline. What will be the magnitude of these changes, either up or down? If investment and government spending exceed the saving and taxes, income will rise until a level of income is reached at which the two totals are equal. Also, if saving and taxes exceed investment and government spending, income will decline until, again, the two totals are in equilibrium.

Case 7.   Income and Expenditures in Prairie City

Since 1945 the steady progress of Prairie City toward a sophisticated cosmopolitanism has become very apparent. Its strategic location near an air base established during World War II provided an original impetus for aircraft-related industries to locate in the community. As flight technology has matured, the original air base has undergone change in functions several times. Currently it is a research and development center for both conventional flight and space technology. Consequently, many additional flight- and space-related industries, electronics industries, and data processing and computer industries have located around the base.

A majority of these related industries are key installations of multiplant, internationally based corporations. Consequently, the orientation of their executives is very cosmopolitan in nature. These men are almost constantly being shifted around the country in various positions as they progress up the professional development ladder. They are well aware of the national and international forces which influence the well-being of the national economy and hence their corporations, which are highly dependent on federal grants and contracts for their livelihood.

Almost without exception the leadership in these major "supportive" industries urges their executives and professional staff to take active roles in local governmental and social activities. Consequently, the points of view of these large corporations with their cosmopolitan executive and professional staffs are reflected in Prairie City's Municipal Council, Board of Education, service clubs, and the like. Although individually they are somewhat transient, these leaders are readily acceptable to the community's decision makers, because such leaders hold points of view on many issues in common with members of the community.

Within such a setting two conflicting points of view have become manifest on the issue of what the nature of the school building expansion program is to be. The "old residents" as well as the "new residents" agree that the school plant must be expanded to accommodate the rather steady growth of the student body. By and large, they also agree that the educational program needs expansion and enrichment in terms of additional courses, newer methods and media of teaching, and expansion of pupil services. Furthermore, they agree that the gradually expanding wealth of the school district will be adequate to support this growth. A conflict, however, centers on how to go about expanding the physical facilities to accommodate the growing pupil population and educational program.

The old residents maintain that such improvements should be financed on a "pay-as-you-go" basis which will expand as the wealth of the district expands. Thus the school district will make additions to the existing facilities as they can be afforded. This position on the part of the old residents became very firm since a slight nationwide recession caused this group to become very interested in holding down expenses.

Leaders among the new residents have taken an opposite stance in this situation. These people, generally speaking, are associated with the flight- and space-related industries. They maintain that the total expansion program should be undertaken immediately and that school tax rates should be increased to pay off the principal and interest on the bonds, which in turn would necessarily have to be sold to finance the new facilities. This group maintains that in a period of national economic dislocation, deflation, and unemployment the country's economy needs a stimulus and the additional school district expenditures are entirely compatible with good economic planning. Advocates of the proposal favoring immediate expansion of the program and facilities maintain that if the community acts favorably on the proposal, it will not only provide a better educational program right away but will also contribute to the resolution of a national problem in economic dislocation.

Questions for Discussion

1. During a period of a slight recession such as that occurring in the Prairie City case, what has likely happened to income? Why?

2. If the old residents' pattern of thinking would be followed on a

wide scale throughout the nation, what economic shifts might be expected in this setting? How would this influence the formula GNP = $C + I + G$?

3. What effect would likely occur if there were general and national acceptance of the new residents' thinking? How would this influence the formula GNP = $C + I + G$?

Case 8. Combating Economic Stagnation in Mohawk Junction

Everyone in Mohawk Junction knew that the local board of education had used nearly every device "in the book" to convince Fred Chapman to accept the position of superintendent of schools. Fred had grown up in this small city, had been an outstanding high school athlete, and was the first boy from that community to play varsity football at the state university. Upon graduation from State, Fred returned to Mohawk Junction as a coach and social studies teacher. However, after only two very successful years in this position, Fred left for a larger city and the development of an outstanding career in coaching, teaching, and school administration. The capstone to his professional career was his eight-year tenure as director of the finance division of the State Department of Education. In this position, Fred distinguished himself not as a financial wizard but as a mediator and consensus builder. The situation previous to his appointment was one of strife and dissension wherein divisions and individuals within the department could not agree on the specifics of the machinery to distribute monies allocated to the state school subsidy program. Fred's broad educational experience, personal contacts with other state officials, and quiet but confident personality enabled him after a short time to join the finance division with the other State Department of Education divisions in a close and productive working relationship. Now, as he was approaching retirement, he was called to revitalize a rapidly withering community.

The influential citizens of Mohawk Junction are by and large of Fred Chapman's generation. Several are members of Fred's high school graduating class and recall the bright future all of them predicted for "the Junction." No doubt that is why many stayed in the city. Today, however, a heavy pall of pessimism hangs over the city.

A few years ago, prominent members of the chamber of commerce were vaguely aware of the unfulfilled promises of prosperity and growth of the community. However, two recent events clearly articulated the unverbalized concern. A dairy equipment plant, long the community's major industry, closed down because of "obsolescence of equipment and processes as well as a declining local market."

The severity of this initial shock and the resulting chamber of commerce drive to attract another industry seemed to offer some promise to the citizens of Mohawk Junction. A prospective industry was located—a milling and cereal plant. After serious "courting" by the chamber of commerce and their own intensive survey, the company tersely refused to consider the establishment of a plant in the city. When pressed for the reasons for this decision, a company representative candidly indicated, "The town has nothing to offer my company, or any other for that matter." More specific reasons included totally inadequate water and sewage facilities, generally shabby and dated public services, limited public school programs, and little apparent public interest to change any of these conditions.

In reassessing the situation, a few key members of the local power structure came to the realization that the city was approaching stagnation. Not only were the charges of the milling company representative correct but also the economic activity in general was gradually slowing down. Retail sales had been in a slow decline for several years, and the last new business in town had been established six years ago. In that same period, one retail business had left town and two others had closed their doors permanently.

Evidence of the problem was irrefutable, the nature of the problem was commonly agreed upon, but the appropriate solutions became major devisive factors among the influentials and the general populace of Mohawk Junction. Three differing points of view predominated, each with the support of one or more of the community influentials led by a second-echelon member of the local power structure and backed by a group of interested citizens. These points of view were:

1. Enhance local spending through the expansion of disposable income. This should be accomplished by local tax reduction through cutting back on public services.

2. Stimulate the local economy by expanding the deficient public services but do so with bond issues and the like which would not substantially reduce disposable income.

3. Stimulate local spending through upgrading local public services but increase local taxes as well.

When Fred Chapman arrived in town and all the ceremonials attendant to the welcoming of a new school superintendent were completed, he knew his first major decision would be that of taking a position on the question of how to revitalize the community. He further realized that his personal background, his experience, and his present responsibility made him the "swing man"—his decision would probably determine the direction the community would move in resolving the problem.

Questions for Discussion

1. Does the financing of public schools ordinarily play a critical role in public finance policy on the local level? Why or why not?

2. What factors other than government spending, tax rates, and disposable income (those mentioned in the three community points of view) would have to be considered in reaching a decision in this case?

3. Are there possibilities of positions fundamentally different from those proposed by the community groups? If so, what are they?

4. In terms of gross national product, what is the influence of expenditures for public schools? What federal policy might be enacted to upgrade the schools of the nation and at the same time increase national income?

Case 9.   Contrasts in State-level Proposals for Income Augmentation

The professional organization for school administrators in an Eastern state has in the recent past behaved like similar associations in most other states. The group, headed by its executive secretary, mounted only a modest pressure group in the state legislature. By and large, its primary interest was in initiating or supporting legislation pertaining to increasing state support for the public schools. Without exception all proposals of this kind were defended on the basis of improving the quantity and quality of education available to the youth of the state.

This group, representing the most respected educational leaders in the state, was apparently enjoying steadily appreciating levels of success. The organization's proposals, as well as the rationale and supporting arguments for the proposals, were accepted as reasonable, and hence they positively influenced the general citizenry as well as the legislators. When, however, the nation as a whole and this state in particular experienced a slight recession, the school administrators' lobby lost considerable influence and power.

Concurrent with the recession and the first reduction of influence of the school administrators' lobby, there emerged a new power in the halls of the state capital—the Committee on Fiscal Responsibility. The group was composed of certain leaders in the industrial and business community, staff members from local "taxpayers" groups, some county and local office holders, and a few private citizens. The general theme of the committee's work was "to expose and highlight waste, extravagance, and the concomitant deficit financing." After each exposé, the group urged reduction in both services and costs of state government. Their basic arguments appeared to be:

1. All state government expenses should be carefully scrutinized in order to assure taxpayers there are no wastes, extravagances, or inefficiencies in that level of government.

2. Efficient and economic government must be administered according to the same rules that are applicable to a successful business or household—it must live within its budget.

3. In times of mild recession when there is apt to be considerable unemployment, deflation, and the like, state government must reduce state spending in order to reduce taxes and so retain more dollars in the taxpayers' pockets.

4. When state revenues are reduced by a recession such as that currently being experienced in the state, it follows that state services must be reduced in order to live within one's income.

5. When reductions in state services are required, priorities of cuts must be made. For example, currently in this state, the growing needs in the Bureau of Unemployment Compensation are much more urgent than that of state assistance for local school districts. The latter program has enjoyed unprecedented growth over the past ten years and has already met its most pressing needs.

In recognizing their rapidly eroding influence among the citizens as well as the legislators and in analyzing the platform of the Committee for Fiscal Responsibility, the school administrators' association shifted the focus of the school financing program for which it sought support. Instead of simply seeking larger state subsidies to local school districts, the association's new proposal incorporated a multistep program to stimulate educational investment. It seeks to integrate stimulative devices on local, state, and federal levels.

Major features of the new plan call for the inclusion of an incentive feature in the state program of assistance to local school districts in order to stimulate greater financial effort on the local district level. Thus, the state would increase its grants-in-aid to school districts which have exceeded an expected expenditure level determined on the basis of local wealth per pupil. A second major element in the proposal is that of providing federal grants to those states which, through this program or any other programs, exceed the combined local and state expenditure levels based on wealth per pupil.

Proponents of the proposal have marshaled the following arguments to justify their positions.

1. It is a legitimate function of the state to use its resources to stimulate increased local school district expenditures through rewards or incentives.

2. Likewise, it is also appropriate that the federal government improve public education by granting incentive rewards to those states willing to expend more state and local monies than expected according to their ability as measured by wealth per pupil.

3. Such a proposal will be complementary to a federal plan designed to increase expenditures on the state and/or local level. The program will thus be integrated and cumulative; e.g., additional local effort is rewarded by additional state assistance. This will reflect a greater combined local and state effort, which in turn is rewarded by additional federal assistance.

4. The plan incorporates a solid approach to local school improvement and in addition implements national policy of stimulating expenditures to affect expanded national income. The resultant increase in income will in turn support much of the augmented expenditures.

Questions for Discussion

1. In all likelihood what effects did the slight recession described in the case have on the income of the state?

2. What was the economic concept implied in the proposal of the Committee on Fiscal Responsibility?

3. What effect would it be likely to have on the formula GNP = C + I + G?

4. What was the concept implied in the proposal of the administrators' organization?

5. What effect would it be apt to have on the formula GNP = C + I + G?

Suggested Readings

Concept C—Income Determination

Benson, Charles: *The Economics of Public Education*, Boston: Houghton Mifflin, 1961; 2d ed., 1968.

————: *Education Is Good Business*, Washington, D.C.: AASA, 1966.

Center for the Advanced Study of Educational Administration: *The Economic Returns to Education*, Eugene, Oreg.: The Center, 1965.

Committee for Economic Development: *Raising Low Incomes Through Improved Education*, New York: The Committee, 1965.

Groves, Harold M.: *Education and Economic Growth*, Washington, D.C.: National Education Association, 1961.

Heilbroner, Robert L., and Peter L. Bernstein: *A Primer on Government Spending*, New York: Vintage Books, 1963.

Lovenstein, Meno: *Economics and the Educational Administrator*, Columbus, Ohio: School-Community Development Study Monograph, College of Education, The Ohio State University, 1958.

McConnell, Campbell R.: *Economics*, 4th ed., New York: McGraw-Hill, 1969, chap. 13, pp. 228–235.

Martin, Richard S., and Reuben G. Miller: *Economics*, Columbus Ohio: Merrill, 1965.

National Committee for Support of Public Schools: *Changing Demands on Education and Their Fiscal Implications*, Washington, D.C.: The Committee, 1963.

Ott, David J., and Attiat F. Ott: *Federal Budget Policy*, Washington, D.C.: The Brookings Institution, 1965.

Poole, Kenyon E.: *Public Finance and Economic Welfare*, New York: Rinehart, 1956.

Samuelson, Paul A.: *Economics*, 7th ed., New York: McGraw-Hill, 1967, chaps. 10–12.

Full Employment

the problem

The progress of educational development is inextricably inter-woven with the economic structure of a society. As a social enterprise, education uses the factors of production and is consequently influenced by the relative abundance of these factors. Thus when goods and services are not available because the labor and resources necessary to produce them are idle, the education process cannot proceed normally. Unemployment therefore jeopardizes education progress. This fact is obvious when there is general unemployment but is also eminently clear when educational resources are not fully employed.

the concept

Few will deny the allegation that unemployment is a most un-desirable condition in our economy. Unemployment of any of our land and capital resources is certainly undesirable, but to have idle human resources is even worse. A moment's reflection will lead us to recognize that the goods which might have been produced today, but were not because the labor and resources necessary to produce those goods were idle, will never be produced. The goods and services that all of us have at our disposal are permanently reduced. The maintenance of as high a level of employment as possible, then, is a very proper economic goal and one which all of us should give serious consideration.

Until but a few years ago it was not considered possible or necessary, in our capitalist economy based upon a free and competitive market system, to be concerned with the level of employment. The "normal" condition, it was believed, was that all persons desiring to work would be able to find employment, just so long as they were willing to accept the wage being offered. Unemployment could only be voluntary, and to some extent frictional, that is, due to the normal layoffs involved while a worker changes jobs. The thesis that full employment is the usual and normal condition was based upon the economic theory called "Say's Law." This theory maintains that in the process of producing goods and services purchasing power is paid to the various factors of production which is just equal to the value of the goods and services produced.

If this theory of markets which was expounded by J. B. Say, a French economist of the early nineteenth century, had been carried no further it would have remained a mere truism, for of course as stated above the thesis is correct. When extended to justify full employment as a normal condition, however, Say's Law encounters difficulties.

No one will deny that businessmen will employ the number of workers needed to produce the goods and services which they will *expect* to sell. If the expected sales are sufficiently high to require all the available workers to produce, then full employment will exist; otherwise it will not. Many factors will influence the businessman in the projection of his expected sales, but probably the most important single factor will be the level of sales in the immediately preceding time period. There is undoubtedly a strong tendency for everyone to believe that what has happened in the immediate past will continue in the immediate future. If all the goods and services produced in the preceding period were sold, it is highly unlikely that the businessman will plan to reduce his production.

As demonstrated by Say's Law, the purchasing power was available to take all the goods and services produced off the market, and those who subscribe to "normal full employment" believe that purchasing power will be used for such a purpose. It has been amply demonstrated, however, that the available purchasing power (or income, for that of course is what it is) need not be, nor is it usually, all spent. Some of it will be saved.

The adherents to the normal full employment thesis of course knew about savings. They maintained, however, that disposable income not spent for consumption goods would inevitably find its way into investment projects. In this way it would become an effective demand on the economy's production. Again, we know that this does not need to be so. Income can be disposed of in any one of a number of ways, and there is certainly no surety that it will ever be used to take goods and services off the market. Say's Law cannot be used to support the contention that full employment is normal.

Instead, full employment will exist only if the level of effective demand, that is, the spending of consumers and investors and governments for newly produced goods and services, is sufficiently high to require the employment of all those who wish to work in the production of those goods and services. If employment is less than optimum, a level of effective demand needed to absorb those goods and services produced will ensure an increase in the number of workers employed. If full employment already exists and the level of effective demand is increased further, the result will be an increase in the level of prices. Further output, by definition, cannot be forthcoming. It is also probable that even if there is some unemployment in the economy, an increase in effective demand will bring about some inflation at the same time that employment is also increased.

Which is the more undesirable, unemployment or price inflation? This may require a value judgment, upon which no two people will agree, but most economists are likely to select a moderate amount of inflation as less undesirable than unemployment. The loss to the economy usually is not so severe.

Case 10.   Expanding Employment of Teachers in Upper Chesney

Upper Chesney has long had a reputation for demanding the best in its public schools. Its inhabitants constituted the "upper crust" of all the adjacent suburbs. The city had the highest per capita income of any municipality in the state besides being first in its size category in the nation. The popular attitude among the inhabitants appeared to be "nothing but the best for our children." Being a very homogeneous community in terms of social and economic status as well as political persuasion, ethnic background, and cultural level, the public schools tended to be looked upon as the community's private schools. In fact for some years the district has not qualified for any state equalization subsidy as it has been in the upper 10 percent in terms of wealth per pupil. The Upper Chesney Board of Education prided itself in having "never taken a nickel of federal aid to education."

It was in this kind of a situation that Elliott Revere found himself as the newly appointed superintendent of schools. Revere's job, as offhandedly described by the president of the board, was to "give us a school that stands with the best Eastern prep schools." Since many of the parents in the school district had attended this type of private school and the majority have always preferred that their youngsters attend Ivy League or Eastern colleges, this was generally accepted.

In assessing the school situation, Elliott Revere found an elaborate and high-quality school plant along with excellent equipment and supplies. The educational program, including curriculum and teaching methodology, was very well thought through and appeared to fit the educational objectives of the community. However, Revere could assess the teaching staff as being no more than good. The first tensions occurred when the board of education (after a slightly shorter than normal "honeymoon" period) starting making rather pointed requests for the superintendent to submit a plan to upgrade the quality of the educational program. Revere recognized that he had only one direction in which to move—that of upgrading the teaching staff. His earlier appraisal of the whole school operation was largely verified. The physical facilities were excellent in terms of space and condition as well as being suited to the desired instructional program. The supplies and equipment were better than the teachers knew how to use. The class size was such that reduction of the pupil-teacher ratio would have no discernible effect on pupil learning.

The teaching staff of the Upper Chesney schools could be termed as a "solid" staff. All teachers met the suggested minimum for academic training, i.e., a baccalaureate degree. Nearly 60 percent, in fact, held the master's degree, and the majority of the remaining group had work beyond the bachelor's degree or were working on the master's degree. However, a large majority of the teachers took their training at the state university in the large city at the center of the urban complex which includes Upper Chesney. Although relatively few of the school district's graduates returned from college to teach in its schools, these few teachers have tended to set the tone. Other members of the staff emulate them since they are very influential with the power figures in the school administration and the city. Thus, the expectations of the Upper Chesney citizenry have been firmly impressed on the teaching staff.

The few teachers employed in the system who have been "other minded" are looked upon as being disturbing elements. Considerable staff and community pressure has been exerted on them to ensure their conformity with the school system's expectations. This type of staff harmony is a matter of considerable concern and pride among most of the teachers.

In order to provide a solid conceptual base to his proposal to improve the quality of the educational program, Elliott Revere predicated his proposal on the concept that underused human resources must be more fully utilized. Investment of more money in the educational program of Upper Chesney must be made in order to be assured of a greater return per dollar, but it is imperative that the additional dollars be invested in the right factor of production. By expending more money for a better qualified staff there would be a fuller employment of available resources. Additional dollars so invested would not only yield greater educational returns but would also have the effect of increasing the production and hence purchasing power and employment.

Questions for Discussion

1. If Elliott Revere's proposal does not intend to add teachers to the staff, how can it increase employment?

2. How will it siphon off available goods and services from the market?

3. In what way was there demonstrated an increased government (in this case the Upper Chesney School District) demand for teachers' services? What effect would this likely have?

4. What effect would this proposal have if there was a severe teacher shortage? If there was a mild inflation?

Case 11.   A State Department of Education Considers Teacher Need and Supply

The State Department of Education in a Western state has long been aware of the chronic shortage of qualified teachers in that area of the country. Even though only a few classrooms have been without teachers, in many instances poorly qualified teachers have been employed and/or the relatively scarce "quality" teachers have been called upon to assume teaching loads which have been clearly excessive.

In order to resolve this problem and also upgrade the quality of instruction in a time of continually expanding enrollments, the State Department of Education checked the figures regarding the number of teachers in training in the state-supported colleges and universities as well as private institutions of higher education. It was found that in the immediate future the state would have more than enough teachers *if* all these college students now taking degrees and/or qualifying for teachers' credentials would indeed enter the classrooms. In checking back over past years the same apparent oversupply was present also, but nevertheless the teacher shortage was acute.

These preliminary findings prompted a more comprehensive investigation involving the state's future needs for classroom teachers, the number of prospective teachers being trained in the state, the number of teachers actually entering the program immediately after graduation, and the number of teachers being attracted from outside the state.

The following table indicates some of the findings as reported by the State Department of Education Research Division. It was observed that:

1. Thirty-three percent of college seniors graduating the previous June (or academic year) who were education majors or other subject

Table 11.1. Teacher Need and the Nature of Teacher Supply, 1964–1965 through 1968–1969

School Year	Estimated Number of Additional Teachers Needed	Actual Number of Additional Teachers Employed	College Seniors Prepared to Take Teaching Positions						Out-of-state Teachers Taking Positions		Non-college Senior In-state Teachers Taking Positions	
			Total		Taking Positions		Not Taking Positions					
			Number	% of Additional Teachers Employed	Number	% of Total	Number	% of Total	Number	% of Additional Teachers Employed	Number	% of Additional Teachers Employed
1964–1965	7,002	6,411	7,120	111	4,984	70	2,136	30	1,164	18	263	4
1965–1966	7,871	7,390	8,002	108	5,521	69	2,481	31	1,339	18	530	7
1966–1967	8,260	7,731	8,422	109	5,895	70	2,527	30	1,311	17	525	7
1967–1968	9,077	8,580	9,160	101	6,046	66	3,114	34	1,520	18	1,014	12
1968–1969	9,420	8,951	9,602	102	6,401	67	3,201	33	1,785	20	765	9

matter majors with qualifications for teacher credentials did not accept a teaching position the following September.

2. Of the 33 percent who did not take teaching positions, 16 percent were found to be unable to do so because of marriage, pregnancy, military service, or health reasons.

3. Of the remaining 17 percent, 12 percent entered professions other than education. Of these 12 percent, 6 percent cited higher pay among the major reasons for their decision.

When the State Department of Education *Report on Teacher Need and Supply* was published, reaction was immediate and lively. The citizenry of the state read and commented on it extensively. However, other than registering surprise at the enormity of the problem and the large number of young people trained as teachers but not taking positions, the public did not speak with one voice nor did it offer any specific proposal. Three "official voices," however, were heard.

1. The State Educational Association issued a statement commending the State Department of Education on conducting a "long overdue study which dramatically illustrates the shameful lack of attractiveness of teaching positions in our state." The state board was admonished to push for the state association's minimum salary proposal.

2. The Citizens for Better Education Committee, a statewide nonpartisan pressure group and consensus-building agency, challenged the State Board of Education to "devise plans to redirect these valuable human resources back into the schools—the institutions to which they were originally and eminently qualified to contribute."

3. In the state legislature there was considerable discussion in the corridors about the report, but official comment was originally limited to proceedings of three standing legislative committees, i.e., the Finance Committee, the Education Committee, and Governmental Operations Committee. Although all three committee reactions were unique and each was geared to its own committee concern, a common theme ran through all. Each called for better utilization of state resources in the publicly supported universities. Each statement either implicitly or explicitly asked the question, Why make massive appropriations to support the teacher education programs supposedly to prepare public school teachers, then have such a high proportion of them enter private business and industry? The problem was thus viewed in terms of a poor financial investment (Finance Committee), lack of utilization of teaching talent (Education Committee), and inefficient governmental coordination (Governmental Operations Committee).

As the discussion of the State Department of Education report increased in tempo across the state, it was apparent that neither consensus nor positive action was about to be suggested. Instead, each interest group read into it a rationale for its own program. Sensing the rapid deterioration of the statewide discussion, the State Board of Education demanded that the state superintendent of public education set forth a positive proposal after having opened this Pandora's box. The board suggested that the superintendent submit a plan based on cold logic to counteract the emotional appeals heard from other groups. This plan was "to identify the real issues and outline a plan of action integrating the many valuable insights provided by individuals and organizations throughout the state."

After some deliberation with his staff and consultation with state government and other personnel, the state superintendent issued a lengthy position paper on the problem of satisfying teacher demands in the state. Excerpts from the rather lengthy paper are as follows:

> The true issue revolves around the concept that education as an enterprise employs the several factors of production. The most effective use of these factors will provide efficiency and maximum productivity.
> It is commonly understood that an additional investment in education will yield substantial benefits—that the point of diminishing returns has not as yet been reached. It is also commonly understood that education increases consumption and demand for goods and services among those people receiving the education. Consequently education increases both production and consumption. Thus if additional teachers are employed, not only will the productivity of the educational system be enhanced but also the state will approach a condition of full employment.
> The recent State Department of Education study indicates that not all our available educational resources are being utilized in our state's public schools. The question becomes, How can we most fully utilize these resources and thus ensure the optimum employment of these teachers?
> It is proposed that additional monies be invested in teachers' salaries in order to utilize these resources which will, in turn, expand the economy far beyond the original investment.

Questions for Discussion

1. What assumptions regarding full employment are suggested in the state superintendent's position paper?

2. What would be the consequences of this proposal if there were a

general condition of full employment prior to the implementation of the proposal?

3. What would be the consequences of the proposal if there were a general condition of less than full employment prior to the implementation of the proposal?

4. What other type of governmental action might be appropriate in a situation of less than full employment?

Case 12.　A Professional Organization Takes a Position on Unemployment

Members of the Resolutions Committee of a national professional organization of school administrators have only recently become aware of the potential influence of their group. In preparation for the annual meeting, the committee has been concentrating its efforts during the last two weeks on formulating resolutions to be presented to the membership for action. At the grass roots level, most school administrators are very concerned about the committee's deliberations, as those superintendents, principals, and others are beginning to feel the pinch of maintaining an adequate educational program in the face of a slowly accelerating economic depression which is being felt all across the nation.

As early as three years ago the general population began to show signs of a lack of confidence in the then favorable economic conditions. The conservative press increased the tempo of its crusade of criticism regarding the "false prosperity" and the "deficit spending that is supporting it." The withdrawal of confidence was reflected at both the state and national levels. In the respective legislative sessions appropriations were generally cut back from their relatively high levels of the previous sessions. Currently many of the earmarks of a full-scale depression are becoming apparent: unemployment, deflation, decreasing consumption, and a general apprehension or even lack of confidence in the stability of the economy.

As a group of school administrators charged with the responsibilty of drawing up a set of resolutions for the national organization, this committee has called and heard expert testimony on the situation concerning the national economy. Two major and contrasting points of view appear to be emerging in the committee.

The first of these, termed the "interventionist" point of view, is predicated upon the following ideas:

1. Intervention by the federal government is required in order to halt the tendency toward recession and to turn the trend back toward economic growth.

2. Educational expenditures should be increased on the federal, state, and local levels, but especially on the federal level. Desirable expenditure programs should:

    a. Expand educational programs on all levels to broaden, enrich, and improve public education. As a valuable side effect such action will provide more employment for teachers.

    b. Expand the construction program for school facilities by additional state and federal assistance.

    c. Expand the work-study program to keep youth in school and increase purchasing power simultaneously.

3. Governmental programs should be initiated to stimulate purchasing and consumption in general, but particularly among the unemployed.

4. A program to stimulate expenditures and investment by domestic industry and business should be undertaken.

The contrasting body of opinion within the Resolutions Committee on the matter of policy pertaining to the national economy is held by those who retain the so-called "conservative" point of view. Major ideas articulated by this group include:

1. The capitalistic, free enterprise system contains the inherent ability to correct artificial imbalances. Consequently, unemployment must be considered as a normal condition, and it is to be expected when there is overproduction due to artificial governmental stimulation.

2. Through the expenditure of reasonable amounts of local resources, local programs can be developed to keep high school youth in school and out of the labor market.

3. Federal deficit financing should be avoided as it will not, in the long run, resolve the problem. Instead it will add to it by inflating prices and providing an artificial economic stimulus.

The committee, now meeting in sessions designed to draw up the statement of prepared resolutions, has heard the expert testimony, the opinion and attitude of the representatives of the school administrators in the field, and the reasoned arguments of the committee's proponents of each point of view. Some kind of action must now be taken.

Questions for Discussion

1. Does the problem situation faced by members of the committee have any relationship to the concepts introduced in preceding cases? If so, what are some of these relationships?

2. What factors would make federal government intervention necessary? What factors would make such intervention unnecessary?

3. What kinds of intervention, if the circumstances dictated it, might be appropriate?

4. Is there a middle ground between the intervention and nonintervention positions? If so, what circumstances must be present to provide for it?

5. On what basis might an administrator in a local school district defend his taking a position on a resolution concerned with the concept of full employment?

Suggested Readings

Concept D—Full Employment

American Association of School Administrators: *The Federal Government and the Public Schools,* Washington, D.C.: The Association, 1965.

———: *Federal Policy and the Public Schools,* Washington, D.C.: The Association, 1967.

Benson, Charles: *Education Is Good Business,* Washington, D.C.: AASA, 1966.

Center for the Advanced Study of Educational Administration: *The Economic Returns to Education,* Eugene, Oreg.: The Center, 1965.

Committee for Economic Development: *Raising Low Income Through Improved Education,* New York: The Committee, 1965.

Galbraith, John K.: *The Affluent Society,* Boston: Houghton Mifflin, 1958.

Heilbroner, Robert L., and Peter L. Bernstein: *A Primer on Government Spending,* New York: Vintage Books, 1963.

Lovenstein, Meno: *Economics and the Educational Administrator,* Columbus, Ohio: School-Community Development Study Monograph, College of Education, The Ohio State University, 1958.

McConnell, Campbell R.: *Economics*, 4th ed., New York: McGraw-Hill, 1969, chap. 2, pp. 23–29.

Martin, Richard S., and Reuben G. Miller: *Economics*, Columbus, Ohio: Merrill, 1965.

Meranto, Philip: *The Politics of Federal Aid to Education in 1965: A Study in Political Innovation*, Syracuse, N.Y.: Syracuse University Press, 1967.

National Committee for Support of Public Schools: *Changing Demands on Education and Their Fiscal Implications*, Washington, D.C.: The Committee, 1963.

Ott, David J., and Attiat F. Ott: *Federal Budget Policy*, Washington, D.C.: The Brookings Institution, 1965.

Samuelson, Paul A.: *Economics*, 7th ed., New York: McGraw-Hill, 1967, chap. 2, pp. 18–23, chap. 39, pp. 766–767.

part 2

The Role of Government and the Character of Public Finance

concepts E–H

Economic Influences on the Role of Government

the problem

The school, as an agency of government, makes decisions within a given concept of its role. The quality of these decisions is measured in terms of how well they implement or expedite the tasks or activities necessary to fulfill the role. Thus, it is necessary to define clearly what the role of the institution is to be.

As is true in most social institutions, the role of government in general and the school in particular is a dynamic one. Since the primary function of any unit of government is to serve people, many questions are raised as to how the school can best serve the community. In order to answer these questions adequately, it is necessary to consider the economic factors which bear on the question.

the concept

> In the particular circumstances of a given age or nation there is scarcely anything, really important to the general interest, which it may not be desirable, or even necessary, that the government should take upon itself, not because private individuals cannot effectually perform it, but because they will not.[1]

The writer of these words is no modern, starry-eyed dreamer; no advocate of a socialist state. John Stuart Mill, rather, was a staunch member of the classical school of economics and a firm defender of the market economy and competition. As a leading spokesman for the classical school, Mill did define the proper role of government quite narrowly (although not so narrowly as did Adam Smith), but both he and Smith recognized that the level of activities performed by government could not remain static over time but should fluctuate with changing conditions.

The reason that the accepted role of government does change is because of the economic needs (or the believed economic needs) of the times. There has been a universal tendency to adopt the economic system, or to make changes in the existing system, which is believed to be most beneficial to those who are in a position to make and enforce the economic decisions. In the final analysis, political ideas usually are subordinated to economic necessity.

[1] John Stuart Mill, *Principles of Political Economy*, book V, chap. 2.

For example, during the seventeenth and eighteenth centuries the economic principles of mercantilism were widely endorsed by most Western European countries, particularly England. Mercantilism was based on the idea that the way for a country to become prosperous was to increase its holdings of monetary metals (gold and silver). One way to accomplish this was to own the sources of the metals, either within their own borders or within their colonies. Spain and Portugal were able to acquire gold and silver in this way.

For a country which did not possess the original source of monetary metal, such as England, the path to prosperity was through trade. If England would manufacture goods and exchange them with other countries for gold or silver, and if this gold and silver would then be kept in England, prosperity would be achieved. Colonies performed two functions in this system by acting as a source of raw materials and as a market for manufactured goods. In all instances the trade of the colonies was to be carried on only with the mother country. The gold and silver, once acquired, were to be retained, for only in this way could a country remain wealthy and prosperous. Such a system required a leading and active role by government. Stringent government regulations militantly enforced were required to keep the gold within the country and to regulate the trade of the colonies.

By the latter part of the eighteenth century it became very difficult for England to remain prosperous under the principles of mercantilism. The country was ready for a new economic system, and it welcomed the ideas advanced by Adam Smith.[2] The "invisible hand" and the "market system" promised levels of prosperity greater than those attained under mercantilism. Germane to this discussion, also, was the greatly reduced reliance on government. This does not imply that Smith did not believe that the economy should be regulated. Quite the contrary, for at one place he states, "People of the same trade seldom meet together, even for merriment and diversion, but the conversation ends in a conspiracy against the public or in some contrivance to raise prices."[3] Smith did not advocate the government as a regulator, however, because of the corruptness and the inefficiency of the government in his time. He was convinced that the economy could not be controlled by the government nearly so well as by the market and competition. For a long time government played a minor role in the economy.

During the latter part of the nineteenth century, however, the balance which was needed for Adam Smith's economic system to work

[2] Adam Smith, *An Inquiry into the Nature and Causes of the Wealth of Nations,* 1776.
[3] *Ibid.,* book I, chap. X, part II.

properly was upset. Large business organizations were formed which were not constrained by the forces of competition, and attempts at forming monopolies which worked to the adverse interests of the rest of the economy were more and more successful.

This tendency could only be counteracted by an increased role for government. Some interested persons have advocated that all business units in excess of a particular size be dismembered into smaller units, but this would require much government interference and regulation. Other persons have campaigned for outright government ownership. The solution selected to keep the economy functioning properly was to maintain or restore competition wherever possible (through the antitrust laws) and to regulate those industries where competition was not deemed in the best interests of the economy (the public utilities). To say that the use of government controls has been perfectly satisfactory would be naïve, but to return to a system of uncontrolled monopoly would be completely unacceptable.

The important conclusion from this discussion is that in all instances mentioned, government has been only a tool used to accomplish the desired economic goals. This is the attitude that most persons hold today; government should be used if it offers the best hope for achieving our needs; it should not be used if it is ineffective or even if it is less effective than other means.

Case 13.   Hot Lunches for Homevale

The new residents of Homevale often referred to their suburban village as a community of cemeteries, golf courses, and fine restaurants. Half joking, but not without considerable pride, these former "big city boys" gently teased each other about moving "out to the sticks."

The characteristics of Homevale lent themselves to this kind of joking since it once had a rural orientation. Most of the present community was originally made up of several large family farm homesteads. When the nearby metropolitan center experienced growth in the early 1900s, it was forced to go out well beyond the immediate boundaries for the space-consuming enterprises such as cemeteries and golf courses. The Homevale farmsteads were natural locations for these enterprises. The big family farms were just on the western edge of the county, were adjacent to interurban train service, and were near a major U.S. highway serving the city.

After four large cemeteries located within the Homevale Elementary School District, numerous small businesses sprang up in the area. In the era of the 1920s greenhouses in close proximity to a cemetery were not only convenient but almost necessary. Since many of the funerals in this early period were something of social affairs, it was very natural that fine large restaurants were established in close proximity to the cemeteries.

The city dweller's demand for recreational facilities resulted in the establishment of two golf courses in the Homevale community. Again, the city's needs for space-consuming enterprises were met in the outlying rural areas.

Homevale and its elementary school district were for the period 1920–1945 primarily identified with former farms largely devoted to cemeteries and golf courses. A large proportion of the people living in the neighborhood derived their livelihood from these businesses.

A significant change in the nature of the community began in the early 1950s when the World War II veterans returned, established households, and bought homes. Homevale was a "natural" for development since it was close to the city yet far enough out to be attractive to GI-financed housing projects. Consequently by 1955 a young, generally middle-class suburban community was superimposed on the original semirural area.

During the early years of community growth in the 1950s, the little elementary school district suffered only the usual growing pains. Many new teachers had to be employed, additions had to be built on the original four room school, and school buses had to bring children in from the mushrooming subdivisions.

Perhaps the most dramatic problem was one related to a unique demand expressed by many of the newcomers to the school district. Soon after these young couples were established and acclimated to the community, many began to express a concern for the lack of hot lunch facilities at the elementary school. Traditionally, the children brought sandwiches from home, bought milk at the school, and ate this lunch in a multipurpose room.

During the summer a delegation of parents petitioned the board of education to establish a hot lunch program in the school. The board, generally aware of the financial implications of the request, expressed some concern over the necessity of establishing such a program. This point was highlighted when it was discovered that, of the delegation representing fourteen families, twelve of the families lived less than a half mile from the school and two lived within two blocks. At this juncture the parents stated that walking distance was not the primary factor. Instead, a supervised, hot lunch program was needed because so many mothers were working or engaged in other activities and therefore the youngsters could not get such a lunch either at home or in school. Sensing the emergence of a serious problem, the board decided to delay a final decision on the petition. Instead, it scheduled a "study session" for itself and a subsequent public hearing for the petitioners.

In considering the course of action during the study session, the board's position was not one of opposition, but instead one of maintaining that the program was unnecessary until it could be proven otherwise. Several of the individual board members as well as the superintendent visited hot lunch programs in neighboring schools. They gathered considerable information on features, costs, organizational plans, and financing arrangements.

By the time the hearing was to take place, an intense community interest had developed. People in the community who had never shown an interest in school affairs before held strong opinions on the topic. At the PTA meeting held just prior to the board-scheduled hearing, several heated exchanges occurred between proponents and opponents of the hot lunch proposal.

At the hearing, the president of the board of education invited the supporters of the hot lunch proposal to present their case. In a carefully worded statement, the spokesman of the group pointed out that the school district was undergoing a change both in size and character. Many more children need this kind of a service. He suggested that now the school was large enough to support a hot lunch program—"long recognized by leading educators as an integral part of a well-balanced educational program which seeks to develop the whole child."

This type of program, the spokesman stated, can be financed by individual lunch charges, state and federal subsidies, and surplus agricultural commodities. Little if any local tax money would be needed.

Immediately after the statement by the supporters of the program, the president of the board opened the hearing for reactions or questions. In the ensuing discussion many opinions, points, charges, and countercharges were made. Although there was much duplication and frequent belaboring of some points, the opponents of the hot lunch proposal centered their dissent around the following points:

1. The hot lunch program is not necessary. A packed lunch with milk is fully as nutritious as a hot lunch.

2. Such a program is expensive since it involves more than just operating costs. Capital outlay for physical facilities and equipment is necessary. Additional supervision of lunchrooms, noon play areas, and/or recreation periods usually involves greater costs since hot lunch programs attract more children than the traditional cold lunch programs.

3. On the basis of the number of children transported, it was deduced that only 34 percent of the children "needed to remain in school during the lunch hour—all the rest could walk home." Since a considerable investment is required for the facilities, it is not fair to tax everyone to support a program that is neither needed nor used by all.

4. Schools which adopt these kinds of programs tend to change from an intellectual function to a custodial function. These schools tend to downgrade their emphasis on academic concerns because of the additional concerns of feeding children, teaching manners, and entertaining them during the noon hour. Such programs make it easy for parents to abdicate their responsibility of much of the upbringing of the children.

When the last point was broached, a bitter discussion ensued regarding the motivation of the parents who requested the program.

"You people want the schools to be baby-sitters for your children. You find it more convenient not to have them come home for lunch. This enables you mothers to get a job or become active in all kinds of social activities."

"It is necessary for our family to have both my husband's and my income to pay for our home and provide our children with what they need. If we are this conscientious in providing for the betterment of our children, I believe the school can cooperate with us and help us do the best for our children."

"I always heard that the best thing a mother could do was to be a mother to her children on a twenty-four hour a day basis. Children need to learn manners, eat different foods, and entertain themselves. The school can't do this job nearly as well as the home. I don't believe any machine or organization can ever replace a mother in the home."

"I am a working mother and proud of it. Furthermore, I'm a good one. Just because kids come home for lunches is no sign they get good food or learn good manners. As far as working mothers go, they have always had them in this community. The greenhouse women work long hours all year around—just because they're in the backyard is no sign they aren't working mothers."

Questions for Discussion

1. What broadly defined social forces might constitute the basic causes of the hot lunch debate in Homevale?

2. What might be the specific economic goals which are influencing the political ideals (hot lunch program) in this community?

3. What implications do the real or believed economic needs of Homevale have on the role of the schools?

4. If economic necessity does govern political ideals in Homevale, what circumstances must be present in order to assure the inclusion of an elaborate hot lunch program in the school?

Case 14.   Legislating for Vocational Education in the Midwest

In recent years the citizens of a rather heavily industrialized Midwestern state were being told that their state was not keeping pace with the "technological revolution." The major industries of steel, heavy machinery, automobiles, rubber, and petroleum products were slow in adopting manufacturing innovations. As a result, production was stable, but it was evident that many of the state's manufacturers were in a cost-profit squeeze and were finding it more and more difficult to compete.

The state is still among the nation's leaders in industrial production, value added by manufacture, and gross state product. However, during the past twenty years, it has slipped several positions in each of these categories. Furthermore, the state's rate of industrial growth is well below that of its East and West Coast competitors, its neighboring sister states, and the nation as a whole.

Several other dimensions of the economic slowdown have been identified. It was found by the state's congressmen in Washington that the biggest part of federal contracts was going to Eastern coast and Western states. Their state was found to be getting only 7 percent of these contracts. University interests in the state followed this disclosure with the fact that although the state was producing more Ph.D.s than most of her neighbors, it was losing a large proportion of them to other states. These highly trained men, by and large, were migrating to either universities or exotic industries located on either the East or West Coast.

It was also found that there was a severe shortage of highly skilled (and trained) technicians used to support the work of graduate engineers. This situation differed however from that of the migrating Ph.D.s. The state provided almost no training for technicians of any kind. Seemingly the state's secondary education program was almost exclusively college preparatory oriented. Post secondary school educational programs were in the main oriented to the baccalaureate degree. Thus a significant gap was found in the total educational program.

The lack of a technician training program was brought into sharp focus when the federal government started enacting legislation in the mid-1960s to reduce technological unemployment and underemployment. The Vocational Education Act of 1963 stimulated some thinking in the state as to what the schools should do to combat the growing unemployment problems. However, the consideration was general in nature, and the program has never been fully exploited in the state. Some of the large city school systems set up programs using the available federal monies but the idea was never fully implemented. The notion of maximum expansion of vocational and technical education simply did not penetrate to the grass roots of the state's educational system. When the federal government's "war on poverty" legislation indicated the eligibility of a surprisingly high number of families in the low-income category, the general population of this state apparently began to appreciate the nature of their problem. The general recognition of the problem plus the knowledge of federal monies available in the several related education bills seemed to stir state legislators, education groups, and other agencies to action.

As a result, the State Education Association and several of its related groups initiated a study of the state's vocational education program. The findings of the study led to the conclusions that (1) the vocational education program was inadequate to meet today's demands and (2) this inadequacy was caused by the inability and/or unwillingness of local communities to support these kinds of programs.

On the basis of the study and the relatively warm reception of it by the people of the state, the Association of Vocational Education Teachers spearheaded the organization of a broadly representative committee. The charge given the Committee for Vocational Education was to "develop specific proposals for the upgrading of vocational education in the state." The committee included educators, industrialists, lawyers, housewives, and physicians.

After a relatively short period of study, the committee submitted its proposal. In general it called for a comprehensive program of vocational education heavily subsidized by the state. It was designed as an additional reimbursable element in the state aid program to local school districts. Despite (or perhaps because of) popular support among educators and those primarily interested in education, the proposal was never introduced as legislation. When it became apparent that the vocational education interests had mobilized enough support to attract "big names" to a Committee for Vocational Education, many other influentials in the state sought to disseminate their ideas of the role and function of vocational education. The most formidable of these groups was a coalition of forces in the state legislature. The leader of this group, a state senator from a rural district, had a reputation of being an outspoken champion of both local control and low taxes.

Although the group was never formalized, it had de facto recognition in the state legislature. Several influential lobbies including the retail merchants, the state small businessmen's association, and several manufacturers' lobbies supplied many data to the group.

The end product which this informal legislative group offered was the introduction of a proposed amendment to the state's school code which required all school districts to provide an adequate vocational education program. This requirement was to be a condition of eligibility for each district's participation in the state subsidy to local school districts.

With the introduction of the bill into the legislature, it was obvious that vocational education in general had considerable support in the state. However, it was also apparent that many questions were raised. There were highly divergent points of view as to what vocational education should be. The question of how any expanded program was to be financed also loomed large.

In the hearings conducted on this bill, the Committee for Vocational Education exerted its total influence in opposition. The major points expressed by committee spokesmen at the hearings on the amendment were:

1. Vocational education is not exclusively a local concern. The quality and extent of vocational education in the local school district influence the entire state since there is considerable mobility of workers before, during, and after vocational education (if any) is provided in secondary schools.

2. Unemployment in one area of the state is an economic liability to the entire state.

3. Wholesome economic growth is dependent on the total and optimum use of all factors of production—especially that of labor.

4. The labor force of the state is largely recruited from youth of high school age. Eighty percent of this group has not completed a recognized vocational education program because (a) they were dropouts or (b) they did not have available or take advantage of a vocational education program.

5. The modern and progressive industry (which the state should attract) will recognize that expenditures for state taxes used to improve education are a form of investment. Good educational programs, especially vocational programs, will increase the productivity of the labor force employed. This will start a cycle of increased consumption–increased production–increased income–increased ability to pay taxes.

In defending their proposal, the forces supporting the state-required vocational education bill predicated their arguments on two lines of reasoning:

1. In order to bolster the economy, more industry must be attracted to the state. New industries are wont to move into a state where state taxation is rising. State financing of vocational education will require substantially more state revenues, and therefore additional taxes must be levied. Furthermore, this would be a continuing and probably an increasing state obligation. Thus, the state's tax climate would become less desirable and continue to be so for the immediate future. The net result would probably be no additional jobs or perhaps even fewer.

2. Public education is primarily a local concern. This is especially true of vocational education since the locality is the best judge of the type of program required in the given school district. If the state provides this program, local initiative and adaptability will be jeopardized. This in turn reduces the effectiveness of dollars invested in vocational education. Local dollars are the most efficient dollars.

In the legislative session being considered, only the state-required vocational education proposal was submitted to the lawmakers. Despite the opposition of the Committee for Vocational Education the proposal was enacted into law. Consequently, every local school district now must provide vocational education with no financial assistance from the state other than the amount formerly allocated to such programs.

Questions for Discussion

1. What evidence is there in this Midwestern state that the citizens will not, rather than cannot, provide for a needed governmental service?

2. What perception of economic necessity was held by the supporters of the state-required vocational education program? By the Committee on Vocational Education?

3. How did each of the above perceptions of economic necessity influence political ideals?

4. What possible benefits could come from the legislation which was finally enacted in regard to benefitting "those who are in a position to make and enforce the economic decisions"?

5. How might the perceptions of the role of government vary between the view held by the supporters of the state-required vocational education proposal as opposed to that view held by the Committee on Vocational Education?

Case 15.   Formulating Legislation to Provide Federal Aid to Education

The recurring concern for upgrading our nation's educational program became evident in a recent session of Congress. As in previous sessions, many and varied points of view were expressed as to the purpose and character of the federal role in public education. In the House of Representatives the predominant theme was the concern with the constantly widening gap between the intensity of social problems and the ability of public schools to contribute to the resolution of the problems. Members of the House of Representatives observed that while problems of urban decay and cultural deprivation grow more severe, the public schools become less able to cope with them. Likewise, while problems of unemployment and underemployment among youth become more widespread, the vocational and general education programs needed to solve these problems improve at a relatively slow rate. Consequently, there is a net loss in regard to solution of the problem. The same situation is present in problems concerning the ability of the school to relate to such phenomena as the knowledge explosion, the civil rights movement, natural resource exploitation and pollution, the population explosion, and ideological conflict.

Without exception, all the special House committees charged with the responsibility of studying these concerns developed recommendations which called for federally assisted educational programs. There was consensus that a unified education bill would be far more effective than piecemeal education programs attached to other major bills. It was further agreed that strong general education legislation was necessary and must be assured before any specific programs could be added as special supplementary activities.

The administration's proposed Omnibus School Aid Act provided a reasonable middle ground which satisfied both concerns. The bill, proposed in the President's message on education, assured to each state "those elements of an educational program which are necessary to upgrade all public schools to a minimum level, adequate to meet certain social needs which the public schools cannot or choose not to handle."

The several titles incorporated in the administration's bill included:

Title I—Extending Elementary and Secondary School Programs

Title II—Providing Instructional Media, Material, and Resources

Title III—Enriching and Supplementing School Programs

Title IV—Providing Research Bases and Coordinating Facilities

Title V—Supplementing Administrative Agencies

Title I of the act carried about 80 percent of the proposed appropriation and had the most visibility. It provided federal grants to school districts to upgrade the education of children in families with incomes below $2,000 and was seen as a major device to combat cultural deprivation through the schools.

The President's message on education and the delineation of the specifics of the administration's education bill consolidated the support for major educational legislation. Regional or group interests among legislators from the majority party became subordinated to the provisions of the bill. Consequently, many of the public school men who were influential with Cabinet members and with the President himself were invited to testify in behalf of the bill. One of these men was Dr. Calvert Devereaux, superintendent of schools in one of the larger cities located in the southeastern quadrant of the nation. Dr. Devereaux spoke not only as a public school administrator of one of the nation's large school systems, but also as a leader in the national professional organization for school administrators, and chairman of the Committee of Superintendents of Major Metropolitan School Districts.

Dr. Devereaux's school district is situated in a city with a present population of over 400,000 and prospects for relatively rapid growth in the future. The economic base of the community has been heavy industry with a recent trend toward electronics and aircraft manufacture. It has characteristics of many other large cities with a spreading central slum. There has been considerable migration of unskilled workers from rural areas into these degenerating neighborhoods.

Since Calvert Devereaux came to the city as a young mathematics department head, he developed for himself an enviable record as both an educational administrator and a leader in his profession. He was active in state and national organizations on several professional levels. Seven years ago, as assistant superintendent for staff personnel, he was elected president of the national organization for educational personnel administrators. Currently he serves as chairman of a national organization of school administrators. In the latter capacity, Devereaux organized a special subcommittee charged with investigating problems of urban education. As a result of the creative thinking exhibited in the subcommittee's report and his expert leadership, Devereaux was invited to testify before the House subcommittee on education of the Committee on Education and Labor. He presented testimony in behalf of Title I of the administration's Omnibus School Aid Act.

The subcommittee met on Monday, February 13, in Room 429 of the House Office Building, Hon. James D. Whittaker (chairman of the subcommittee) presiding. A quorum of representatives was present. These legislators were drawn from both political parties. Representatives present were Allison, D'Angelo, Cadwell, Place, Carter, Shoger, Hochschneider, and Gast. Also present were personnel from the office of education and counsel for the subcommittee and minority counsel for education.

Chairman Whittaker called the committee to order, indicated that a quorum was present, and then proceeded to welcome Calvert Devereaux.

"I certainly want to extend our welcome to you, Dr. Devereaux, to testify before this subcommittee in behalf of the Omnibus School Aid Act.

"For the benefit of my colleagues in the House who are not familiar with our nation's educational leaders, I wish to state that Dr. Calvert Devereaux is one of the most productive and responsible school administrators in the land. For many years now, he has held national office in his various professional organizations and presently serves as superintendent of schools in the largest city of his state. He is also chairman of one of the most influential educational groups, the Committee of Superintendents of Major Metropolitan School Districts.

"We welcome you here, Dr. Devereaux. You may proceed in any manner you prefer."

Devereaux thanked the chairman, introduced himself by name and position, then indicated he had a prepared statement he wished to have inserted in the record.

Chairman Whittaker acknowledged the receipt of the statement, declared it would be inserted in the record, and then called on Devereaux to summarize his statement.

The school superintendent began by indicating that the intent of his statement was one of supporting the Omnibus School Aid Act in behalf of the Superintendents of Major Metropolitan School Districts, an organization representing the fifty largest cities of the nation. He communicated the gratitude of the literally millions of people living in these cities for the recent federal legislation which made space age education possible. Special recognition was given to the National Defense Education Act and the Vocational Act.

Dr. Devereaux proceeded to point out that education in urban centers now possesses some compelling and unique needs. Several interrelated social movements have combined to produce knotty problems in metropolitan areas. Technology has revolutionized the nation's production patterns and in turn has reduced employment in jobs which require little skill. The unskilled, unemployed workers tend to migrate to cities where they concentrate in slum areas. All these factors produce a self-perpetuating cycle of ignorance–poverty–crime–social alienation–ignorance–poverty. Education is recognized as the best hope of breaking this cycle, but the type of education needed in these urban centers differs from conventional school programs in purpose, approach, and financing. Legislation to provide this type of education is in the federal province since it is both in the nation's interest and within the nation's ability to resolve the problem of urban education.

The superintendent of schools concluded this summary of his statement with a plea that Title I of the Omnibus School Aid Act be passed in order that "the federal government help the public schools to help themselves."

Chairman Whittaker thanked Devereaux for his cogent statement of a complex and compelling problem.

"Your statement is both a source of concern and comfort. We are concerned with the enormity of a confounding situation. But at the same time we are comforted with the realization that you and the other educational leaders from our large cities are cognizant of it and have determined a way you may join hands with your federal government to resolve it."

Following this acknowledgment, the subcommittee chairman recognized Representative Allison.

"Mr. Chairman, I have several questions of a fundamental nature which I would like to explore with Dr. Devereaux.

"Dr. Devereaux, I am certain that you recognize that as superintendent of schools you are responsible for the administration of one of the most important local governmental units. It is my observation that the strength of these and other local government units is derived from the fact that they are independent and not subject to control by other units. If local programs must be expanded to accommodate people with these problems, why can't this be done by the cities themselves? Generally speaking, they have more taxing ability than most school districts in the states."

Calvert Devereaux hesitated a few moments before he responded.

"Congressman Allison, there isn't a major city in the United States that hasn't set up some kind of a locally financed program in its schools to combat cultural deprivation. None of these, however, is anywhere near adequate. In the study of our fifty major metropolitan school districts we found several reasons why cities couldn't do this on their own.

"First, there is no prototype. In order to provide the needed creative approach, we must have research and development. Sophisticated and basic research into the problem requires time, organization, and money.

"A second reason which is closely related to the first is that since the considerable outlay required is controlled by the local people—usually by a vote for additional tax money—we must first convince them of the necessity of it before we can obtain it. In most cities where the problem is critical—and here I am generalizing—it is very difficult to convince the unemployed, poverty-stricken, and the culturally deprived resident that we must raise taxes to solve his problems. In most cases, he is apathetic rather than antitax in attitude. Sometimes these people feel that they would be better off if the schools were closed. They are that alienated, they are that much 'antieducation.'

"A third reason that these monies cannot be raised exclusively on the local level is that it is also hard to convince the nondeprived voter his money should be spent to upgrade education for the culturally deprived. Many times our good solid citizens are of the opinion that these new arrivals came to us with inferior school experiences. Thus, city residents reason that the fault and the consequent responsibility lie in the school district of origin of these deprived people.

"Lastly, property owners in major cities frequently do not themselves live in the city proper. Thus, we do not have the leverage of saying, 'If you do not vote additional taxes, it will adversely affect your child's education.' Consequently many of these property owners choose not to support locally financed educational programs designed to combat cultural deprivation."

"Would you cite the same reasons for the inability of the state to finance these programs?" asked Representative Allison. "Supposedly, if the programs go beyond the locality, we should next look to the state."

"In general," replied Devereaux, "the same reasons may be given when one asks the question of why the state cannot provide the financing for these programs. However, several other situations also mitigate against exclusive state support for them.

"In our state, as is true in most, the classical interpretation of the state school foundation program or the state school aid program is used. In essence, this sets up a minimum program or a minimum cost per pupil that the state guarantees for each school district. Realistically, no state includes a program to combat cultural deprivation in its financing plan.

"Another factor responsible for the lack of state support for these programs stems from the rural-urban split we find in many of our state legislatures. By and large, rural legislators will not support legislation which is aimed at predominantly urban problems. Even though many of the city slum dwellers come from deprived rural environments, the problem does not become obvious until they congregate in the city."

Representative D'Angelo was recognized by the subcommittee chairman. After making reference to Dr. Devereaux's demonstrated ability for maximizing educational outputs for each dollar expended, he asked the following.

"Will this federal legislation reduce local and state incentive to maintain and upgrade educational programs?"

"No, it will not. The legislation requires that local school districts maintain at least their past year's level of expenditures, so federal money will not replace state and local money. Although the legislation does not call for increases in state and local expenditures, I believe that federal money will provide a powerful incentive for local districts. Because it will enable the local districts to make more decisions, not fewer, local control will be enhanced, not depreciated. In my experience, when a community is given more decision-making power, it has an incentive to make greater investments in education."

Seeing there were no more questions, Chairman Whittaker thanked the witness and expressed the appreciation of the subcommittee for the appearance of Dr. Devereaux. Representative Whittaker then recessed the hearing until 10:30 A.M.

Questions for Discussion

1. How does the proposed Omnibus School Aid Act illustrate the dynamic role of government?

2. What economic considerations might be entertained as one explores the desirability of federal aid to education for the purpose of combating cultural deprivation and poverty?

3. In Dr. Devereaux's testimony, what economic considerations might explain the attitude of the local power structure in opposing the use of local revenues in combating cultural deprivation and poverty?

4. If the federal government assumes the role as suggested in the Omnibus School Aid Act, what roles might the federal government also assume in the near future?

5. What major shift in the role of the federal government will occur if the Omnibus School Aid Act is passed? What shifts might be affected in the role of the local school district if the act is passed? What shifts might be affected in the role of the state if the act is passed?

Suggested Readings

Concept E—Economic Influences on the Role of Government

Allen, Hollis P.: *The Federal Government and Education*, New York: McGraw-Hill, 1950.

American Association of School Administrators: *The Federal Government and the Public Schools*, Washington, D.C.: The Association, 1965.

————: *Federal Policy and the Public Schools*, Washington, D.C.: The Association, 1967.

Center for the Advanced Study of Educational Administration: *The Economic Returns to Education*, Eugene, Oreg.: The Center: 1965.

Committee for Economic Development: *Fiscal Issues in the Future of Federalism*, New York: The Committee, 1968.

————: *A Fiscal Program for a Balanced Federalism*, New York: The Committee, 1967.

————: *Modernizing Local Government*, New York: The Committee, 1966.

————: *Modernizing State Government*, New York: The Committee, 1967.

————: *The National Economy and the Vietnam War*, New York: The Committee, 1968.

————: *Paying for Better Schools*, New York: The Committee, 1959.

————: *Raising Low Incomes Through Improved Education*, New York: The Committee, 1965.

Galbraith, John K.: *The Affluent Society*, Boston: Houghton Mifflin, 1958.

————: *The New Industrial State*, Boston: Houghton Mifflin, 1967.

Gardner, John W.: *Creative Federalism*, Washington, D.C.: Department of Health, Education, and Welfare, October, 1966.

Groves, Harold M.: *Education and Economic Growth*, Washington, D.C.: National Education Association, 1961.

Heilbroner, Robert L., and Peter L. Bernstein: *A Primer on Government Spending*, New York: Vintage Books, 1963.

Hirsch, Werner Z., et al.: *Inventing Education for the Future*, San Francisco: Chandler, 1967. (Master article)

James, H. Thomas, J. Alan Thomas, and Harold J. Dyck: *Wealth, Expenditures, and Decision-making for Education*, U.S. Department of Health, Education, and Welfare, Office of Education, Cooperative Research Project No. 1241, an Extension of Cooperative Research Project No. 803, Stanford, Calif.: Stanford University, June, 1963.

Lovenstein, Meno: *Economics and the Educational Administrator*, Columbus, Ohio: School-Community Development Study Monograph, College of Education, The Ohio State University, 1958.

McConnell, Campbell R.: *Economics*, 4th ed., New York: McGraw-Hill, 1969, chap. 6, pp. 92–104.

Meranto, Philip: *The Politics of Federal Aid to Education in 1965: A Study in Political Innovation*, Syracuse, N.Y.: Syracuse University Press, 1967.

Munger, Frank J., and Richard F. Fenno, Jr.: *National Politics and Federal Aid to Education*, Syracuse, N.Y.: Syracuse University Press, 1962.

Ott, David J., and Attiat F. Ott: *Federal Budget Policy*, Washington, D.C.: The Brookings Institution, 1965.

Samuelson, Paul A.: *Economics*, 7th ed., New York: McGraw-Hill, 1967, chap. 8.

Tiedt, Sidney W.: *The Role of the Federal Government in Education*, New York: Oxford University Press, 1966.

Economic Dimensions of Public Finance

the problem

The primary goal of any social institution is to meet a given societal need. However, institutions must be concerned not only with ends, but also with means to attain these ends. It has been observed that the methods which an institution uses have a marked influence on the way in which the end is met. The school as one public agency is influenced by all others in the social system in terms of both the ends it seeks and the means utilized in attaining the ends.

The study of public finance explores ways that governmental activities are financed and ways in which governmental activities influence the total community. Decision makers in education are faced with problems not only in determining the appropriate role of the school but also what is the best way to finance the services necessary to implement the role. However, because other governmental activities influence the total community including the school, educators must also address themselves to the question: What other policies of government which are noneducational in nature are most appropriate to further societal goals in general and educational goals in particular?

the concept

In a previous discussion (income determination) the influence of spending for newly produced goods and services was stressed. It does not matter, it was emphasized, whether this spending is made by consumers or businesses or governments; the effect on income (measured as gross national product) is the same. This is true, but a more detailed analysis of government spending is in order.

The income-influencing activities of government can be divided into three principal parts: spending, taxing, and borrowing. The latter, in turn, can be divided into two subparts: borrowing from the public and borrowing from the banking system. Each of these activities has a different and distinct influence on the economy.

Government spending has a direct influence on income. As spending is increased, income is increased. If the government decides to reduce the level of spending, gross national product will be reduced. If government could confine its economic activities to spending alone without resorting to either taxing or borrowing, it would be a simple matter to fix the level of government spending at the amount necessary to attain the optimum gross national product. Taxing, however, reduces gross national product by reducing the funds available for spending by the consumers and businesses who pay the taxes to the government. Borrowing, if the funds are obtained from the public, will also reduce the funds available for spending. If the borrowed funds are obtained from the banking system, however, the result is to increase the amount of money in the economy and so may have an inflationary influence on prices. The conflicting effects of these activities complicates the efforts designed to use government outlays to achieve a gross national product sufficient to provide for full employment. As a result, public finance, which is the study of the spending, taxing, and borrowing activities of government, is difficult for the average layman to understand. Its importance for the economy, however, cannot be overstressed.

The idea that public finance activities can and should be used to influence the level of gross national product was first popularized by John Maynard Keynes.[1]

Many economists have developed further the ideas of Keynes in the years following the publication of his book, but no one has presented them more provocatively than Abba Lerner.[2] In this article, Lerner argues that government spending should be used purposely to maintain the level of gross national product needed to achieve full employment. Taxes, on the other hand, should never be imposed, says Lerner, unless it is desired that consumers or businesses spend less money. These two policies might very often lead to deficits requiring that the government borrow. Such borrowing should be from the banking system unless it is desired that the public hold less money, in which case the securities could be sold to nonbank investors. It was Lerner's contention that through following these policies it would be possible to maintain full employment without inflation and at the same time to achieve at least the minimum desired level of economic growth.

The undeviating adoption of the Lerner proposals would make the sole function of government an economic one, which of course is not practical. Government has many necessary tasks which cannot be reduced in emphasis in spite of the inflationary effects such activities might have. The obvious solution is a combination of taxing, spending, and borrowing which will permit government to carry out the functions it must and at the same time have the maximum effect on employment, income, and price stability.

---

[1] John Maynard Keynes, *The General Theory of Employment, Interest and Money,* Harcourt, Brace and Company, Inc., New York, 1963.
[2] Abba Lerner, "Functional Finance," *Social Research,* September, 1943.

It must also be stressed that the income-influencing activities of consumers and businesses have the same four parts as for governments, and each part affects income and employment in the same way. Any program designed to influence such income and employment concentrates on the economic activities of government, however, because only the activities of government can be altered to any practical degree. Little control can be exercised over consumers and businesses.

It must be emphasized further that the program proposed by Lerner will work if we are willing to adopt it. The tax cut of 1964, an attempt to increase income and employment through the deliberate fostering of a deficit in the federal budget, was a distinct success. Attempts during 1966 and 1967, however, to increase taxes with the stated purpose of easing the existing inflationary pressures, were staunchly resisted by a majority of Congress, and it was not until 1968 that a tax increase was finally passed. In the minds of the individual congressman, at least, the public did not believe that the alternative to a tax increase was a rise in prices which would reduce real income by as much as the tax increase. The effects of the tax cut would be visible; the effects of inflation would not be so noticeable. For fiscal policy to be effective in controlling the economy, we must be willing to accept tax increases as well as decreases. In view of our most recent experience in this area, it would seem that we are not yet ready to adopt the program proposed by Abba Lerner.

Case 16.   A Platform for Economic Vitality

When Thomas Henderson made the decision to run for the governorship of his state, it was clear that his stand on certain economic issues would become important planks in his platform. People, both within and outside the state, were aware of the state's economic problems. The state was eligible for sizable grants from the recent "Appalachia" legislation and other measures associated with the war on poverty program.

The state has had a long-standing reputation for being a chronically depressed area. The first problems of this sort became nationally visible during the depression of the 1930s. Farmers working submarginal and subsistence farms were unable to draw a living from their mountainous acreage. The coal mines, by cutting production, induced unemployment which in turn precipitated widespread and bloody strikes. These in turn (according to the mine management) contributed to the eventual shutdown of many more mines. Industrial production in the state was gradually reduced.

However, with the advent of World War II heavy demands for

war goods and supplies for the Allied powers and the consequent labor shortage and economic boom breathed new life into the state's economy. This stimulus was temporary and shallow. Shortly after the war, the old economic problems returned and appeared even more formidable. Unemployment became prevalent among the semi-skilled as well as the unskilled, the submarginal workers, and the "hard core unemployables." Industrial plants of the state which were operating on military contracts could not meet the competition of larger and highly automated industries when they switched over to peacetime consumers' goods. Substantial numbers of the more able and employable workers emigrated to several nearby states which retained flourishing economies. Thus, a segment of the population with the ability and need to spend left the state at the time they were most needed.

As the economic decline progressed, the public schools of the state received less and less financial support. In some sections of the state, local property values declined markedly and thus reduced the amount of local tax monies available to the schools. It also became more difficult to obtain state revenues, while demands increased for more and larger state programs. Most conspicuous among these were welfare, unemployment, and similar programs.

As a life-long resident of the state, Thomas Henderson felt he knew and appreciated the problems of such regions. He also believed himself qualified to propose and implement a program to resolve them.

Tom Henderson was born and reared in a small county-seat town near the state capital. His grandfather served twenty-two years as an elected county judge and his father held the same post for the subsequent sixteen years. Tom received an appointment as a U.S. Senate page, attended the state university, completed a baccalaureate degree in political science, accepted a commission into the Air Force, and flew combat missions over Korea. Upon his return to civilian life, Tom Henderson completed a law degree, was admitted to the bar, and accepted a partnership in a law firm in his hometown. After five years with the law firm Tom was elected to the State Assembly and served three terms. During this period he assumed the leadership role for economic development programs and established his reputation as an expediter for the legislation necessary to qualify for and to implement jointly financed federal-state projects.

Thomas M. Henderson announced his candidacy for nomination as governor of the state shortly after a vigorous, young candidate for the presidency of the United States opened his own campaign for nomination. When the presidential candidate emphasized his commitment to "getting the nation moving again," Tom Henderson gladly accepted identification with such an attractive national figure.

Playing on this identification, Henderson described the economic problems he saw in the state. He observed that the state's unemployment rate was not only much higher than the average of the nation as a whole, but was also increasing faster than the rate for the nation.

Data regarding the value added by manufacture in the state for the last decade illustrated that proportionally the state was falling behind the nation and particularly several surrounding states. Supportive of these data were figures which showed not only relative but absolute reduction in capital outlay by industry over the past few years. Henderson thus concluded that the state could anticipate a continued decline in economic activity unless strong and positive action was taken soon.

The tax picture presented by the candidate was also gloomy. The present "patchwork of stop gap taxes, poorly conceived to solve an ill-defined problem" was, according to Henderson, contributing to the problem rather than resolving it.

Tom Henderson suggested that major problems existed also in the financing of state programs. Not only were many of these undersupported, but also some serious imbalances were present. He pointed to inadequate expenditures for education on both local and state levels. Relationships between educational support levels and economic productivity were noted among other states. Henderson implied that increases in economic productivity could be expected when "additional investments in education were made."

The "politically expeditious" methods of borrowing money for state programs, especially capital improvement projects, were hit by the gubernatorial candidate. This dimension of the state's public finance program was condemned on the basis of its scope and timing as well.

In terms of the platform planks to be recommended, Thomas Henderson suggested that the party consider giving primary emphasis to those relating to the state's economic plight. He proposed that:

1. The state government should launch a positive program touching on all dimensions of public finance.

a. State government expenditures should be markedly increased so as to raise levels of both employment and income among the workers of the state.

b. State government programs singled out for substantial budget increases were public education and related activities which tend to increase both capacity to produce and proclivity to consume.

c. The taxation program of the state should be modified so as to effect an overall delay in applying taxes. Since it is important to raise the level of spending in order to raise incomes, it is equally important initially to protect this increase in income. Thus, taxes to support these expanded programs will not be imposed on a pay-as-you-go basis but will be levied after the economy generates some momentum. This will of course result in some early deficit spending which will be absorbed later by taxing the expanded economic base.

d. The gap between spending and income derived through taxation should be met by means of government borrowing. State legislation aimed at channeling increased state borrowing through the banking system should be developed so as to minimize the income-reducing effect of borrowing.

2. The state government should closely relate its public finance policies to those of the federal government. The federal tax cut of 1964, designed to stimulate economic growth, should be augmented and supplemented on the state level so as to take full advantage of the economic upsurge generated by this federal legislation.

3. The state should provide leadership to the consumer and business community in order to demonstrate best the viability of these public finance concepts. State leadership should suggest the applicability of the basic concepts to the private sector as well.

a. The state should promote public confidence in the economy so as to expand consumer spending in order to raise the level of employment and income within the state.

b. Business interests of the state should be encouraged to make long-term investments in their productive capacity through use of credit extended by banks. This will also have the net effect of increasing spending and hence employment. Naturally, a greater increase of consumer and business spending will make possible a lower proportion of government spending.

As the date of the primary election approached, Tom Henderson felt confident his "public finance and economics" platform was sound.

Questions for Discussion

1. In a state such as the one in which Thomas Henderson lived, what specific state spending programs might be considered as appropriate? Why?

2. What means might a state use in order to stimulate greater spending in the private sector among businesses? Among the consumers?

3. What might be the immediate effects of greater expenditures for public education? Why?

4. What might be the long-term effects of greater expenditures for public education? Why?

Case 17. Fiscal Coordination in Cooperston

Cooperston is an upper-middle-class suburb situated adjacent to the capital city of one of the Rocky Mountain states. The population, now at or near 18,000, is drawn primarily from the professional or artisan class. When compared with similar communities on the East Coast or in the Middle West, Cooperston is a new community having been settled during the last fifty years.

Perhaps the most outstanding characteristic of the city and its inhabitants is the spirit of independence. Although they do not scorn tradition and most openly respect a conservative point of view, these people also prize "rugged individualism." This is demonstrated among individuals and also in the actions of the governing boards of the several local taxing units. Members of each board are strongly committed to the notion that a public trust has been placed with those who were chosen to formulate policy for the various governmental functions. Members of each board are proud of the economy and efficiency shown in the running of their own particular agency. There is an admittedly "wholesome competition" among the boards governing the city's school district, municipal government, and park district. Seldom does a service club luncheon go on without there being some good-natured joking regarding one agency outdoing another. Each seems determined to show that it can give more service to the city per taxpayer dollar than any other agency.

Almost since its original settlement, Cooperston has enjoyed prosperity. Even when the nation as a whole was in recession or depression, the community maintained a relatively healthy economy. Now, in the midst of a booming national prosperity, Cooperston reflects these conditions to an even greater extent. The city has enjoyed high employment but now there appears to be an actual labor shortage—especially in certain high skill and professional fields. There has always been a brisk demand for goods and services in the community but now shortages in certain commodities have appeared. Prices on consumables in the city have for some time been a bit higher than elsewhere in the area but recently costs of living have increased faster than the earnings in the community. The professionals living in

Cooperston have become much concerned since the recent increases in their salaries have not been sufficient to offset the rising spiral of the cost of living.

This concern has permeated the thinking of the several governing boards of local government. The issues, for which the boards have the responsibility of decision making, are now being considered in light of the severe local manifestation of a national problem.

The Cooperston City Council must make a decision as to paying off an issue of callable bonds. Six years ago a forward-looking city council developed a long-range and comprehensive master plan for the city. This plan included provisions for the installation of sewers to accommodate the future growth of the city. Sewer lines were extended into then undeveloped subdivisions which, according to predictions, would not be built up for another fifteen or twenty years. Now these areas are nearly saturated, and the system is functioning as anticipated.

Not only has the mechanical plan for the sewer project proved to be adequate and efficient, but also the financing plan has functioned very well. The schedule of special assessments, hookup charges, and sewer rates as well as the tax rates to operate the system were well conceived and have provided an adequate financial base. Consequently, the opportunity has now presented itself wherein it appears feasible to pay off a block of the callable bonds issued six years ago. This would necessitate an increased tax rate but would reduce the long-term debt of the city. Members of the city council recognize that paying off the bonds would call for immediate sacrifice to gain the long-term advantage of not paying interest on the bonds if they were allowed to remain outstanding. They are also aware that in the present inflationary trend the general population is calling for lower taxes to offset higher prices of goods and services.

The Cooperston School District was represented on the committee which was responsible for the development of the city's master plan. Since the completion of the plan, the board of education has taken full advantage of the data and the consultant's advice in such matters as the location of the school buildings. Small but expandable buildings were constructed on the large sites. The several school buildings which have since been built have had neighborhoods fill in around them, pretty much as the master plan had assumed. Thus, the school district has enjoyed an orderly growth and today, although all schools are nearly filled to capacity, no school is drastically overcrowded.

A key decision that the Cooperston Board of Eductaion must make is the method of constructing and financing new school facilities as these are needed. Even though there is no severe overcrowding presently, it is apparent that additional classrooms, cafeterias, and gymnasia will be needed within two years. Since the anticipated growth will probably have an even distribution throughout the district rather than being limited to specific "open areas," the board members are of the opinion that construction should be limited to additions to and renovations in present school buildings. This contention is further supported by the fact that the original buildings were flexible in design and situated on sufficiently large sites to accommodate schools of maximal size for the given type of organization (elementary, junior high, senior high).

There are several alternate methods of financing the anticipated school construction. In this state the most popular method is that of floating a bond issue to obtain the large amount of money needed for constructing the facilities. The issue would be paid off by semiannual payments of principal and interest. Thus, money for construction is available immediately, new facilities of large scale can be provided very readily, and the financial obligation is liquidated on a deferred payment basis.

A second method which has been getting considerable attention in the state is the establishment of a special tax levy designated for the construction and renovation of school facilities. This pay-as-you-go building fund must be approved by qualified electors as it is over and above the regular tax program to operate schools. It provides monies for construction each year, the amount being determined by the tax rate extended against the assessed value of real property in the district. When this method is compared with bonding, it usually produces less money for construction in a given year, but it assures an annual flow of smaller amounts that will increase as the real property valuation of the district increases.

A third method is that of using the capital outlay classification in the regular operating budget. This budget item is merged with others to form the operating budget of the school district. However, tax limitation laws in this state, as in most others also, are restrictive to the point that it is feasible to undertake only the most modest renovation projects and still maintain a respectable instruction program. Consequently, this alternative provides only a small amount of money annually for minor construction and renovation.

In assessing these problems and the alternatives available to resolve them, the Cooperston Board of Education has become aware of several factors which bear on the decision.

The inflationary character of both the national and local economy has considerable influence on the board's decision. It is felt that in an inflation the community will get "less school building per dollar spent" because of the high prices on labor and materials. There is a concern that because of inflation on the national level, the money supply will "tighten up" and higher rates of interest will be charged on the bonds sold in order to finance the construction projects.

The character of school building needs is also a factor considered by the board members. It is assumed that a program of construction and renovation is inevitable in maintaining good quality in the educational program. However, careful analysis of need suggested the feasibility of a modest but long-term program of construction rather than a single massive program of building one or two entirely new school plants.

A third major factor which is thought to bear heavily on the decision is that related to the opinion of the voters on the question of how to finance the construction program. It appears that many people are of the opinion that because of inflation they simply cannot stand a marked increase in property taxes. Of those who favor adding physical facilities, most prefer modest tax increases to finance a bond issue rather than a higher tax for direct capital outlay expenditures. Consequently, it is assumed by the board that there would be considerable resistance to a heavy tax to finance school construction.

The Cooperston Park and Recreation Board has only recently gained prominence among the city's public servants. Until last year the board had the responsibility of overseeing the management of a dozen small neighborhood parks, the Veterans Memorial Center, the Municipal Stadium, and the city's summer recreation program which was conducted in cooperation with the board of education. However, last year the park and recreation board accepted title to a 360-acre parcel of land bordering the Municipal Stadium site. This plot was designated as a wilderness area to be used for camping, hiking, nature study, and similar activities. Community enthusiasm was high and there was immediate public pressure to open it for use. A small additional tax levy was approved for the anticipated expense of operation, but according to the projections of rent and use charges nearly all the operating costs could be covered by these nontax monies.

A major problem developed, however, when it was recognized that a full year would elapse before the additional tax monies would be available. The rent and use charges would be collected during the initial season and hence would not be available for the preparation of the area. The cost of preparing the wilderness area also exceeded original estimates. Considerable labor was involved in opening trails, clearing out debris and noxious weeds, pruning, trimming, and opening streams. Consequently, the park and recreation board spent its entire budget for personnel services during the first quarter of the fiscal year. Revenues from taxes as well as rents and charges were almost assured, but they were not collectable for several months.

Two obvious alternatives were considered by the board. Tax anticipation warrants could be issued to cover salaries for the next few months or a bank loan could be secured. The members of the park and recreation board had never done either of these previously, and so it seemed entirely natural for the members to consult with their friends on the school board and on the city council.

When the first informal conversations began among members of the three governing bodies, it became obvious that the problems were not simple or mechanical in nature. Members of the council and the board of education cited the factors which they felt must be considered in the resolution of similar problems. As a result of a few informal conversations, it was decided that a joint session involving the three governing bodies should be convened. At the meeting, all the most pressing financial problems were reviewed and analyzed. From the latter process it was determined that solutions to the problems of specific bodies could not be effectively resolved without considering the whole local environment as well as the national scene.

All three groups recognized that there were needs to expand public services and all these services required expenditure of public monies. It was also recognized that the inflationary nature of the rapidly growing national and local economy posed real problems for Cooperston as it expanded public services. It was obvious that the additional services should be provided without adding substantially to the inflation. The best way to finance these public services would be through an immediate rather than a deferred tax program. When it was necessary to borrow money, it would be least harmful if loans were obtained from the public rather than the banking system.

As a result of these discussions, the three Cooperston governing bodies have established guidelines for decision making in their own problem areas. The city council is seriously considering paying off the bonds which are callable, thus reducing the long-term debt as well as counteracting inflation.

The Cooperston Board of Education is considering the pay-as-you-go plan for financing renovation of old buildings and the construction of additions to existing buildings. It is proposed that this plan should be used until the inflationary threat is over.

The park and recreation board will shortly act on a proposal to issue tax anticipation warrants to cover operating costs until tax monies are received. This alternative is supported by the argument that borrowing from banks will stimulate inflation whereas borrowing from individuals will retard inflation.

Questions for Discussion

1. What is the likely effect on income in Cooperston if the several local projects are undertaken by the three local units of government?

2. Why does the source of the needed revenues for the projects become important?

3. What are the relative merits of financing government expenditures during an inflationary period through:
   a. Pay-as-you-go taxation
   b. Issuance of bonds
   c. Government borrowing through the banking system

Suggested Readings

Concept F—Economic Dimensions of Public Finance

Allen, Hollis P.: *The Federal Government and Education*, New York: McGraw-Hill, 1950.

American Association of School Administrators: *The Federal Government and the Public Schools*, Washington, D.C.: The Association, 1965.

————: *Federal Policy and the Public Schools*, Washington, D.C.: The Association, 1967.

Burkhead, Jesse: *State and Local Taxes for Public Education*, Syracuse, N.Y.: Syracuse University Press, 1963.

Committee for Economic Development: *Fiscal Issues in the Future of Federalism*, New York: The Committee, 1968.

————: *A Fiscal Program for A Balanced Federalism*, New York: The Committee, 1967.

————: *The National Economy and the Vietnam War*, New York: The Committee, 1968.

Corbally, John E., Jr.: *School Finance*, Boston: Allyn and Bacon, 1962.

Gardner, John W.: *Creative Federalism*, Washington, D.C.: Department of Health, Education, and Welfare, October, 1966.

Groves, Harold M.: *Education and Economic Growth*, Washington, D.C.: National Education Association, 1961.

Hirsch, Werner Z., et al.: *Inventing Education for the Future*, San Francisco: Chandler, 1967.

McConnell, Campbell R.: *Economics*, 4th ed., New York: McGraw-Hill, 1969, chap. 9, pp. 136–137, chap. 14, pp. 247–264.

Meranto, Philip: *The Politics of Federal Aid to Education in 1965: A Study in Political Innovation*, Syracuse, N.Y.: Syracuse University Press, 1967.

Musgrave, Richard A.: *The Theory of Public Finance*, New York: McGraw-Hill, 1959.

National Committee for Support of Public Schools: *Changing Demands on Education and Their Fiscal Implications*, Washington, D.C.: The Committee, 1963.

Poole, Kenyon E.: *Public Finance and Economic Welfare*, New York: Rinehart, 1956.

Samuelson, Paul A.: *Economics*, 7th ed., New York: McGraw-Hill, 1967, chap. 19.

Taylor, Philip E.: *The Economics of Public Finance*, New York: Macmillan, 1953.

Education—Public or Private

the problem

The public nature of our public schools demands dedication to both the needs of the community as well as the moral and financial support of the community. Consequently the structure of the public school system frequently reflects two apparently conflicting or incompatible values. On one hand, the school system seeks to establish a high minimum standard of education available to all children in the state. On the other hand, however, a high value is placed on promoting local initiative wherein a given community inaugurates and finances a specific educational program which is supplementary to the basic or minimum program.

The same problem is manifest on the level of the individual citizen. He has a pattern of choice regarding educational opportunities to be made available to his child. He has a vote in determining which educational facilities are to be provided through the school system. He also determines which facilities his child will obtain through private means. In order to make these decisions adequately, the educator and the layman must consider the economic bases of private versus public support.

the concept

Elementary and secondary education has been typically a public function in the United States for many years. An adherence to the principle of universal school attendance, regardless of place of residence, wealth, or individual ability, with such attendance financed by the public treasury, has been the American pattern. It has also been the pattern for the schools to be operated as a public enterprise.

The undeniably higher levels of personal productivity, together with the accompanying higher levels of personal and national income, and the improved functioning of our democratic institutions, do not permit a logical questioning of universal education. Nor can the principle of public financing of education be a serious topic for debate. It does not necessarily follow, however, that the schools need be operated by the government. It is pointed out that if the school is operated by a governmental unit, attendance must be to the school operated by the government unit in which the student lives. This fixes the quality of the education provided at that level desired by the majority of the voters residing in the district, and greatly reduces the freedom of choice available to each family. Unless a family is sufficiently affluent to pay private school fees in addition to the taxes levied by the local school district, that family must be satisfied with the quality of education provided.

Recognizing that many families would be unable to afford the outlays necessary for even a minimum level of education and being well aware of the vital concern the general public has in an educated society, no responsible person advocates an abandonment of public financing. However some persons, notably Prof. Milton Friedman of the University of Chicago, advocate that the government provide tuition credits to be spent with the private school chosen by the student. The credits provided would be in the amount necessary to provide the minimum level education desired by the electorate; if a family wished to supplement the amount available from the public treasury to provide a better education for its child, it could do so. The additional cost would not be so great as at present, however.

Friedman would have the schools operated by private enterprises for profit or by private nonprofit institutions; and the role of government would be limited to the establishment of minimum educational standards, to the provision of funds needed to purchase this minimum standard for each school child, and to the inspection of private schools to be sure that the minimum standards are being maintained. Friedman maintains that this program would work as well as the federally financed educational program for veterans following World War II. He wants the program to be limited to elementary and secondary education, however, for it is his belief that higher education is totally for the benefit of the student, and he should pay the entire cost.

Friedman recognizes that in some sparsely populated areas it is practical for only one school to exist, that this program would tend to accentuate class distinctions, and that the establishment of an acceptable minimum standard would be difficult. All these objections Friedman feels are outweighed by the widening of choices available to the student.

Freedom of choice is highly desirable; whether it is worth the price that Professor Friedman is willing to pay is questionable. The proliferation of schools would undoubtedly mean substantially higher costs, as the economies of large-scale operation would be eliminated. Even more important, the Friedman program would almost certainly establish a class system which could conceivably lead to a substantial alteration of our democratic system. Such a price would be much too high.

The limitation of public involvement in only the elementary and secondary educational levels can also be challenged. Society benefits from an educated population, higher education as well as elementary and secondary. It is not even certain that the student benefits more from a college education than does the society as a whole. Public financing of higher education can very logically be supported on economic grounds; in fact the trend toward increased student fees at state universities is a movement which should be resisted.

In spite of the advantages of the public schools, efforts should be made continually to meet the objections against the publicly operated system. The student should be presented with as great a variety of choices as possible, and the advantages of public operation should be improved constantly, e.g., the savings from large-scale operations and the tendency to eliminate class distinctions. Such actions will bolster and strengthen the public school system.

Case 18.   Decision at Southgate

Southgate City has fulfilled the destiny of its name in many ways. Situated on both slopes of a gap which breaches a long ridge, it was until a hundred years ago the state's most convenient gateway to the South. This state, always considered as a border state, has served as a buffer between the rural, agricultural South and the urban, industrial North. Consequently, Southgate City has developed the character of a unique border city in a unique border state.

In its role as an intermediary between North and South, the city has profited commercially and culturally to a much larger extent than have the farmers and villagers living out in the hills and hollows of the more remote parts of McNabb County. The state as a whole has been considered somewhat poor economically since it does not have the endowments of natural resources to enable it to be wealthy in either industry or agriculture. Considering these limitations of natural resources, the state legislators decided that the best way to expand the economy of the state was to upgrade the productive capacity of its people through education. In assessing local school systems, it was obvious that the state as a whole was well below the national average on nearly all measures. It was observed, however, that certain school districts in the state were above the national average and well above the state average on these measures. Nearly all "above-average districts" possessed a unique resource or offered a unique commercial service. Southgate City and Addiston, one of its suburbs, were frequently mentioned examples of the latter classification. As a consequence, when legislators were seeking ways to finance an upgraded state educational program, a proposal was made to reorganize school districts on a countywide basis and thus eliminate small inefficient districts and somewhat equalize tax bases. Despite the fact there was solid opposition from the wealthier communities, the measure passed and was enacted into law.

After several years of operation under the new county school district pattern of organization, criticism of the reorganization did not abate. The more wealthy communities continued to be most vocal in their opposition. In Addiston, Carl Olson was the leading opponent of the reorganization. His criticism carried considerable weight since he was the former president of the Addiston Board of Education and was an outspoken advocate of "excellence in education." As an executive in a multistate trucking firm, Olson had been promoted to the managership of the Southgate Terminal from the Cleveland, Ohio office. While in Cleveland, the Olsons lived in an upper-class suburb which prided itself in the "best schools in this part of the country."

Carl Olson's values had been clearly reflected in the policies of the former Addiston school district. Addiston was a relatively homogeneous upper-class community which demanded a college preparatory type school program. Since it also was exclusively residential, the community taxed itself quite heavily to provide excellence in education. Thus, prior to the reorganization, the property tax rate for schools in the Addiston district was the highest of all districts in McNabb County.

When Carl Olson began a campaign of criticism against the reorganization legislation, it was not based on the usual reasons of a rising school tax rate. Indeed, for the residents of Addiston, school taxes had gone down since the district was absorbed into the new county school district. Instead Olson was saying the following:

> "Addiston residents no longer have the choice of providing excellence in education for their children. Now, they have to be content with the level of mediocrity approved by the whole county."

There appeared to be considerable data to support Olson's argument. Before reorganization, the Addiston school district expended $726 per pupil; after the organization of the new McNabb County School District, this expenditure was $483. The average pupil-teacher ratio was increased from 26 to 1 before reorganization to 31 to 1 following reorganization. Expenditures for supplies and equipment in Addiston's schools were reduced also.

Carl Olson's most dramatic argument centered on the school tax rate.

"We couldn't pay more taxes for our schools if we wanted to! In this community we know we need to spend more than $483 per pupil to equip our children to compete with their peers across the nation. Let's face it, the rest of the county does not need or want the kind of schools *we must have.*"

In summing up his argument, Olson concluded that the concept of big government was now being applied to public education with the result that individual interests and local control were being ignored. This power grabbing, he contended, deprived the people in local communities, who best know their own educational needs, of the opportunity to make these choices.

"The situation has now become so acute that only through drastic measures can we regain our rights."

The proposal Carl Olson posited was considered by many to be drastic. Its major features included a major overhaul in the state constitution and state education code. It provided for government tuition credits to be given to pupils to be spent in private schools of their own choice. The amount of the credit would be in the amount necessary to provide the minimum level education as set by the people. If a family wished to supplement this amount, it could do so in order to provide an education exceeding the minimum level.

In defending the proposal, Olson maintained the following.

"This is not an idle dream of a crackpot. The idea was originated by a reputable scholar in one of America's leading universities. The idea is a fresh but logical approach in supporting the public education program. This concept assures both excellence in education and preservation of our traditional freedoms in providing it."

Members of the McNabb County Board of Education had long known Carl Olson's point of view. Most of them had considered him as an outspoken and fair critic of the reorganization. Since the formation of the county school district, Olson played the role of "the school board's conscience—he won't let us go off half-cocked!" Now, however, for the first time, members of the board felt he posed a serious threat to the school district and its program. Olson's novel argument and drastic proposal could undermine the people's confidence in the board and the school district. And it was not beyond the realm of possibility that the whole state reorganization movement could be placed in jeopardy.

The board members were in unanimous agreement that they would eventually have to make a public statement as to their reaction to Carl Olson's proposal. Informally and through incidental discussion, the following arguments emerged to counter those which Olson used to support his case:

1. Public education is a natural monopoly. A system of private choice would carry with it many more disadvantages than advantages.

2. There is a long standing interpretation of the courts to the effect that the function of public schools goes beyond providing training of youth in academic skills. It has the function of preparing youth for democratic living. A system of private schools will jeopardize the democratizing process now found in public education.

3. The Olson proposal will lead to the establishment of many small private schools, each catering to a unique group. Consequently, the excessive competition will result in high cost and low quality.

4. The redistribution of income function of the public school finance program will be lost.

5. Minimum standards of education as decided on by the people will be excessively general in order to be applicable to all groups. Thus, the minimum educational level will be so low as to endanger the concept of universal education.

6. The function of public education is not to bestow benefits on the individual but instead to enable the state to survive.

Armed with these arguments, the President of the McNabb County Board of Education was almost relieved when the program chairman of the Southgate Women's Club asked him to serve on a panel to discuss the Olson proposal and "clear the air about this thing."

Questions for Discussion

1. What are assumed to be appropriate choices of parents regarding the education of their children under the present concept of our compulsory education system?

2. How might these choices be affected if the Carl Olson or Milton Friedman proposal were to be implemented in McNabb County and the state?

3. What is the implied function of publicly supported education in the Carl Olson proposal?

4. What concepts of financing an individual school among several others in a given school system might prove helpful in providing for the unique needs of a given group of pupils?

Case 19.   *Educational Crossroads on the Great Plains*

State appropriations for public education in a Great Plains state have shown only token increases over the past three biennial sessions despite a general demonstration of interest to promote major additions to these funds. Any number of highly respected experts in the field of education have issued statements of pressing educational needs. Recently there has been considerable public clamor for the state legislature to do something about these educational inadequacies. Yet, the state legislature has not responded with any significant increases in state funds.

Educational leaders in the state have attributed the apparently disinterested attitude of the legislators to three primary causes: (1) the lack of real conviction on the part of the people of the state to invest more in public education, (2) sharp divisions of opinion among the state educational lobby groups as to needs and means to meet these needs, and (3) the inability of any one group to galvanize the support of all the educationally oriented groups to back one given educational support proposal.

When the most recent legislative session adjourned with a "last minute patching" of the state aid formula, the officers of several of the educational lobbies agreed to meet and talk together about their concerns to upgrade the school support program. As a result a Conference of Organizations for the Support of the Public Schools was organized for the purpose of "identifying the needs of public education in our state and ways to meet them." This was a grass roots type conference with representatives from the PTA, board of education, and teaching and administrative staff of every school district throughout the state. On the basis of a mail-out questionnaire, a preliminary poll of education concerns was taken. The concerns most frequently mentioned became topics of formal presentations made by experts on the given subject. Following each presentation, "buzz sessions" were held wherein reactions from the conference participants were recorded. By this interaction, the conference planners hoped to develop some consensus and identify areas of agreement.

At the conclusion of the conference when the buzz-session reports were compiled, it was apparent that the groups developed rather close agreement on the nature of the educational needs. However, it was equally apparent that there was much divergence of opinion on how these needs were to be met.

Participants agreed that the pupil-teacher ratio should be reduced, the state minimum and average teachers' salaries should be raised so as to be competitive with any neighboring state, additional school services should be added—especially in the areas of counseling and special education for handicapped children—curricular opportunities should be broadened, and more monies should be expended for public education.

In regard to means to effect the above changes, however, little consensus could be obtained. Although several proposals were made regarding specific changes in the state financing program to provide for meeting these needs, none could be agreed upon by the majority of the conferees. It was on only a few innocuous guidelines that any agreement on means seemed to appear. It was the consensus of the group that a state financing program should assist in implementing a state-required minimum program of education; that local initiative for program expansion beyond the minimum should be stimulated; that innovative and high quality "lighthouse" school districts should be given incentives through the state program; and that broadened citizen participation in determining methods of school support should be encouraged.

As the steering committee for the conference considered the problem of defining an action program to meet the educational needs, it was decided that the guidelines which were agreed upon did suggest an approach. The committee decided that each of the organizations represented in the conference should develop a position paper on a state financing program which would (1) be based on the agreed-upon needs, (2) utilize the agreed-upon guidelines, and (3) incorporate the specifics of a state educational financing program.

Up to the time of this event, Bob McKelvey had shown little interest in statewide activities of the Association of Boards of Education. As a member, he dutifully attended the annual conferences but never assumed a leadership role. However, when the call came for members to contribute their ideas for the formulation of the association's position paper on a proposed state finance program for the public schools, McKelvey became very articulate. Initially, he shared his personal ideas on the subject with other board members he knew from his area of the state. Upon getting favorable and enthusiastic response from many of these members, he was "drafted" to present his propositions to the ad hoc committee charged with the formulation of the association's position paper.

In his presentation, McKelvey observed that the lack of enthusiasm and the lack of a sense of direction for public education in the state were due to the "suppressive dominance of a lockstep state school aid program which has dictated mediocrity. This program has dictated the same pupil-teacher ratio, the same administrative and supervisory staffing pattern, the same vocational education program, the same teacher qualifications, and many other uniform practices."

Because of these factors, McKelvey concluded, the public has lost all initiative in controlling public education. Since they could not make decisions in these crucial areas of school program, it is no wonder they have been apathetic. He maintained that because of this apathy, local school district programs are becoming more and more inadequate.

When pressed to suggest a positive approach, McKelvey proposed that the association adopt within the restrictions of the present law, a plan based on the ideas of Milton Friedman.

"The Friedman concept," argued Bob McKelvey, "is certainly applicable to our state today. The lockstep educational program specified by the state has sapped local incentive. We must return to the people their right to make educational choices. Naturally, within the present law we cannot totally adopt the Friedman plan. We can, however, propose a program which moves in the direction of the Friedman concept. If we can sell this program and get it into operation, it will demonstrate the feasibility of Friedman's basic ideas. Once proven, we shall then have a good chance to change the state school code to move closer and closer to the original Friedman idea."

McKelvey further noted that the guidelines agreed upon by the conference were viable and could indeed be used in developing the specifications of a proposed state school financing program. These guidelines or criteria would be apparent in his proposal: state support for a basic program, state stimulation of local initiative, state stimulation of "lighthouse" school districts, and encouragement of broad citizen participation.

The specific features of McKelvey's proposal included a state minimum program based on "the fundamental academic skills." McKelvey observed that the primary educational function of the state is to provide that educational program needed by all—and the basic skill areas are the only ones that meet this criterion. All the rest are unique and thus should be designed and provided by the local school district. Eventually, the decisions on this part of the school program would be moved from the local school district back into the hands of the people themselves. This latter move would partially attain one of the goals of the Friedman proposal—private control of publicly required education.

Reaction to Bob McKelvey's thinking and the proposal he enunciated was immediate but not violent. The Association of Boards of Education had a long tradition of honoring the varying points of view of its members. Seldom was a resolution passed without vigorous debate.

Many of the members of the association had long championed the cause of more state involvement in public education—in both higher educational standards and greater financial support. Most of these members maintained this point of view and identified themselves with Dr. Eldon Schmidt, a physician from one of the many small rural communities of the state. Dr. Schmidt had become well known in the association in the last few years as being a leading exponent of the "education is our best investment" argument. His story of a poverty-stricken childhood, the affection, attention, and inspiration given him by a teacher, his overwhelming ambition to become a physician, and the tremendous contribution which public education made to his career, had been heard as a keynote speech at several professional meetings throughout the state.

During the past few months Dr. Schmidt had devoted considerable study to ways of financing a broadened state educational program. It was natural, then, that he would attract many of the members who would not support the McKelvey point of view.

Dr. Schmidt endorsed the belief that education in the state needed to be upgraded. He supported the general guidelines for improving the state's program as agreed upon by the Conference of Organizations for the Support of the Public Schools, i.e., state financial assistance in implementing a state-required minimum program, stimulation of local initiative to exceed the state minima, incentives for local lighthouse school districts, and broadened citizen participation in determining methods of school support. To counter the McKelvey proposal, Dr. Schmidt submitted a proposal to be considered as the Association of School Boards' position on the question of how the state program of educational improvement is to be supported.

It was noted with interest that although Dr. Schmidt started with many of the same value positions that McKelvey used, the Schmidt proposal in the final analysis was almost diametrically opposed to that of McKelvey. Dr. Schmidt suggested that a simple foundation program be developed around three major components: (1) a teacher salary allocation determined by salaries found in a state-approved schedule multiplied by the number of state-approved teacher units; (2) a $170 per pupil allotment; and (3) an allotment of $1,200 for each school operated by the school district. The total dollar amount of the foundation program for each school district was to be determined and from this the yield of 8 mills of local property tax would be subtracted. The latter tax is to be based on the state-mandated 50 percent assessment ratio. The balance would be the amount of state assistance going to the local district. However, one other key feature was included. In order to stimulate local initiative and provide freedom of choice to the local school district, Dr. Schmidt suggested that the state provide a bonus of $5 per pupil in average daily attendance for each mill of property tax the local district levies for school purposes over the required 8 mills.

Supporters of both the McKelvey and Schmidt plans busied themselves in gathering data to defend the approaches of their own choice. Both groups recognized that there were deep philosophical differences between the two positions. The hearings held by the ad hoc committee of the Association of School Boards for the purposes of drafting their proposal would be quite influential in determining the future direction of public education in the state.

Questions for Discussion

1. What observations can one make about the proposition that increasing private (citizen) control over publicly required education will increase differentiation and private (citizen) interest in this educational program?

2. McKelvey based his arguments on the assumption that uniformity in program was the major contribution to mediocrity in program. What other factors might have contributed to it?

3. What arguments might be stated to counter McKelvey's conclusion that basic skills should be the basis for the state minimum program and all other program components should be designed and provided by the local school district?

4. How might Dr. Schmidt's proposals meet the criteria set by the Conference of Organizations for the Support of the Public Schools? How do these differ from the McKelvey proposals?

5. To what extent should communities be forced to operate schools better than they actually want?

Suggested Readings

Concept G—Education—Public or Private

Freeman, Roger: *Taxes for the Schools*, Washington, D.C.: The Institute for Social Science Research, 1961.

McConnell, Campbell R.: *Economics*, 4th ed., New York: McGraw-Hill, 1969, chap. 6, pp. 97–99.

Education as a Government Function: Implications for Role and Financing

the problem

Public education as a community concern does not exclusively reside at a single level of government. Each of the three levels of government—local, state, and federal—has certain educational interests, needs, and responsibilities since taxpayers and school patrons are citizens of their state and nation as well as their local school district. Thus, each level of government seeks to promote and provide financing for some dimension of the educational program.

The kind of program is determined not only by the educational need felt on that level but also by the financial capability of the given unit of government. Some programs because of their unique features, are better done at one level of government than at another. Thus, the role of each level of government must be studied in order to provide educational programs most effectively.

In considering the financing of public schools, it is necessary to recognize and to appreciate the interrelationships among the sources of school support. The actions of one level exert a marked influence over the actions of the other levels. Thus, it is imperative that the roles of each of the three levels of government be appraised as they pertain to public education before firm decisions are made on educational programs and financing plans.

the concept

It is not sufficient merely to reach the conclusion that education, in the large, should be a government enterprise, that is, that the role of government should not be confined to financing. The role of each *level* of government must also be determined. Traditionally, elementary and secondary education has been financed and supervised by local school districts. In recent years, however, considerable debate has been held concerning the efficacy of federal aid to public education. In addition, most state governments for many years have provided to local school districts the financial support designed to provide a minimum educational program. Whether either the federal or state program of aid to public education is justified is a proper topic for consideration, and a determination of the proper role in the educational process for all levels of government needs to be made.

Traditionally, public education has been a function of local government. Conceptually, it is financed by local taxes (in the main, the property tax) and supervised by a locally elected board of education. The first deviation in this pattern was the establishment of minimum standards of performance by the state governments. State aid in financing was a later development. The question is, How much involvement by state and federal governments can be justified? Furthermore, as an enlargement of this same question, when is state and federal participation in any government function justified?

Much can be said for executing governmental functions at the local level. The local electorate best understands the problems and the needs of the local government. The voters apparently are more interested in government if the financing and supervising functions are carried out at the local level. Also, if the voters know that with the approval of each new government activity their taxes will be increased, it is probable that they will be more hesitant before giving such approval. On the other hand, the advantages of centralization which are usually present in manufacturing industries are seldom attainable for governments in the performance of their services.

There are at least two substantive economic reasons for not executing every function of government at the local level. At times there is a need to equalize the tax burdens among a number of local units of government. All local units are not equally able to finance certain programs, but the need for the service or program is just as vital in the poor as in the wealthy tax district. By shifting the financing of a particular program from a local unit to a higher level—for instance, a state—the burden and the quality of the service tends to be equalized throughout the larger unit. The taxpayers in the wealthy districts contribute more to the central fund for financing the program than that district receives from the central fund. On the other hand, the taxpayers in the poor districts pay less than is received by their district.

The other justification for financing a particular service at either the state or federal level is the frequent existence of "spillover" or "neighborhood" effects. Very often the activities of one government will have significant effects on the citizens of another government. When this occurs, there is a justification for financing or controlling those activities by a larger government which encompasses all the affected areas. It periodically floods in the second state, but those floods can only be stopped by building dams and other flood control structures in the first state, where there is no flood problem. It cannot be expected that the citizens of the first state will tax themselves to build those structures needed for the benefit of the citizens of the second state. Nor can it be expected that the citizens of the second state will tax themselves to finance projects outside the boundaries of their state. Only by the federal government taxing the citizens of both states (and all other states) and undertaking the improvements as a federal project can relief be obtained.

Does this principle have applicability in the field of education? Very definitely. A great many people benefit from a particular individual's education, including that person's employer, and with the increasing mobility of our population, there is a reduced possibility that an employer will contribute to the costs of educating his future employees. It might be argued that while the taxpayers of one district bear the costs of educating the future employees for employers in some other district, those employers (as taxpayers) will be doing the same for those persons who will move into the first district. However, there is never an even exchange. Many districts, particularly those in the rural areas, consistently experience a net loss of population. These districts regularly are educating students who will be employed elsewhere in the country but receiving no in-migration in exchange. Also, under the pattern of complete local control and financing, the employer has nothing to say about the quality of the education provided his future employees.

In this discussion the relationship between education levels and income is also important. This relationship is a positive one, so that the higher the level of education, the higher the level of income. It is also obvious that the higher the income, the higher the level of spending, and the better such an area is as a market for this country's goods. Producers, then, have a very positive economic interest in the level of education in all parts of the country. This interest is of such a magnitude, in fact, that it would be to their benefit to bear a portion of the costs of education throughout the country.

All this is an overwhelming justification for at least a partial financing and supervision of the educational function at a higher level of government than the local district. To a considerable extent this is a proper function of the state, and to an increasing degree of the federal government. The loss of complete local control, the reduction in interest in the operation of the local schools by the local citizens, and perhaps even the increased standardization of the schools over much wider areas than at present, these may be developments which we consider undesirable. But the economic gains are overwhelming. Increased financing of education by the state and federal governments is inevitable if the economic role of education is to be developed to the fullest.

Case 20.   Changing the Role of the State in Public Education

During the latter half of the nineteenth century, waves of immigrants from northwest Europe rolled into the region of the upper Middle West. These people were of hardy rural stock who took great pride in working the land and building up fine farms. Consequently, in this part of the country agricultural concerns clearly dominated the whole way of living. By the end of World War II, a new social character had developed. One state in particular demonstrated this dramatic change as it reconsidered the state's role in public education.

Although this particular state was still predominantly agricultural in terms of geographical area, the population had now become more than 50 percent urbanized. Most of the urban population was concentrated in a series of cities situated along the shores of one of the Great Lakes. This in turn provided access to the Atlantic Ocean.

During the early 1950s the state's traditional school aid program was closely and critically examined. Not only were the specifics of the aid program questioned but also the popular acceptance of the concept that public education is primarily a local responsibility was challenged. At this time, the state imposed only a few requirements on the local school districts, e.g., a minimum number of days in the school year, teacher certification requirements, and the minimum number of credits plus a few courses required for graduation.

The state's financial program for supporting public schools was patterned after the "weak district aid" model. It provided a small flat grant per pupil to all school districts and a variable grant supplementing local district monies raised by a small state-mandated property tax. If the local district was not able to raise $242 per pupil with the mandated millage, the state made up the difference.

By the end of World War II urbanization and advancing technology had caused a rapidly widening gap between the rich school districts and the poor ones—at least as measured in terms of ability to pay local property taxes. Inadequacies in the educational programs of the local school systems became more and more obvious. At the same time marked demographic changes were also occurring. As the manufacturing and commercial enterprises flourished in the cities along the lake, agricultural production on the inland farms grew but with opposite results in terms of manpower requirements. Cities with growing industries attracted young people who were not needed on farms. Farm labor was in surplus whereas factory labor was in shortage. As the economy of the state and nation boomed, this demographic trend accelerated.

As the trend deepened, it became apparent that these two needs were not offsetting as originally thought. The rapidly expanding industries were expanding because of technological advances. This in turn required many highly skilled technicians. The whole labor force, both within the urban areas and coming from the farms, showed an excess of unskilled and semiskilled labor. Thus there was a condition of unemployment of these workers but at the same time a shortage of highly skilled operators, technicians, and professionals. The element needed to cause the two demographic trends to offset themselves was the appropriate kind of education and/or training.

It was apparent that the existing pattern of control and financing of public schools was inadequate to meet these needs. It had been known for some time that the educational program of the small rural school districts was inadequate in preparing youth for urban vocations. Now it was recognized that there was no real alternative—few rural youth were needed in highly mechanized agriculture and only 20 percent of them went on to college. Thus the majority had to go into industrial or commercial vocations.

The rural problem was further compounded with another condition—the decreasing ability of residents in agricultural areas to pay property taxes to support the local schools. Because of automation and the consequent piling up of surplus agricultural commodities, farm income levels had fallen far behind the income levels of other occupational groups.

Urban centers felt the problem as well. Industries were hampered in attaining efficient production because of the scarcity of skilled workers. Problems of marketing were apparent also since the consumption of manufactured goods and services by the unemployed was relatively low. Industrial and commercial leaders recognized that in order to continue industrial expansion and high production, it was necessary to strengthen markets and maintain a high level of consumption.

All these points substantiated the conclusion that a major social dislocation had occurred. It appeared that new relationships must be established in order that the whole state could prosper. As a result of public unrest growing from this awareness, the state legislature created five study commissions to consider the situation. These commissions were authorized to study problems in economic development, state taxation, unemployment and welfare, urban planning, and public education. The commission on the study of public education was charged with several specific responsibilities which "in summary shall provide the bases for the redefinition of the role of the state in public education." The study was financed by the state and conducted by the Bureau of Educational Research of the state university. The whole group of study commissions utilized a common pool of professional consultants and technical and clerical personnel. As a result there was considerable interchange of both ideas and data among the five study teams.

The report of the study commission on public education was comprehensive as it was designed "to consider the dramatic social changes which are prerequisite to recognizing the inadequacy of the present state role in public education. The study of these social changes is also useful in pointing the direction to a new concept of the role of the state in public education."

The study was organized around five major considerations. These considerations included the philosophical, social, political (legal), educational program, and economic factors. Within the latter group of factors, attention was given to the economic interdependence among regions, industries, and social groups within the state.

The phenomenon of spillover effects of education was also considered. It was found that the benefits of education accrue to many other individuals and regions outside the school district where a given individual is educated.

Because of the spillover effects, consideration was given to the equalization of tax burden. It was found that considerable variations of ability and effort did exist among local school districts within the state. In light of spillover effects as well as social justice a case for equalized tax burdens was explored.

An analysis of the relationship between educational level and income indicated that during recent years the increase in the educational level of people in a given community corresponded to the increased income. The converse was also demonstrated.

On the basis of these and other findings, the commission recommended that the state exercise its plenary power in public education and that it provide a basic educational program. It was also recommended that the state specify the role of the local school district to be one of supplementing with and making local application of those areas of permissive activity as provided by the state.

The commission developed only general guidelines to implement its recommended redefinition of the role of the state in public education. It recommended that the state describe a basic educational program which would be required for every student within the state. In order to implement this minimal program, a foundation program was recommended wherein the state would bear a major share of the cost of the required program. It also provided that the state and the local school district would share equally the costs of the locally initiated features to supplement the basic or foundation program.

Questions for Discussion

1. What were the implied roles for state and local governments in regard to public education before the establishment of the commission on public education in the case study?

2. What might have been the major arguments in defining state and local responsibilities for education in this manner?

3. In the concept statement two economic reasons are given for not executing every function of government at the local level. How are each of these reasons demonstrated in the case study?

4. In the state described in the case study what are examples of spillover or "neighborhood" effects?

5. How has a state's plenary power in matters of public education been exercised to enlarge or accelerate development of educational opportunity? To diminish or retard development of educational opportunity?

6. What are some ways in which the commission's guidelines would shift responsibility from the local level to the state level?

Case 21. Reconceptualizing Local Control

If it is true, as many New Englanders would have one believe, that the last vestiges of real grass roots democracy are practiced only in the rural parts of this region of the nation, then Marlenborough is a case in point. This small community, located near the western border of one of the New England states, enjoys the rich heritage of the town meeting concept of government.

Although the public schools are governed by school committees, the spirit of the town meeting is strong since there is much community interest and involvement in public school affairs. The actions of the school committeemen reflect the attitudes of the people of the town.

Committeemen openly solicit the opinion of the laymen when knotty problems and controversial issues face the school committee.

For more than ten years residents of the town of Marlenborough have been aware of the school reorganization movement. Most of the more densely populated areas of the eastern third of the state and the region around the capital have already reorganized according to the guidelines suggested by the State Department of Public Education. These guidelines stated that every school district must provide a program covering grades one through twelve, that every secondary school enroll at least three hundred pupils, and that schools meet designated standards in areas of teacher preparation, curricular offerings, facilities (laboratories, libraries, classrooms, auditoriums, etc.), population, geographic size, and wealth of the school district.

These "guidelines for recognized school districts" worked very effectively in the eastern part of the state. Many small school districts were reorganized into larger consolidations or were merged with already larger districts. Although there was an implicit threat that financial assistance would be withheld if a school district was not "recognized," other factors provided the real motivation for school reorganization.

The nature of the population in the eastern section was far more cosmopolitan than in the western part of the state. With the bustling manufacturing and commercial centers, the large and famous universities, and the clustering of research and development agencies which interrelate with both industry and higher education, the population included many well and broadly educated people. The demands for the best in public education were almost constant. School committeemen sensitive to these demands eventually saw that only with large school districts could one hope to provide the breadth of program which was demanded by these people. It was also necessary to maximize the efficiency of the operation in order to provide the money to support the broadened program.

The people of Marlenborough clearly set themselves apart from the "easterners." The former did not consider themselves cosmopolitans —their families had settled the area generations ago. There were few external pressures for broadening the school program.

The standards of tradition dictated the nature of the educational program. If these standards were met, the program was good! Thus, as long as the state guidelines were not enforced but suggested only, they had little influence in Marlenborough.

In assessing the status of school district reorganization, the state legislature found that the eastern part of the state had responded well to the guidelines. Through mutually agreed upon annexations and consolidations, most of the small school districts had been merged with others to form units of adequate size. Almost nothing along these lines had been done in the western half of the state however. As a result, the legislature enacted a law which prevented the distribution of state school aid to those districts which did not comply with the standards set for "recognized school districts."

When news of the enforcement of the guidelines for school reorganization reached the Marlenborough School Committee, the reaction of the members ranged from an apathetic "it can't happen here" to one of righteous indignation. Aaron Adams, a long time member of the school committee and member of one of the fine old families of the town, was the chief protagonist of the latter point of view.

> "Those people at the capital," he argued, "can't do that. They can't take the control of schools away from us. These schools belong to the town, we know how to run them, and we use our own taxes to operate them."

Because of his cogent and direct argument and his social standing in the town, Adams marshaled considerable support for his position of resisting school reorganization. It was apparent to all concerned that he would be influential in determining the position of the school district reorganization.

John Pennyworth had served as superintendent of the Marlenborough schools for nine years. He was born and reared in this section of the state but could not claim the distinction of being a native son of Marlenborough. John was respected as an educator in the town but was not influential in community affairs.

Despite the fact he shared a somewhat similar background with Adams, Pennyworth was convinced that school district reorganization was the key to educational improvement in the area. The superintendent also believed that the state should play a more aggressive role in setting and enforcing high educational standards. Having had considerable contact and some teaching experience in other parts of the state, he maintained that more than just local leaderhip was necessary to upgrade educational programs throughout the state.

Pennyworth also recognized that his professional judgment would not carry the weight of that of the school committeeman. The townspeople would certainly follow Adams's lead. The superintendent concluded that the only way to avoid a "showdown" between the forces of Aaron Adams and the state legislature was to convince Committeeman Adams that a reasonable if not advantageous role for the local school district could be incorporated in the state's reorganization plan.

The confrontation of Adams's and Pennyworth's views came when the Marlenborough School Committee was notified by the State Department of Public Education that as a school district which did not fully meet the state standards, it must file a letter of intent regarding its plans to meet the standards. The letter, having been received by John Pennyworth, was included in the agenda for the forthcoming school committee meeting. Consequently, it was no surprise that when this item was reached in the meeting, Aaron Adams read a prepared statement. The major points were those which Adams had articulated many times.

1. The schools belong to the people, and therefore the local people should make decisions regarding standards as long as they maintain schools as required in the state constitution.

2. The public schools are supported by local property taxes which are levied by the school committee, collected and retained by local agencies, and dispersed by the local school committee. This fiscal control should remain in the hands of locally elected officials.

3. Since the local schools educate local youth, the unique needs of these youth are best determined by the local school committee. Local decisions are better than those made a hundred or more miles away in the state capital. Local control makes schools more sensitive to the needs of the people.

4. The state's requirement of adherence to the standards under the threat of the loss of state aid to the local school district clearly states a critical choice.

> "Men and women of Marlenborough, the possessors of the proud heritage of defenders of civil liberties, must soon make an important choice. They must support or reject the privilege and responsibility of making their own decisions pertaining to education—and then live with the consequences.
>
> "I propose that the Marlenborough School Committee, by reflecting the wishes of the town, indicate its intent to retain its own control of public school affairs; that it not submit to the state standards; and if necessary that it forego the state subsidy and operate the Marlenborough schools with local resources only."

Despite the fact he had prepared himself emotionally for this moment, John Pennyworth realized the half apologetic tone in his voice as he asked permission to respond to Aaron Adams's proposal.

"Mr. Chairman, I would like to speak to the question of the committee's position on the letter of intent. These are my thoughts as a professional educator whose primary responsibility is the execution of policy developed on both the state and local levels, but whose secondary responsibility is that of professional advisor to his superiors."

Having declared his role in the consideration of the question, John Pennyworth spelled out in a clear and confident manner his interpretation of Adams's arguments. He also added a few other observations which he felt bore on the question. His major points were:

1.   The schools belong to the people, but since public schools are agencies of the state, a community cannot jeopardize them because of a conflicting local value.

2.   Public schools in Marlenborough, and most of the state, are not supported by local option with exclusively local money. Approximately 30 percent of current expenses is derived from state support. Even the 70 percent of the operating budget obtained from local property taxes is not "local" in the purest sense. First, this tax is mandated by the state. Local property taxes must be used for the support of local government, including schools. No other tax can be used. Also, the state requires that every school district levy at least 6 mills to support the local schools. This is really a state-required tax which is administered on the local level.

3.   Although the inhabitants of a local school district no doubt know the pupils personally much better than anyone outside that district, this does not ensure that the needs of these youth are best met through local decisions. All the pupils attending Marlenborough schools will not spend their adult lives in Marlenborough. The fact that people are mobile requires a far broader base of educational experiences to prepare them adequately for future training and vocations.

"Because of the rapidly growing demand for broadened educational experiences, several points are significant. First, in my judgment, a state-based decision will generally be better than a locally based decision since the former offers a broader perspective of needs. Second, the resources needed to support such a broadened educational experience are far greater than can be normally expected to be raised in a school district dependent only on local resources. Third, since mobility patterns indicate that many persons other than those residing and paying taxes in Marlenborough will benefit from this town's schools, the tax base should be broadened."

4. There is a fallacy in the argument which maintains that local decision-making authority is reduced any time state authority is increased. The state regulations and the concern of the state legislature with school district reorganization illustrate this point. A small school district with limited resources really has few decisions it can make. It must provide those basic elements of an educational program required by the state, so it can make no choices in that regard. However, if the state intervenes, some decision-making power is added as well as some lost because of the requirements of the state. A reorganized school district, for example, would gain local control because the addition of state money to the budget would enable its school committee to make decisions as to what additional programs it might provide.

> "The fact that the reorganized school district would be a larger operation could enhance local control. It is more efficient to operate a school district three times the size of Marlenborough than it is to conduct our schools. This is especially true in offering a broadened program. Our advanced courses in science, mathematics, foreign languages, and the like are usually very small—frequently only six or eight in a class. Teachers' salaries account for the biggest item in our budget—about 80 percent. Thus, a larger school district would make more efficient use of its personnel and could divert the 'saved' money into other programs which would in turn add to its ability to make decisions.

> "When states specify and support a state program, the local school district is given the opportunity to use local taxes for optional programs. This, I believe, would add to local control rather than detract from it."

At the conclusion of his presentation, John Pennyworth was not certain whether he as superintendent still held the confidence of the Marlenborough School Committee. He was sure, however, that the direction which the committee would take on the letter of intent was still an open question.

Questions for Discussion

1. In the Marlenborough case, what was the apparent justification of state involvement in public education?

2. What was the implied role of the local school district in the statement presented by Aaron Adams? In that presented by John Pennyworth?

3. How could the concept "the schools belong to the people" be compatible in both the Adams and the Pennyworth positions?

4. What are some inherent problems of rationalizing state involvement in public education on the bases of both financing and supervising public education as it operates on the local level? On the basis of either financing or supervising alone?

Case 22.   Shaping National Policy from State and Local Needs

Although the national legislative session which ended several years ago had been called the "education congress" because of its passage of the Elementary and Secondary Education Act of 1965, many members of the Congress were certain that much remained to be done in the area of public school legislation. Two of the most visible leaders of this group were Senator Paul Anholdt from an agricultural state in the central South and Representative Anthony Pucinni, from an urban district of an East Coast industrial state. These two men, despite almost complete divergence in age, appearance, background, and experience, held many common views about the problems of the nation and the role of the federal government in resolving them.

Having served on several joint Senate-House committees which considered education legislation, the two men shared concern for the same problem but viewed it from two different perspectives. And interestingly enough, the two legislators had arrived at the same conclusion regarding the measures needed to resolve the problem.

Anholdt and Pucinni were both concerned over the inability of their respective states to cope with the problems of providing adequate living and working conditions for their citizens in the lower socioeconomic classes. Anholdt's rural state was commonly termed an "economically depressed area." To him, however, the problem extended beyond jobs, wages, and grocery bills.

> "My state suffers from more than economic depression. It suffers from a fatalism which threatens to allow the rest of the nation to grow away from it. Our problems have been of such long duration that now they have become part of our way of life. Somehow, we must be brought from this backwater into the mainstream of the nation."

The state has lost population for more than a decade. The small farm agriculture could not compete with large-scale units operating in nearby states. Consequently, more and more marginal land has been taken out of production. Young men, unable to find employment in the state, have left to hunt jobs in the cities of the upper-Midwest or the Pacific Coast. The few remaining industries, as well as the manufacturing plants themselves, have become increasingly obsolescent. Many of the products no longer command much demand on the market, e.g., cotton textiles, wood and forest products, and low-grade tobacco. Thus employment opportunities have decreased since few new industries have located in the state.

The per capita income of the state has reflected the bleak employment picture. The state's rank slipped from forty-seventh to forty-eighth in the nation. While the United States average per capita income has exceeded $3,200, Anholdt's state income per capita is $2,351.

Public education has always been poorly supported in the state. In recent years when other states were expanding their programs and budgets for the schools, this state did little more than maintain the low level of support previously afforded the schools.

The federal programs under the Elementary and Secondary Education Act have provided more hope than lasting and dramatic changes. Considerable immediate assistance was provided under Title I, and the supplementary centers under Title III have whetted the appetites of educators for even broader programs. However, additional financing from the state and localities has not been forthcoming, and so the major dimensions of the problem have remained. Consequently, Paul Anholdt has looked to the federal government.

Anthony Pucinni was born and reared in the then largest city of the nation. His immigrant parents were frugal, hardworking people. Pucinni's father supported his family of ten through employment in a brass foundry of a plumbing supply factory.

As Anthony Pucinni grew up he became aware of the changing character of the city. His own neighborhood changed from a relatively homogeneous lower-middle-class section of modest but neat three-flat apartment houses to a polyglot neighborhood of recent immigrants. The first of several groups moved in from other parts of the city, then others came from the Deep South, and later from Puerto Rico.

In the meanwhile the plumbing supply factory which employed the elder Pucinni encountered major problems. Competent foundry workers became increasingly difficult to hire. Skilled machine operators needed in the rest of the plant also were in short supply. As the profit margin shrank, the plant management invested less and less in new equipment. Finally, in 1962 the business was sold to a large diversified industry. The old factory was closed and the plant was relocated in a suburban community some 40 miles from the city.

Because of these demographic and economic changes, other major social problems emerged. As the employment patterns of the city shifted, the migrants who entered the city experienced more and more difficulty in finding jobs. Unemployment rates soared and were paralleled by crime rates. Consequently, demands for public services rose sharply. The deteriorating neighborhoods required more police and fire protection. Congestion in the core of the city demanded more public transportation facilities. The high incidence of unemployment, disability, and dependent children required vast additions to the welfare programs. As the city's needs increased, its ability to support these needs decreased.

In analyzing these problems, Pucinni concluded that the public schools, the one agency with the capability of contributing to the long-term resolution of the problem, were receiving little or no additional resources to do the job. Many of the recent migrants to the city do not appreciate the value of education in this matter, and so local tax increases are unpopular. The state as a whole has been wont to spend "state money" on one city, and so nothing has been done to bring about a long-term solution to the problem.

As Anholdt and Pucinni shared their concerns and analyses of these problems, the framework of a piece of legislation seemed to emerge. The rationale and principle of the legislation are based on the fact that broad social forces are operative in the country which cause severe economic and social dislocations. The dysfunctions which result from these dislocations are of such a nature that neither local nor state governments have the capability of correcting the dysfuncton. Since this dysfunction has national influence and since only the federal government is capable of resolving the problem, it is appropriate that the federal government enact a program providing assistance to states and cities.

In generalizing on the difficulties of financing adequate educational programs in the settings of a given city and a given state, Paul Anholdt and Anthony Pucinni identified several major problems which they felt are a proper concern of the federal government:

1. Fiscal inability of some states to support an adequate educational program—public education is a national concern, and there are commonly accepted norms for adequate educational programs. It is obvious that certain states cannot provide an adequate program without exorbitant sacrifice on the part of the taxpayers. The federal government should provide poor states with some assistance in meeting a

minimal expectation and leave some discretionary income to the tax-payers.

2. Ability-effort discrepancies—many of the states with meager financial resources expend a relatively greater effort to support education than do the wealthier states. Financial assistance from the federal government should be given to states which exceed reasonable expectations. Thus extraordinary effort is rewarded which stimulates program improvement.

3. Adjustments for spillover effects—since the benefits of education often accrue to states other than the one which provided the worker with his schooling, the federal government should provide some kind of compensatory arrangement. Thus, when workers are educated in a poor state but subsequently migrate to an economically prosperous state to find employment, the latter state gets the benefits at the expense of the former. However, frequently the reverse is true. Prosperous states attract many workers who are not adequately trained for employment in modern industries. Consequently these unemployables congregate in neighborhoods which in turn deteriorate and thus require greatly expanded public services including unemployment compensation, police and fire protection, welfare services, and the like.

Thus, spillover has both negative and positive effects. Federal assistance to states supplying poorly educated workers for other states is justified since the sending state must be encouraged to upgrade educational standards.

The negative effects of spillover are felt largely by specific cities and not as much by the states. Thus the federal government should provide assistance to these cities either directly or indirectly through the states to the cities. The unique educational problems of the large city are of national import and thus deserve federal assistance in order to bring about a solution.

4. Alleviation of the economic causes of educational problems—many of the problems of public education are precipitated or directly caused by economic conditions. Because of the complex nature of the economy, the federal government is the only logical agency to intervene. Automation and technology have drastically changed the educational and manpower requirements of the nation's economy. Without federal intervention, a chain reaction of consequences will result: (a) traditional public school programs cannot satisfy these new demands; (b) unemployment and limited consumption will result; (c) economic growth will be hampered by a shortage of highly skilled employees to operate new industry at or near capacity; and (d) recession and deflation could result. Federal intervention in assisting states and localities in providing adequate vocational education will stimulate employment and economic growth; federal activities to increase income will stimulate consumption and thus reduce the possibilities of recession and deflation.

In reviewing their action program, the two legislators became aware of the enormity of their task. For the federal government to meet these needs on a long-term basis, a new role would have to be defined for it. Anholdt and Pucinni realized that this was the most formidable task of the whole program. If this federal program for public education must wait for a major crisis as did all other significant pieces of federal legislation, the two legislators wondered what nature of catastrophe would usher it in.

Questions for Discussion

1.   The rationale for the legislation prepared in this case study rests upon the fact that broad social forces have caused severe economic dislocations which cannot be corrected at the state or local level. How does this rationale relate to the economic Concept H?

2.   The economic problems described in the case study are a concern of the nation as a whole. How many of these problems are, or were, present in your state? What other economic problems are present in your state which should be acted upon by the federal government?

3.   In what way would part of the tax burden for public education be shifted if the Anholdt-Pucinni proposal were to be enacted?

4.   What general statement of the role of the federal government in public education is implied by the Anholdt-Pucinni proposal and its several components?

Suggested Readings

Concept H—Education as a Governmental Function: Implications for Role and Financing

Allen, Hollis P.: *The Federal Government and Education*, New York: McGraw-Hill, 1950.

————: *Federal Policy and the Public Schools*, Washington, D.C.: The Association, 1967.

Bailey, Stephen, et al.: *Schoolmen and Politics*, Syracuse, N.Y.: Syracuse University Press, 1962.

Committee for Economic Development: *A Fiscal Program for a Balanced Federalism*, New York: The Committee, 1967.

————: *Paying for Better Schools*, New York: The Committee, 1959.

————: *Raising Low Incomes Through Improved Education*, New York: The Committee, 1965.

James, H. Thomas, J. Alan Thomas, and Harold J. Dyck: *Wealth, Expenditures, and Decision-making for Education*, U.S. Department of Health, Education, and Welfare, Office of Education, Cooperative Research, Stanford, Calif.: Stanford University, June, 1963.

Lovenstein, Meno: *Economics and the Educational Administrator*, Columbus, Ohio: School-Community Development Study Monograph, College of Education, The Ohio State University, 1958.

McConnell, Campbell R.: *Economics*, 4th ed., New York: McGraw-Hill, 1969, chap. 9, p. 143.

Meranto, Philip: *The Politics of Federal Aid to Education in 1965: A Study in Political Innovation*, Syracuse, N.Y.: Syracuse University Press, 1967.

Munger, Frank J., and Richard F. Fenno, Jr.; *National Politics and Federal Aid to Education*, Syracuse, N.Y.: Syracuse University Press, 1962.

National Committee for Support of Public Schools: *Changing Demands on Education and Their Fiscal Implications*, Washington, D.C.: The Committee, 1963.

Tiedt, Sidney W.: *The Role of the Federal Government in Education*, New York: Oxford University Press, 1966.

part 3

Differentiation of Functions
Among Levels of Government

concepts I–J

Powers and Functions of State and Local Governments

the problem

The common perception of democracy implies self-government—a government of, for, and by the people. It is recognized, however, that all the people cannot be directly involved in all governmental decisions. So, three levels of government were established in order to allocate decisions as to both the type and the degree to which the individual was represented in the political decision-making process.

We have observed that making choices or decisions is an inherent part of living, and this is particularly relevant in economic matters. Choices or decisions are made in a collective sense on the federal, state, and local governmental levels. The allocations of governmental decisions among the three levels are defined by the unique powers and functions assigned to each level. This assignment of powers and functions thus determines "who does what."

The federal Constitution is the basic document which provides for the assignment of such powers and functions. In the Constitution the states delegated certain powers to the federal government and reserved all others for themselves. Public education per se is commonly accepted as such a reserved power. However, in recent years it has become apparent that public education does not operate in a vacuum. Many activities carried on in the public schools have a bearing on the rights of individuals and groups as ensured by the federal Constitution. Furthermore, the federal government has used the public school as a site to accomplish the functions assigned to it by the Constitution. Thus, the powers and functions of the state government are not static or stable. The federal-state relationship must be constantly redefined and clarified.

The state-local relationship must likewise be assessed. As states are plenary or original in power in matters of public education, there should be a constant search for the most effective way for them to discharge their educational responsibilities. Given the dynamic society of today, the problems and thus the programs of public education are constantly changing. Consequently, the exercise of power between the state and local levels of educational government is in flux and must continually be redefined.

the concept

The federal Constitution, from which the federal government derives its powers, also is an important determinant of the limitations of power for state and local governments. States derive most of their authority from the police power, which gives states the right to legislate in the area of health, safety, and morals. In this legislation they are limited only by the restrictions imposed by the federal Constitution and by those limitations which they have placed in their own state constitution. The police power evolved from the common law and included all the regulation necessary to the virtue, peace, and wealth of the community. This doctrine was further upheld by numerous court cases so that today the ability of a state to act in the interests of the general public is far-reaching.

The limitations of state power may be stated either expressly or by implication in the same manner as are the powers of the federal government limited. Thus a state is prohibited from coining money because Article 1, section 10, of the federal Constitution forbids it; and also a state is prevented from taxing property owned by the federal government or in any way taxing directly that government, because the federal Supreme Court has interpreted that the federal Constitution implies such limitation. One limitation is just as effective as the other.

Local governments are limited in their operations by the same restrictions as are placed upon state governments by the federal government, and in addition by those restrictions imposed by the appropriate state government. Local governments are created by the state and are under the complete control of the state. Furthermore, the state at any time may change or destroy any existing local government; there are no inherent rights to local government.

Beyond the legal and constitutional limitations on the power of state and local governments there is also a fiscal control which can be exercised by the federal government. The principal source of revenue for the federal government is the personal income tax, which is a very flexible and productive tax. Furthermore, insofar as this tax is collected through the withholding provisions of the revenue laws, it is a relatively painless tax to pay. The other principal sources of federal revenue, the corporate income tax and the federal excises, are even easier to collect and to pay, for these taxes are not a burden on the person who pays the levy to the government but are shifted by him to someone else. (In the case of a portion of the corporate income tax there is evidence that the tax causes a reduction in the price of the corporate stock.)

State governments derive most of their revenue from consumption taxes (called "consumption" because it is expected that the consumer of the taxed good will bear the burden of the tax). These taxes are very productive, although somewhat less than the federal levies. It is much more difficult to adjust the state taxes to changing economic conditions than is true with the federal taxes.

Local taxes are even less flexible, for local revenues are mostly confined to taxes on property. Property taxes can be changed, as can state consumption taxes, but at the present time when there is an increasing need for state and local revenues and the state and local taxes seem to be at the bearable limit, such change is very difficult.

The scarcity of state and local revenue, and the relative abundance of federal revenue, has made it possible for the national government to influence state and local policy through the offering of grants-in-aid for certain state and local projects. The justification for this type of control need not be considered here, but the power of the federal government to influence policy must be recognized. The ability or even the desirability to resist the offer of a large grant in exchange for meeting a certain set of standards seldom rests in a state, and particularly a local, unit of government. The existence and exercise of this federal power constitute a definite limit on the power of the local and the state governments. Furthermore, this limitation will conceivably grow in the years to come.

Case 23. Interpreting Powers of Local Government

Gillennon County has frequently been referred to as being typical of the larger region of which it is a part. This section of the southwestern quadrant of the nation has a rather colorful character despite its relatively modest resources. The agriculture of the region requires large acreage in order to support an individual enterprise. Crops of fiber and foodstuffs are raised, and cattle raising is profitable in some areas. Although parts of this region of the nation have rich mineral resources, Gillennon County is not so fortunate.

The county is truly in the "wide open spaces" of the Southwest. Although there are many small towns in this and surrounding counties, there is no large city within 100 miles.

Even though Gillennon County is far from being poverty-stricken and is certainly not economically depressed, community leaders for years have been interested in bringing in business or industry to provide balance to the predominantly agricultural economy. Until three years ago, efforts were largely in vain since they were usually uncoordinated, shotgun approaches used by many individuals and groups. The only positive result was the setting up of a few modest businesses in the county. However, because of the outcome of the last elections for national congressional seats and the presidency, much of the success of the dominant political party was attributed to the hard work of the local party organization in Gillennon County. Since Gillennon was a pivotal county in the state and, in turn, a state win was instrumental in the party's national victory, the work of the county's party organization was recognized by many highly placed government officials.

Gillennon's party visibility came shortly after the decision to fund a U.S. Department of Agriculture program to establish a series of regional centers. These agencies were to gather, abstract, and diffuse information regarding agricultural crops, production practices, products, processes, marketing, and consumption. As a result of intense and systematic work by the State's congressional delegation, Gillennon County was selected as the site for one of the four regional agricultural data centers.

The construction of the physical facilities for the center provided a substantial economic stimulus for the county. These having been completed, the initial phase of operation was undertaken. The primary task here was the recruiting and employing of a staff of several thousand. Although nearly a hundred highly trained agricultural specialists, scholars, and researchers were recruited from the Department of Agriculture in Washington and from all over the nation, the majority of employees were to be recruited from the immediate area of the center. These personnel were classified as clerks, stenographers, typists, office machine operators, data processing technicians, and the like. Several hundred maintenance and service personnel were also to be recruited from the immediate area.

The state's congressional delegation which had worked so hard and effectively in having the center located in Gillennon County was vitally interested in the success of the center. The congressmen were concerned not only for their political reputations but also for the possible expansion of the center under a proposed Phase II project.

As a consequence of periodic reports from and visits to the center, a major problem in the operation became apparent. Although the center had no difficulty in attracting sufficient numbers of applicants for the clerical and technical positions, there was a real problem in finding enough personnel who had the skills demanded by the federal specifications. There were adequate numbers of high school graduates from the area, but very few of these had a background of or experience with the relatively sophisticated machines and equipment being used in the center. Most of these applicants came from the small high schools found in the rural areas and towns of the region. Only a few of the applicants had any post-secondary school training in the several private business colleges located around the state. The distance, tuition, and questionable quality of the schools made this type of training impractical for most high school graduates of the area.

This problem was quickly recognized by the residents of Gillennon County, but it was the pressure of the area's congressmen which drove them into action. The congressmen found local leaders to press a proposal that the community provide post-high school training in the required technical skills so as to qualify applicants for employment in the center. Initially, two major alternatives appeared, i.e., a post-secondary school program to be set up and maintained by the county or the incorporation of such a program in the senior high school currently being operated in the Gillennon County School District. Since the county and the public school district were coterminous, the same geographic area, population, and tax structure would be involved in either alternative.

The county board of commissioners was first to act on the alternatives. The members were unanimous in their decision not to become involved in such a program. Furthermore, they urged that the project be seriously considered by the county board of education since it was an educational enterprise.

Even before the commissioners passed the final form of their resolution not to become involved, the county board of education initiated its study of the proposal. Informal discussions of the problem were being heard in board meetings almost immediately after the congressmen had expressed concern about adequate staffing of the agricultural data center. Dexter Irvine, president of the board, introduced a motion to consider "initiating a post-secondary school program providing for the training of business and management technicians."

Dexter Irvine had been an influential and effective board member. He was a partner in the law firm established by his father, who in turn was the son of one of the original settlers in the area. The Irvine family, although not wealthy by many standards, did own or control a significant sector of the Gillennon County economy. The family always had been influential in county affairs, but no member had ever held a major public office. Many residents in the county were of the opinion that Dexter was about to change that.

Under Irvine's prodding and subsequent leadership, an ad hoc committee of the board was charged with the responsibility of looking into the feasibility of the proposal. The committee began work immediately by scheduling consultation with the prosecuting attorney who was the ex officio legal advisor to the board. Irvine, who knew the state statutes providing for public education, was not surprised with the prosecuting attorney's response to the feasibility of the question. In essence, the state statutes required boards of education to provide free public education for all youth six to sixteen years of age. Boards had discretionary authority to provide a public education program for youth five years of age and for youth through the secondary school. Other statutes incorporating discretionary authority empowered boards of education to provide an education program for youth with various handicaps, to adults for citizenship education, to adults for basic literacy, and to adults for regular high school completion.

The state statutes made no further mention of the powers of the boards of education for providing public education. However, the state constitution listed education among discretionary powers of municipalities. It stated that municipal corporations may provide those instructional and training programs necessary for the welfare of the community, providing they were not offered by other governmental bodies.

It was the opinion of the prosecuting attorney that there was no possibility for the school district to provide post-secondary training under the present interpretation of the law. Instead, there appeared to be clear authority for only the county commissioners to do so.

At the next regular meeting of the Gillennon County Board of Education, President Irvine, as chairman of the ad hoc committee, presented a progress report on the preliminary investigations of the committee. The thorough and well-organized report was centered on the citation of specific paragraphs of the state constitution and the state statutes. To these Irvine added the interpretation of the prosecuting attorney. In summarizing the findings of the committee, Dexter Irvine added his own assessment of the situation.

"And so, gentlemen, from the strict interpretation of the state constitution and the statutes which implement it, it would appear that school districts are not empowered to provide the program we contemplate. However, let me remind you of one additional factor. Our constitution and statutes are man-made; they represent the guidelines and facilitating machinery which were deemed necessary to operate state and local governments as they existed over a half century ago. Both have been changed in the past, and both contain the machinery to change them again."

Dexter Irvine described briefly some of the significant changes made in the state constitution and illustrated with several cases some rather dramatic changes in the state statutes. He summarized this statement with a charge that all responsible citizens and officeholders have the duty not only to execute the law, but also to test and seek improvements in the law.

With his conclusion, some of the alert but less articulate board members asked Dexter just what he was "gettin' to." Just as forthrightly, Irvine responded. He stated that Gillennon County had the opportunity to make a valid and dramatic case for changing the state constitution in such a way as to enable local school districts to provide post-secondary school training to adults.

After considerable discussion it was agreed that Irvine should prepare a statement of rationale for a case to test the constitutional restriction. The board would decide whether the action should be undertaken after it heard Irvine's statement.

When Dexter Irvine presented the rationale for testing the state constitution on the matter of providing adult technical training in the public schools, one could easily detect his ability to communicate matters of public policy to a lay audience. His presentation incorporated three basic ideas expressed clearly in terms readily understood by the board. It was apparent that Irvine had carefully selected the arena in which he would seek state visibility in order to launch his political career.

The basic components of his rationale were:

1.   The issue is an appropriate one to be addressed by the board since it is educational in nature. If successful in its case, the board would contribute to unifying the educational function of the state. By obtaining explicit power to provide technical training for adults, boards of education could provide integrated educational policy, administration, and financial management for all segments of the educational enterprise. This would be a distinct improvement over the present situation of divided responsibility.

2.   There is logic, precedent, and a substantial body of legal opinion to provide a conceptual base for such a decision. The several steps of logic are as follows:

    a.   The federal Constitution provides for the delimitation of power for both the federal government and the separate state governments. State power is largely derived from the concept of police power which enables states to legislate in the area of health, safety, and morals. State power in this area is limited only by those powers specifically delegated to the federal government or those in which the state wishes to limit itself through its own constitution.

b. Local governments are created by the state and are given authority by the state itself. The state is plenary or original in power and thus can grant to or withdraw authority from local government.

c. There are essentially two types of local governments: municipalities and school districts. A "municipality" is a corporation created by the state for the primary purpose of local government. While it is in part a state agency for the conduct of government, its primary function is to regulate its own concerns. It has been said that local advantage and interest are characteristic of municipal government rather than execution of state policy. Thus it is vested with broad legislative and administrative powers.

The second type of local government created by the state is a school district which is substantially different from the municipal corporation just previously described. A "school district" is strictly defined as a quasi corporation. It is created by the state in order to execute state policy. It is an arm of the state with power limited by statute to the execution of a given function.

3. School districts, clearly recognized as quasi corporations, are responsible for the execution of state educational policy. The state constitution lists as discretionary the authority of municipal corporations to provide "instructional and training programs necessary for the welfare of the people." Thus, the provision of adult technical training is appropriate. The only question is whether this should be provided by the municipal corporation or the school district as a quasi corporation.

Legal precedent indicates that there are varying interpretations of municipalities. Courts have found that the word could apply to school districts, e.g., *Curry v. District Township of Sioux City, 62 Iowa 102, 17 N.W. 191.* Thus, the Gillennon County Board of Education might very well be considered a municipality with the authority to provide adult technical training.

Dexter Irvine concluded his statement with the admonition that, as school board members and consequently state rather than local officials, they could perform a significant service to the whole state by initiating action to test the intent and reasonableness of this law.

Questions for Discussion

1. If reallocation of power or authority among local governmental units is the basic problem in this case study, on what authority may the state take action?

2. In a 1966 statement by the Committee for Economic Development entitled *Modernizing Local Government*, the committee recommended that the number of overlapping layers of local government should be severely curtailed. What action might this suggest in the Gillennon County case? How could this be justified?

3. What is the interest of the state in seeking to reorganize local governmental units?

4. What implications does your statement answering question 3 above have for the concept of "local control"?

Case 24.   Fiscal Dependence in Bayshore

Tom Meredith and the Bayshore Board of Education seemed to "hit it off" from their very first encounter. Tom had just enough of the alert, somewhat brash appearance of the "new breed" intellectual to create the image of dynamic leadership. However, he also maintained many of the mannerisms of his Midwestern home environment to provide the board with the assurance of his sensitivity and stability.

Both his professional career and academic record qualified him for the superintendency in this upper Middle West city. Meredith grew up in a neighboring state, attended the university there, and taught and held administrative posts in the public schools in that state. After a total of six years in two superintendencies in small communities, Tom accepted a research assistantship on a school finance project at the state university near Bayshore. During his 2½-year tenure on the project, Tom completed his Ph.D. degree and served the last year as assistant to the director of the project. As a part of his responsibility, Tom communicated regularly with the superintendents and boards of twenty-two cities in the state, including Bayshore.

Consequently, when the Bayshore superintendent retired, Tom Meredith was highly recommended for the position by several influential agencies and individuals.

As a young school administrator committed to making the superintendency his career, Tom actively sought the Bayshore position. The job was a good one since the city was situated in a metropolitan and industrial belt stretching along the shore of one of the Great Lakes. The majority of its population of 90,000 derived its livelihood from the huge single-plant major appliance industry located in the city. Residents of Bayshore were predominantly blue-collar, many being second-generation immigrants. Since the major industry had been steadily automating its production for the past twenty years, the proportion of highly skilled technicians and engineers had markedly increased.

During the twelve-year tenure of the retiring superintendent, Bayshore was a "status quo" school system. A close working relationship among industrial, community, and school leaders had been affected fifty years ago with the establishment of a prototype vocational high school in addition to and separate from the original "academic" high school. In the late 1920s Bayshore Vocational High School characterized the best of its type of education. For many years after, the community rested on its educational laurels. However, for the last fifteen or twenty years the vocational program was maintained not as an educational model but as a training center for the city's major industry. Because of this as well as the changing technology, the vocational high school program and its enrollment have been steadily shrinking for the past ten years.

The rest of the school program during this period did not change in character either. When vocational education enrollments dropped, a larger proportion of students enrolled in the traditional college preparatory program. This caused little or no community concern until the last few years when a disturbingly high percent of Bayshore high school graduates were not admitted to the state university.

In assessing his new position, Tom Meredith tried to relate this apparent educational problem to community attitudes. Relations between school and community seemingly had been wholesome for years. After a careful examination of the records of tax levies and expenditures plus some informal chats with "old-timers" in both the school system and the community, Meredith concluded that the school system's educational and fiscal programs were largely determined by a loosely defined power structure. The origin of this practice lay in the industry-community-school alliance which was formed fifty years ago when the vocational high school was being initially promoted. The approval of the budget by the power structure was necessary to get the support of the industrial and community leaders to mount and maintain such a program. The practice of having the budget approved by these leaders became institutionalized and was followed ever since. As a result, tax rates and expenditures for the school system were always held to what these leaders would accept. Thus, there were never any overt disagreements regarding the rather static school programs or finances.

This situation was particularly significant since Bayshore, with its 90,000 population figure, was in a classification of cities which the state had designated as fiscally dependent; i.e., the school budget, after being developed by the board of education, had to be finally approved by the city council. Since the community leaders had already been informed of the expenditures and had given the tentative budget an informal nod of approval, the budget review by the city council was, with few exceptions, a perfunctory act. Occasionally, a minor change was made in order for the council to show the board of education "who was boss."

The School Board of Bayshore, after having worked with Tom Meredith's conservative predecessor for several years, was ready for dynamic leadership in its new superintendent. Consequently, when Tom initiated proposals for upgrading the college prep curriculum as well as broadening the general education program, the board was supportive. Both Tom and the board members knew this would involve a considerable increase in the budget. It was almost taken for granted that such additional expenditures would also generate considerable opposition among the taxpayers. Thus, it was agreed that community leaders must be consulted on the budget.

Two board members held executive positions in the appliance works and were influential in obtaining a statement of support from the corporation's board of directors. Other civic leaders were contacted and reaction was generally favorable. The mayor indicated that he could not openly support the additional expenditures but he promised not to oppose them. The several councilmen, however, were clearly shaken when they were originally contacted on the matter. The majority of the council had been elected during the past three years and were none too sure as to their function in this situation. The few "old-timers" never had to cope with the problem of such a substantial increase in the budget. Consequently, as individuals, each councilman adopted a noncommittal attitude toward the informal contact made by Meredith and the board regarding the budget to be submitted to the city council.

The constitution of the state within which Bayshore is located provides that on or before January 15 the city board of education must submit to the city council a tentative budget for the next fiscal year. The council is authorized to reduce or add to the total amount of the budget but not to the line items in the budget itself. On or before March 15 the council must return the approved or modified budget to the board of education. The board of education may appeal the council's action and request a public hearing which must be held prior to April 30. If, after the hearing, the board of education wishes to appeal again, the district judge hears the appeal and makes the final decision on the school budget.

The Bayshore Board of Education submitted its tentative budget to the city council on January 9. The council received it at its regular meeting of January 11 and placed the budget into the traditional review machinery. It was evident to the board of education, however, that this year's review would not result in the typical prefunctory approval.

The city council did not return the approved budget document to the secretary of the board of education until March 14. When the budget was examined, it was found that over $800,000 had been cut out of the original $3,550,000 budget!

Upon receipt of the reduced budget, the secretary of the board of education called a special session for purposes of reviewing the council's action. In looking at the reasons for the action, it was generally agreed that the council had responded to pressures exerted by citizens resisting additional local taxes and representatives of small industries and small businesses who claimed to be in a costs-profits squeeze. It was apparent that the $800,000 cut from the budget represented the cost of the proposed additions to the school program.

When the question was posed as to next steps, the board was unanimous in favoring resubmission of the original budget to the council at a public hearing.

The daily newspapers of Bayshore as well as other large cities throughout the state had a field day. The major focus of the news and editorial coverage appeared to be the question, Who should make fiscal decisions for the schools: the board or the city council? The legal authority of the city council to cut the budget was fully documented and interpreted.

One newspaper ran a series of features on the Bayshore situation. A professional educator and a political scientist were interviewed in order to identify the major points of disagreement. Arguments for both fiscal independence and dependence were stated. The major points made by the professional educator were those which favored fiscal independence.

1. Public schools should be free of partisan political control.

2. Education is a state function, and the intervention of municipal control makes it impossible for a local board of education to be responsible only to the state.

3. Fiscal control contributes to de facto control of educational policies.

4. Fiscal independence promotes greater stability and continuity in educational planning.

5. Fiscal dependence promotes municipal-school friction by overt competition for the tax dollar.

The political scientist identified four basic arguments supporting fiscal dependence:

1. Fiscal dependence promotes coordinated planning.

2. Fiscal dependence promotes rational and concerted programs and thus prevents disjointed financial structures and overlapping functions.

3. Fiscal dependence promotes the visibility of government by reducing fragmentation of decision making.

4. Fiscal dependence promotes the weighting of the relative merits of various local public services including education.

Both authorities, however, agreed there was no clear empirical evidence as to whether either fiscally dependent or independent school districts were more efficient or economic in operation.

A feature common to most of the news stories, stated or implied, was the question, "Is a city council the appropriate body to approve school budgets when a board of education is responsible to the people for the quality of the educational program?" Thus, the concept of fiscal dependence was thoroughly analyzed by the metropolitan press during the period between the council's original return of the budget and the requested public hearing.

Both the city council and the board of education prepared carefully for the public hearing. As provided by the law, both agencies compiled statements and introduced testimony to support their school budget proposals. A large group of interested citizens was also present.

The city council defended the reduced budget on the following bases:

1. The proposed public school budget would raise the school portion of the city property tax from 20 to 24 mills. The rest of the municipal budget (16 mills) would remain at the same level. Thus, the increase in school taxes was responsible for the total increase in city property tax from 36 to 40 mills.

2. Other city programs planned for the following year would be jeopardized because of the increased tax rate this year.

3. The proposed school budget would "disturb the traditional balance in quantity and quality of municipal services available to and paid for by the citizens."

4. Several items of the proposed school budget appeared to be "frills—less necessary than certain other municipal programs being contemplated by the city council."

The president of the board of education, as spokesman for that group, made the initial statement for the board. He presented a brief and general review of the current school program, the nature of educational needs in Bayshore, and the proposed budget to meet these needs. Special emphasis was given to the new and additional programs. The president was very positive in citing the way in which "the board considered these needs and exercised its judgment, appropriate to a body elected by the public to serve this function."

The testimonies presented by the council and the board were essentially supportive of the council's budget and the board's budget, respectively. Among the organizations which testified in favor of the council's budget were the Bayshore Taxpayers' Association, the Commercial Club of Bayshore, and two of the city's four neighborhood property owners' associations. In addition several speakers who identified themselves as "interested citizens" made informal statements supporting the reduced school budget.

It was quite apparent that the board of education had the advantage in both the number and the relative prestige of groups and individuals giving testimony. All the "power structure" who were originally and informally contacted early in the budget development process were there and gave testimony. They left no doubt that these educational and expenditure plans were approved by their organizations. The chamber of commerce, which was dominated by personnel from the appliance works, presented an official statement of support. The local AFL-CIO affiliate of the appliance works also sent a spokesman who indicated that organization's support of the school board's budget. The Bayshore Council of PTA gave supportive testimony for the original budget also.

These formal statements of support were supplemented by a large group of interested citizens who spoke on behalf of the board's budget. Without exception, these were parents of school children concerned about upgrading the city's educational program.

After all testimonies were heard, the mayor, as presiding officer of the hearing, charged the city council with its next task of reconsidering the school district budget and filing the reconsidered budget by the mandated date. The mayor then adjourned the hearing.

In an informal "executive session" which followed, Tom Meredith and the board members reflected a feeling of optimism about the way in which they mobilized broad and impressive community support for their budget. All felt the question of the appropriateness of the school budget in terms of needs was positively answered. Several of the members felt the original school budget would be approved. All felt at least a major part of the additional funds would be approved.

However, the group displayed a haunting doubt despite the apparent overwhelming success of their "power play." Several members of the board expressed concern over the issue cited during the last few weeks by the metropolitan newspapers, "Is a city council the appropriate body to approve school budgets when a board of education is responsible to the people for the quality of the educational program?" Bernie Mayfield, an accountant elected to the board two years ago, was of the opinion that the hearing aptly demonstrated the council's lack of knowledge of school problems.

> "We showed them we were right and that we could back up our budget, but are we going to have to do this every year? If the law says we are to determine what the schools need, I can't see how a group which knows very little about schools should override us."

> "But Bernie," Tom Meredith began, "the law in the state has made boards of education fiscally dependent, and this. . . ."

> "I know, I know, Tom," Bernie interrupted, "I heard it all a hundred times. The real question is whose judgment will prevail. Tonight I believe the board's judgment prevailed, but it did so after expending an awful lot of time and energy which should not have been necessary. Somehow, there must be a better way to balance school needs against other municipal needs—and I don't mean that we should abdicate our responsibilities, either."

Bernie Mayfield's statement touched off a lively discussion on the concerns of powers of local government, authority of elected bodies, and responsibility of boards of education. However, each time a member's comments ventured off into abstractions, it was Bernie Mayfield who brought the discussion back to Bayshore with the following question.

> "That's all right, but how is that going to help us avoid all this again?"

Because of Mayfield's prodding, the Bayshore board members isolated three alternative positions which might be taken in speaking to the issue of fiscal dependence:

1. The board could employ the power play and dominate the city council if the latter again reduced the board of education budget.

2. The board could co-opt the council by soliciting and gaining its support for the school budget prior to its actual submission.

3. The board could exercise leadership in the state to abolish fiscal dependence of boards of education through a state constitutional amendment.

Questions for Discussion

1. How does the concept of fiscal dependency relate to the plenary power of the state?

2. What might be the state's interest in creating fiscally dependent school districts?

3. What problems does fiscal dependency create? What kind of legal provisions might a state provide in order to eliminate or relieve these problems?

4. What actions might be taken in Bayshore by individuals or groups which favored a fiscally dependent school district? What are the legal bases for these actions?

Case 25.   Curriculum Balance in Sequoia Valley

School officials in the Sequoia Valley School District received the news of the passage of the National Defense Education Act with mixed feelings. The school district was in dire need of financial assistance, and personnel representing the district had been supporters of various federal aid to education proposals for several years. However, the national urgency of "catching up with the Russians" in the space race as occasioned by the launching of Sputnik in 1957 was not felt as markedly in Sequoia Valley as it was in other parts of the nation. Some rather severe local problems tended to take the edge off questions related to how the United States would go about surpassing the Soviet Union in space activities.

For several generations nearly all residents of Sequoia Valley and the surrounding area derived their livelihood from many relatively small, privately owned lumbering operations. The countryside had been liberally dotted with small sawmills and a few lumber-related processing plants and industries. However, automation influenced this segment of the West Coast lumbering industry also, and for the past ten years its character had been changing.

Large corporations, having worked through the more productive lumber regions, turned to areas like Sequoia Valley for new timber cropping tracts. Not only did they take over the small private enterprises, but they also brought in the more efficient machinery and methods which characterized big companies. As a consequence, many of the jobs maintained in smaller, less-sophisticated lumbering operations were eliminated.

No mass unemployment resulted from this shift, however. Coincident with the moving in of the big lumbering interests was growth of other more diversified enterprises. A long-dormant fishing industry was revived. The small and modest resort and tourist industry experienced a sudden spurt of growth. Truck and fruit farms were developed and expanded to fill the rapidly increasing national demand for such foodstuffs.

LeRoy Holmberg, superintendent of the school district, and Kermit Albern, the high school principal, had both been residents of the school district for more than twenty years prior to 1958. Holmberg had been brought in as high school principal twenty-two years before. For the past fourteen years he had served as superintendent of schools. Albern, appointed to the principalship when Holmberg was elevated to the superintendency, had served as a teacher in one-room schools in up-river lumber camps, and as a high school science and mathematics teacher in Sequoia Valley. Both men knew the community and commanded respect as schoolmen in the area.

With the apparent shifting of the local economy in Sequoia Valley, both Holmberg and Albern were concerned over upgrading vocational education in the local high school. The state program was essentially the same Smith-Hughes program adopted a generation ago. It was clearly inadequate for local needs in Sequoia Valley, and the school district had little tax leeway to provide its own locally financed vocational and technical training program.

The publicity which accompanied the National Defense Education Act of 1958 prompted many of the residents of Sequoia Valley to expect massive federal grants to upgrade the school district's science and other programs with little or no local effort being required. However, when the provisions of the act were publicized and interpreted, it was apparent that substantial state and/or local effort must be expended in order to qualify for this instructional bonanza.

The act itself contained ten titles with the majority providing funds for elementary and secondary education. Other titles provided for loans to students, the conduct of institutes, fellowships, state supervisory and statistical services, area vocational programs, and related programs.

Title III, the most significant of the ten titles, provided for assisting instruction in mathematics, modern languages, and science in secondary schools. Grants under Title III made monies available to local school districts for materials and equipment to upgrade instruction in science, mathematics, and foreign languages and to finance minor remodeling of space for these purposes.

In order to take into consideration the varying ability of the several states, the NDEA allotted the monies to the states on the basis of a formula which took into account school-age population (ages five to seventeen) and the state's "allotment ratio." These ratios varied inversely with the average income per school-age child. The ratio was derived from the following calculation:

$$100-50 \times \frac{\text{State income per child of school age}}{\text{U.S. income per child of school age}} \quad .$$

However, a 33⅓ percent minimum value and a 66⅔ maximum value were placed on the allotment ratio. Thus, the ratios ranged from 1⅓ times the nationwide average for poor states to ⅔ the nationwide average for wealthy states.

Each state, having been allotted a variable share of the monies appropriated to the NDEA, was obligated to match its federal allotment with state and/or local monies. State plans for the dispersing of these monies were subject to general federal guidelines but provided considerable flexibility to accommodate unique conditions found among the individual states.

Since allotments to the individual states varied directly with school-age population and inversely with income per child of school age, the residents of Sequoia Valley recognized that their state would receive a relatively generous grant. The state's ratio of school-age youth to adult population was considerably higher than that of the United States's average while the income per capita was somewhat lower than the average. Thus, on both factors the state qualified for an allotment larger than the majority of states.

Although the state qualified for a generous amount of federal aid under the act, this posed a problem since an equal amount of state and/or local money was required to match the federal allocation. Just two years prior to the enactment of the NDEA, this state had increased its sales tax to provide more assistance to local school districts. Consequently when the state program for administering the act was drawn up, there was virtually no legislative support for using state monies to match the federal allotment in Title III. Instead, the state program called for matching monies to come from local sources.

As information pertaining to the development of the state program to implement the NDEA reached the Sequoia Valley school administrators, it became apparent to them that major readjustments would have to be made in order to claim the federal monies to which the school district was "theoretically" entitled. Superintendent Holmberg was particularly anxious to design a plan to utilize all available monies. The school district, never a wealthy one, was undergoing a change which required a considerable modification of school program. Both Holmberg and Albern, the high school principal, agreed that the change from small mill lumbering to a more diversified economy had made the high school program increasingly obsolete. In former years, the traditional college preparatory course took care of the few youngsters that went on to college, and the apprentice-type experience provided in the small mills and on the farms took care of the vocational training of the non-college-bound boys. Beyond these two program "tracks," there was little community concern. By 1958, there was not only a demand for a "beefed up" college preparatory program, but also for a more adequate program to prepare both boys and girls for the various service industries, technicians, training programs, stenographic training, and the like.

For the three years prior to the actual implementation of the NDEA, Mr. Albern as high school principal had requested the expansion of the business education program and the addition of a course in speech. The major point in his supporting argument was that now many of the youth of the community must find employment outside "the Valley" since the mill operation changed. In order to do this, additional skills in both communication and preparation for the operation of, or further training in, complex equipment was necessary. Finally because of his persuasive argument and persistence, Holmberg and the school board agreed to increase local taxes and the budget to accommodate these additions.

However, before Albern could start the search for personnel and begin to develop a program, the word was received first by the "grapevine" and then by State Department of Education directive that all Title III allocations must be matched with local monies. It came as no surprise to Albern when LeRoy Holmberg informed him that his "projects and other lower priority items would have to wait." The funds originally earmarked for them would instead have to be diverted to cover the matching required to obtain new furniture, demonstration tables, audiovisual equipment, and other items for the science department as well as some minor remodeling to assure better usage of the equipment.

In defending this action, Holmberg stressed the following points:

1. The school district was getting "more mileage" from its total ex-

penditures by using local matching monies to obtain an equal amount from the NDEA.

2. The imbalance caused by siphoning monies out of the speech and business education programs was temporary since the NDEA equipment and remodeling expenditures would not require additional local outlay in the near future.

3. Although equipment obtained was to be used primarily for science instruction, much of it could be used to upgrade instruction in other teaching areas as well; e.g., the electronics equipment purchased for the physics classes could be used in industrial arts, the calculators obtained for the mathematics room could be used in business education classes, and the furniture replaced in the science room could in turn replace the older furniture in the English department.

4. By prompt action, the local school district could perhaps obtain a supplementary NDEA allocation since some school districts in the state did not take advantage of the program. Thus, the districts which did participate could receive (with additional matching monies, of course) an additional grant since the state's allocation was based on 100 percent participation.

Kermit Albern was somewhat skeptical of the all-out move to obtain the NDEA money. He proposed several counterarguments to the action:

1. A severe curriculum imbalance would result not only from the additional emphasis on science and mathematics but also because other curriculum areas were contracted in order to provide half of the additional support given the former.

2. Several of the curricular areas cut were the very ones which needed upgrading the most, i.e., business education and speech.

3. The additional emphasis and public visibility given the science and mathematics areas will make it increasingly difficult to mobilize public support for areas originally felt to need immediate help, i.e., business education and speech.

4. Some of the equipment to be ordered is of such a sophisticated nature that it outstrips the teacher's ability to use it effectively. Although it is a "bargain" in terms of the outlay of local money, it is perhaps false economy in terms of what it will add to the program.

5. There is no assurance that the minor remodeling proposed for the science room is economically feasible since such a specialized facility will be used only two or possibly four periods a day. The school district will have to maintain and operate it as a single-use facility whereas before it was a classroom used by different instructional groups.

Kermit Albern knew his arguments would not influence the immediate decision to obtain NDEA funds. He was hopeful that his thinking would enter into broad philosophical and policy considerations to be entertained later.

Questions for Discussion

1. How was the NDEA an example of the exercise of federal police power at the state and local level of government?

2. Cite an example of the fiscal control which the federal government exercised in the Sequoia Valley Case.

3. In what way did the NDEA influence state policy in this case?

4. What specific local policy in Sequoia Valley did the NDEA influence? What might be secondary or "chain reaction" effects of this policy?

5. Can you cite any other federal legislation that has had a similar impact on state and local policy in education?

Suggested Readings

Concept I—Powers and Functions of State and Local Governments

Advisory Commission on Intergovernmental Relations: *Measures of State and Local Fiscal Capacity and Tax Effort*, Washington, D.C.: The Commission, 1962.

Bailey, Stephen, et al.: *Schoolmen and Politics*, Syracuse, N.Y.: Syracuse University Press, 1962.

Committee for Economic Development: *Modernizing Local Government*, New York: The Committee, 1966.

——: *Modernizing State Government*, New York: The Committee, 1967.

The Council of State Governments: *Local School Expenditures: 1970 Projections*, Chicago: The Council, 1965.

McConnell, Campbell R.: *Economics*, 4th ed., New York: McGraw-Hill, 1969, chap. 9, pp. 137, 143.

National Education Association: *Guides to the Development of State School Finance Programs*, Washington, D.C.: The Association, 1959.

Samuelson, Paul A.: *Economics*, 7th ed., New York: McGraw-Hill, 1967, chap. 9, pp. 162–166.

Tax Foundation, Inc.: *State Tax Studies: 1959–1967*, New York: The Foundation, 1967.

U.S. Department of Health, Education, and Welfare, *State Programs for Public School Support*, Washington, D.C.: The Department, 1965.

concept j

Powers and Functions of the Federal Government

the problem

Public education has traditionally been seen as a local function. However, it is important to recognize the genesis and nature of this function. In order to analyze the rationale and propriety of the concept, it is fruitful to consider the general powers and functions of the federal government as well as those specifically related to public education. After determining the proper functions of the federal government in education, it is then possible to ascertain the appropriate educational programs to be determined at the federal level. From this, one can also determine the kind of financial support the public schools should have at this level of government.

The student of "practical politics" is quick to sense that the ultimate power of any governmental unit is not necessarily limited to that designated in a constitution. The ability or means available to exercise the delegated power is also significant. One of the most important means of exercising power is economic or financial means. Thus, one must consider the extent to which a governmental unit can implement or put into effect the legislated power it holds.

These are appropriate concerns for the student of educational government for two major reasons. First, it is a major task to clarify the duties and functions of the three levels of government in any area of endeavor.

The second reason is related to the most remarkable feature of our governmental structure (particularly the federal Constitution), i.e., its flexibility to adapt to a changing culture. Thus powers and functions stated generally change form as they are applied to a changing society. In the concept statement and the cases, one will recognize implicit problems in both interpretation and application of the powers and functions of the federal government in public education.

the concept

The powers and functions of our federal government are all based on the national Constitution. A relatively short document, this Constitution contains not only grants of power, but limitations on power. In fact, a great deal of the efforts of the Constitutional Convention of

1787 was directed toward determining ways to prevent any one of the three branches of the federal government from dominating the other two.

The general limitations on power are three. First, the balance of power, by which the functions and powers of the national government are divided among the administrative, legislative, and judicial branches, with each branch supreme in its own sphere. Second, the due process provision, which provides that no person shall be deprived of life, liberty, or property without due process of law. Fundamentally, this means that every person has the right to appeal any government action taken against him to the courts. And third, our federal system of government. A federal government is a dual system in which the powers are divided between the central (national) and local (state) authorities, with each supreme in its own sphere.

In the years since the Constitution was adopted in 1789, this document has been changed and modified in many ways. It has been modified by custom, by amendment, by legislative statute, and by judicial decision. The largest body of changes is in the form of the legislative actions; the most important body of changes is in the form of the judicial decisions. The task of interpreting the Constitution, now a responsibility of the Supreme Court, was not explicitly assigned in the Constitution. There is evidence that the matter was discussed in the Constitutional Convention, but it was not settled. The Court assumed this task, however, in the case of *Marbury v. Madison*. This is an example of the axiom that important law is often decided in unimportant cases, for this case involved the efforts of Mr. Marbury to obtain a commission appointing him justice of the peace. The Supreme Court (with John Marshall as Chief Justice) did not grant Mr. Marbury his plea, but it did assume for itself a power not previously settled: the power to declare acts of Congress unconstitutional.

Powers, and the limitations on power, may be granted expressly or by implication. The existence of implied powers is hinted at in the Constitution (Article 1, section 8), but this hint was not firmly established until 1819 and the Supreme Court case of *McCulloch v. Maryland*. This case involved the attempt of the state of Maryland to place a discriminatory and confiscatory tax on the paper currency issued by the Baltimore branch of the Second Bank of the United States. Mr. McCulloch, the Baltimore cashier, refused to pay the tax and appealed the case to the United States Supreme Court. The Court made two rulings. First, that no state has the right to tax an instrumentality of the federal government, and second, that there are implied powers of the federal government. Even though the Constitution makes no explicit grant of power to the national government to establish and operate a bank, Congress must be given the right to choose whatever means they desire to carry out those powers which are explicitly granted. Concomitantly, there are also implied limitations on the powers of the federal government.

The existing pattern of explicit and implicit powers and limitations on powers, together with the prevailing customs and practices, has established the current functions of the federal government. Just as the Constitution has been changed and modified, so have many government functions become more or less important than in previous years. Some new functions have been added and some have even been discarded. Most of the additions to the list of federal governmental functions were made during the depression days of the 1930s, and this period has sometimes been described as the "start of the march of power to Washington." Another description, which may be just as accurate, is that there was witnessed during the decade of the 1930s a "flight of responsibility to Washington."

The functions of the federal government, however, have remained basically the same in the period since the beginning of the century. The change has been in the relative importance of specific functions and the degree of participation in a particular function by the federal government. For instance, national defense has always been an exclusive function of the federal government, but this has grown so much in relative importance that it now accounts for over half of the federal budget. Also, the federal government for many decades has been involved to a slight extent in the financing of education (the Smith-Hughes Vocational Education Act is an example), but in recent years the importance of the federal participation relative to the role of the state and local governments has been rapidly expanding.

Since the period before World War I, the percentage of total government outlays expended by the federal and local governments has been reversed. That is, in 1900 local governments as a group were responsible for 55 percent of the total government expenditures, and the federal government was responsible for 34 percent. In 1966 the local governments accounted for 20 percent of the total, and the federal government accounted for 63 percent. The relative position of the state governments has remained largely unchanged.

It is sometimes futile to speculate about the future, but it does appear that the force of circumstances will dictate a continuation of the developments of recent years, that is, the increasing dependence of one part of the country upon the other parts, and the growing difficulty of financing local government functions. The result will be increased demands for federal participation; there seems to be no logical alternative.

Case 26.   Redefining the Issue: Dollars for Education or Roles of Government

As a social studies teacher in Ramsey Senior High School, Richard Fulton's major concern was that of awakening in his students the realization of their rights and responsibilities as political activists. Dick Fulton characterized these beliefs in his own behavior. As an undergraduate, Dick was active in student government, in the Current Issues Forum, and on the college debate team. After college, he took a teaching job in the social studies department in Ramsey Senior High in 1957 where he taught courses in world and American history and civics. He also served as coach and advisor to the high school debate team.

Outside of school Dick Fulton was active in local politics—something previously unheard of among Ramsey faculty members. Although he did not run for office, Fulton was a very visible supporter for the men and issues he favored.

His political commitment was also demonstrated in his activities in the state and local professional organizations. After serving on numerous committees for four years, Fulton was named legislation chairman for the Dodge County Education Association in 1963.

During the summer of that year Dodge County as well as the rest of this Great Plains state and the whole nation was carefully watching the national Congress. A unique and comprehensive bill had been introduced which, if enacted, would provide millions of dollars for a broadened program of vocational education. By October, it was apparent that there was sufficient support to bring it to the floor for debate and probably a vote.

Education interests which supported the bill set up programs to expedite the moving of the bill through the Congress. One specific program was that of designating representatives from the state education associations as contact men for each member of that state's congressional delegation in Washington. Consequently, Richard Fulton was asked to present the case for the proposed bill to Congressman Anderson Millington.

Dodge County was a relatively populous county in this Great Plains state. The state was of a generally conservative tradition although it had always supported federal farm programs and the like. By and large, other forms of federal aid were not enthusiastically supported unless they provided specific benefits to the state such as flood control or highway construction.

In the matter of federal education bills, little support could be mustered for any type of general aid proposal such as the Murray-Metcalf bill. Even schoolhouse construction measures were unpopular.

The state's congressmen did support, however, the School Lunch Program bill, and Public Laws 815 and 874 for federally impacted school districts.

The State Department of Education and local educational jurisdictions reflected the same kind of attitudes. Both of these types of organization were locally oriented. The State Department of Education delegated considerable authority to the local school districts in matters of staffing, curriculum, and the like. Most educational innovations had always been initiated on the local level. Little more than coordination was provided by the state department. Consequently, local school districts developed and maintained their own educational programs supported in the main by local property taxes. The state, through essentially a flat grant plan of state aid, contributed only 15 percent of public school revenues.

With relatively few state restrictions, the original Smith-Hughes vocational legislation was well suited to this state. Most of the programs which were actually implemented in the many small rural school districts of the state were of a relatively modest vocational agriculture type. Without pressure from the State Department of Education, little change had taken place in the program for more than forty years. Consequently, in more recent years, even though fewer and fewer youth were being employed as full-time farmers upon high school graduation, the vocational education programs remained primarily agriculture-oriented. Occasionally pressure mounted in a community to provide some kind of technical, trade, or industrial education, but since these were high-cost programs and because of only modest state aid, the additional local tax burden which would be necessary was usually cited as a major deterrent to such an addition.

The state's congressional delegation reflected the inherent conservatism of this region. Anderson Millington, the senior U.S. representative, came from the congressional district which included Dodge County. Thus, Richard Fulton was charged with the responsibility of contacting the congressman to discuss the proposed legislation.

The mechanics of the contact were arranged by the State Education Association. At the appointed time, Richard Fulton of Dodge County presented himself at the office of Representative Millington. He was greeted and ushered into the congressman's inner office. After the usual amenities and inquiries as to Fulton's hometown and his job, Millington took the initiative concerning the proposed Vocational Education Act.

"I understand, Mr. Fulton, that your organization—the State Education Association—is pushing for this vocational education bill."

"Yes sir," replied Fulton, "but I am here on behalf of the Dodge County Education Association and on my own behalf as well. I am of the opinion this legislation is badly needed in our state. I believe it is important for you to be aware of the beliefs of some of your constituents on this proposed legislation. It is also important that you know the reasons for their positions on the legislation."

Acknowledging a nod from the distinguished congressman, Dick Fulton recited a long list of arguments favoring passage of the proposed bill. Although he was certain the legislator had heard them all before, Fulton cited the changing industrial and economic base of the state; the passing of the family farm from the scene; the technologically unemployed farm youth; the underemployed factory workers; the scarcity of properly trained technicians; the inability of local school districts to provide the needed educational programs for in-school youth, to say nothing of the out-of-school youth and adults who desperately needed it; and finally the inadequacy of the State Department of Education in handling the problem.

When he finished, Dick Fulton braced himself for the anticipated rebuttal by Congressman Millington. The venerated legislator started out slowly.

"Yes, Mr. Fulton, those are appropriate arguments for mounting a comprehensive program in vocational education. They are convincing—and I have been aware of most of them for several, if not many, years. Further, I agree that action must be taken to correct or at least alleviate the most serious of them. But, I must ask you, does the proposed legislation provide the only path to the resolution of these problems?

"I'll answer my own question: No, we must look at several other factors which bear on the question. First, what kind of problem is this? It is educational in nature. I will grant that the federal government is and should be interested in education, but our Constitution and heritage tell us public education has always been and should be a vital responsibility of the state and local levels of government. Without strong local and state government, public education can never be strong. If we continue to initiate and finance education programs through the federal government, we will cause educational concern at the state and local level to wither and die. Today we have seen too much of this already —local and state authority and powers degenerate when not exercised.

"Although we see the immediate maladjustments, the problem, I believe, requires a long-range look. Let us find ways to strengthen state and local governments so they can handle their own educational problems—that is the best service the federal government can perform."

Dick Fulton realized that Congressman Millington had redefined the issue. The new issue pertained to the appropriate role for the federal government in the matter of vocational education. This would require the use of different data and perhaps a different approach.

Questions for Discussion

1. In what way might one use the Vocational Education Act of 1963 as an illustration of a given federal function changing not in purpose but in importance?

2. What were the apparently differing points of view held by Richard Fulton and Congressman Millington regarding the role of the federal government in the question of this vocational education act?

3. What was the constitutional basis of the act? Was it an expressed power or an implied power?

4. What counterarguments might Richard Fulton use to rebut Congressman Millington's statement regarding the continued federal initiation and financing of education programs and its consequent effect of killing state and local concern for these programs?

Case 27.   A Statement on School Finance Pathology: Causes, Symptoms, and Cures

As a school board member, Angelo Tolletti shared many of the same concerns as the 800 or more school board members who were attending a regional school boards conference on school finance. He had children of his own in school and realized the necessity and value of a good education.

Angelo's father migrated to the United States early in the century, settled in an East Coast city, took a job in a refinery, started night school, married, and raised a family. Because of a natural leadership among his fellow workers and his rapid grasp of the language and customs of his adopted country, the senior Tolletti became spokesman, then union steward for the refinery workers in the plant.

Angelo was reared in an environment where a close family relationship set firm goals and expectations for members of the family, but also developed a social conscience regarding the individual and his relationships to social institutions. Angelo was one of the few young men from his neighborhood to go on to college following his high school graduation. While enrolled in one of the smaller state universities near his home, the younger Tolletti became interested in social work and eventually completed his degree in that area of study. After a hitch in the Army, Angelo returned to his hometown and took a position with a privately funded social agency. After several years, Angelo Tolletti had progressed into a "middle management" position with the agency where he supervised caseworkers and planned with community leaders.

During the past year or two, Tolletti's attention had been almost wholly devoted to work with intercultural groups. He was instrumental in developing and preserving a delicate armistice among several potentially explosive factions within the city. In his work with the city leadership, Angelo had developed the reputation for being fair but outspoken, and volatile but logical. Many of his fellow school board members knew him from his accomplishments with the agency, rather than his contributions to the school boards group. Consequently, many of these representatives were not surprised to see Angelo Tolletti ask for the floor in the final or summary session of the conference on school finance.

"At a session where we are supposed to suggest ways of implementing all we have learned these past 2½ days, I suppose I'm a heretic to say that I'm convinced we're wasting 90 percent of our time at these finance conferences. We talk of how school boards are to relate to other local taxing bodies, how we can influence the Governor to modify certain features of the state aid formula, how to tax house trailers, and how to minimize federal controls through careful proposal writing. We're dabbling with details of little consequence. Other than venting our frustrations, little good has been accomplished in these deliberations.

"Our concern with minutia has, I believe, blinded us to the real and significant problems of public education. Not only have we been preoccupied with details—we have been largely concerned with the details as they trouble us in our own school districts.

"Nearly all openly profess or covertly imply that we are concerned with public education across the whole nation and by this, best serve the youth in our own state, town, and school. But, our actions are nearly always turned inward to our own local situation. We say the federal government does have a responsibility in public education but we never bother to define it. We concern ourselves with the local symptoms of educational problems. We urge the adoption of compensatory programs for the children in slum neighborhoods in our large cities. We have Headstart, cooperative work-study programs, school breakfast programs, school lunch programs, Upward Bound, and many other specific programs. We adopt thin, stop-gap programs where well-conceived and well-financed programs are necessary.

"Why? What is the basic problem? One part of the problem is that we want an adequate educational program for all our children, but at the same time we don't want to force programs requiring exorbitant taxes on areas where financial ability is modest.

"Another dimension to the problem is that there are some basic inequalities in this country, and we are afraid to recognize them and correct them. Where does this inequality come from? It's basically one of economic ability. Look at the personal income for each child of school age. New York has $13,604 while Mississippi has $4,945! New Mexico has only $6,725 and South Dakota has $6,923!

"What happens? Without decent education we start a cycle of unemployment, poverty, and then even poorer education. When people can't make a living in Mississippi or New Mexico or South Dakota, they head toward the big cities of the North or the East, or the far West. It is here then that even more symptoms of the problem crop up—unemployment, slums, crime, and huge welfare costs. Much of the problem is the same—it has just moved and concentrated.

"I say we're wasting 90 percent of our time when we talk about our own symptoms of the problems. Instead we should start working to provide an adequate education for every child in the country—not just those in our own school district or our state. If we solve the major or key problems, we won't have to chase around trying to decide what symptom we should treat next and how we are going to do it.

"For a long time we have worked to assure every man a vote. This was good—it made everyone the same. But this is only quantitative. Each man has a vote but the quality of that vote is unequal because some voters are being short changed on the education which is needed to make them use it effectively. Now we have to provide equal education opportunity to make that vote qualitatively equal.

"There's only one agency that can be used to gain effectively this kind of equality in education—and that's the federal government. In the past few years, it has done this in many other fields—social security and unemployment insurance, the Civil Rights Act, Medicare, and many others. It's time that all the states were given equal opportunities to provide a good education for all their children. There's no reason we can't develop legislation to achieve a national purpose—we always promote laws to meet state or individual purposes!"

The chairman of the summary session thanked school board member Tolletti for his comments. Several other "for the good of the order" suggestions were made, but it was apparent the majority of delegates present understood Tolletti's message and the few suggestions which followed his speech highlighted his concerns. Despite a lack of apparent agreement, Angelo Tolletti's argument would be widely discussed among groups of school board members.

Questions for Discussion

1. Angelo Tolletti identified inequities in educational opportunity throughout the nation as his primary concern. What inequities other than education has the federal government sought to alleviate? What powers has it exercised to do this?

2. What was the basis of the inequity identified by Tolletti? How have basic problems caused a shift of responsibility from state and local governmental levels to the federal level?

3. What is the role of the federal government in education as implied in Tolletti's comments?

4. What rationale did Angelo Tolletti use to involve the federal government in the resolution of the problem of educational inequities? Is there any other rationale that could be used? If so, what might it (they) be?

Case 28.   A Reconsideration of the Role of Federal Government

Since his election to the United States Senate from a traditionally conservative state in the Northwest, Robert Thomson was known as an "unlikely liberal." Not only did he originate from a conservative area but also Thomson was raised in a family of successful small town merchants of a conservative bent.

As a student in the state university, young Robert Thomson soon abandoned his plans (and those of the senior Thomson for Robert) to take his undergraduate degree in commerce. Instead Robert gravitated toward the Arts and Sciences College and eventually took his degree from that college with majors in both political science and economics.

Probably as something of a compromise, young Robert returned home from the state university and became involved in the management of the small group of Thomson's department stores. However, his interest in political science drew him to support a minority point of view regarding a federal conservation bill which had considerable implications for the logging and paper mill interests in the state. His activities in supporting the bill and his identification with the point of view of several liberal leaders on the national scene gave him a great deal of visibility in the liberal party in his own state. The party had been a potent political force before and during World War II, but since the late 1940s had lost appeal to voters in the state and became impotent and attracted few young activists. Consequently, Robert Thomson had little difficulty in getting the party's nomination for senator to the state legislature. Thomson lost the election, but during the following year he was appointed to fill out the unexpired term of the senior senator who died in office after serving twenty-five years in that body. As a member of the state Senate, Robert Thomson worked quietly and methodically very much in the style of his predecessor.

The majority party was in firm control of both houses and the governorship, and so Thomson's views and proposed actions as a minority party member in the Senate were not considered a threat. Thomson worked behind the scenes and did manage to provide a moderating influence in much legislation coming from the state Senate.

Near the end of this first term, a severe intraparty conflict erupted in the majority party. Sharp regional and doctrinal differences split the conservatives. Bitterly fought primary elections widened the breach, and despite monumental efforts to unite the party for the fall senatorial elections much ill feeling pervaded in the party and confusion reigned in the ranks of the voters. As a result, Robert Thomson was elected as a state senator largely on the basis of support from apprehensive voters who lost confidence in the majority party.

Thomson built on his image of stability and used it to complement both his identification with a liberal point of view and his ability to work with the opposition. By 1958, he had been reelected to a second full term in the state Senate and provided leadership in revitalizing the minority party to the point where it was again considered a serious contender for being the party of the majority.

The state chairman and other leadership figures in Thomson's party supported his nomination in 1961 for a U.S. Senate seat. He was successful in the nomination race and emerged a winner in the 1962 November election.

Thomson's election as a U.S. Senator broadened the focus of his liberal views. He was appointed to committees and subcommittees dealing not only with conservation and areas of his early interests but also with matters pertaining to education and welfare. In these positions he supported his party's policies and soon began to emerge as a party spokesman. In general, he took the position that the federal government must do what local and state governments could not or would not do. Thomson became a leading proponent of the most extensive "federal aid to education" bills which were being introduced in one form or another in every session of Congress during the 1960s and 1970. He constantly brought to the Senate floor his observations and supporting data pertaining to educational and welfare deficiencies of the nation along with proposed federal remediation for these ills.

Early in the recent session, the Senate Education Committee had under consideration a massive federal aid to urban education program. Thomson's party and the administration saw this as a piece of key legislation. Urban decay and core city education were major concerns throughout the nation and were bound to be important election issues at the forthcoming presidential election two years hence. Interparty differences were centered on how the problem was to be resolved rather than whether a significant problem existed. The bill under consideration by the committee provided compensatory education, a core city teachers' bonus, and an urban education enrichment program. The news that Senator Thomson cast the deciding vote to kill the bill in the Senate Education Committee came as a bombshell!

In pressing for a statement from Thomson, newsmen asked why he seemingly reversed the position he had consistently held for over twenty years on federal aid to education and why he rejected one of his party's key pieces of legislation.

In replying to the newsmen and to his constituents, Thomson indicated his recent action was based on several principles:

1. Government authority is divided between the federal unit on one hand and the state and local units on the other. Each has its own unique function. Authority exercised by each must be commensurate with the responsibility assigned to the given unit and its function in the total process of government. The authority patterns of the several units should be complementary. Each unit, as it exercises its authority, should make the others more effective.

2. The authority or power of a given unit of government is not solely determined by the theory of government and the constitutional provisions which originally created it and which currently direct it. The power of a unit of government is also determined by its ability to obtain resources necessary for it to execute its function.

3. Changes in the capability of a unit of government to gather revenues reflect changes in the power balance among the several governmental units. This is illustrated by changes in the proportions of total tax revenues gathered by federal and local governmental units over a period of years.

"The basic problem as I see it is that considerable power has shifted from local and state government to the federal government. We find that more problems need to be resolved at the federal level; it is more feasible to do this since only the federal government has the resources to do the job. There is an eminent danger of further power shifts since under the present taxation system state and local units cannot perform their unique functions with their limited revenue-gathering capability.

"Now is not the time for the federal government to intervene directly and use its power and resources to resolve a problem that occurs all across the nation. Rather, now is the time for the federal government to use its power and resources to strengthen state and local government to resolve immediately and eliminate ultimately this nationwide local problem. To do otherwise will encourage state and local governmental units to abdicate their responsibility.

"The federal government acting to strengthen state and local government—often tagged as 'creative federalism'—does indeed suggest the recognition of an additional federal responsibility. This new responsibility is that of upgrading state and local government power and authority. Such an action will make these units more effective and will in turn maintain a viable division of powers among the several levels of government."

Questions for Discussion

1. What rationale for creative federalism can be developed from that part of the concept statement which deals with the general limitations on federal government power?

2. What arguments might be cited to counter the Thomson proposal to resolve urban problems by the federal government acting to strengthen local and state governments?

3. In what kinds of problem situations might the Thomson proposal be more appropriate?

4. How is the general versus categorical aid differentiation related to the concept of creative federalism?

Suggested Readings

Concept J—Powers and Functions of the Federal Government

Allen, Hollis P.: *The Federal Government and Education,* New York: McGraw-Hill, 1950.

American Association of School Administrators: *The Federal Government and the Public Schools,* Washington, D.C.: The Association, 1965.

————: *Federal Policy and the Public Schools,* Washington, D.C.: The Association, 1967.

Committee for Economic Development: *Fiscal Issues in the Future of Federalism,* New York: The Committee, 1968.

————: *A Fiscal Program for a Balanced Federalism,* New York: The Committee, 1967.

————: *Paying for Better Schools,* New York: The Committee, 1959.

Gardner, John W.: *Creative Federalism,* Washington, D.C.: Department of Health, Education, and Welfare, October, 1966.

Heilbroner, Robert L., and Peter L. Bernstein: *A Primer on Government Spending,* New York: Vintage Books, 1963.

McConnell, Campbell R.: *Economics,* 4th ed., New York: McGraw-Hill, 1969, chap. 9, pp. 136–137, 140.

Meranto, Philip: *The Politics of Federal Aid to Education in 1965: A Study in Political Innovation,* Syracuse, N.Y.: Syracuse University Press, 1967.

Munger, Frank J., and Richard F. Fenno, Jr.: *National Politics and Federal Aid to Education,* Syracuse, N.Y.: Syracuse University Press, 1962.

National Committee for Support of Public Schools: *Changing Demands on Education and Their Fiscal Implications,* Washington, D.C.: The Committee, 1963.

Ott, David J., and Attiat F. Ott: *Federal Budget Policy,* Washington, D.C.: The Brookings Institution, 1965.

Samuelson, Paul A.: *Economics,* 7th ed., New York: McGraw-Hill, 1967, chap. 8, pp. 139–146.

part 4

The Tools of Government

concepts K–Q

concept k
Public Finance Theory: Shifting and Incidence

the problem

It is recognized that in the final analysis all taxes going to support public services, such as public education, are finally paid by individuals. In order to develop the most intelligent and rational public policy on such taxation, it is necessary to determine which individuals or groups of individuals in the society ultimately bear the burden of taxation for the given services and the relative amount of the burden. This is important to know since the tax burden will have certain effects on the individual, on the total economy, and on the program supported by the tax.

Economic tools have been developed in order to analyze the taxation phenomenon. In the following concept statement the authors address themselves to the questions:

1. How is the burden shifted from the person originally taxed to the one who bears the ultimate burden?

2. What are the factors that determine this phenomenon?

3. What are the differences in shifting phenomena among the various taxes usually employed in supporting public education?

The concept of tax shifting and incidence is relevant to the study of public school finance for several reasons. Such a study will enable one to make better decisions regarding who should pay for public education. It will also be helpful in making decisions regarding how the burden for public education should be distributed among the various groups in the society. A knowledge of the shifting phenomenon will assist in determining what is the most appropriate pattern of tax vehicles to achieve the proper allocation of burden.

the concept

With respect to any tax, it is of considerable interest to determine just who bears the final burden. The assumption that every tax causes a reduction in income for the taxpayer by the amount of the tax paid is erroneous; nothing could be farther from the truth. It is important, then, to understand just how the burden of a tax can be shifted from the person who pays the money to the government and just who does suffer the loss of income.

To understand how a tax may be shifted by the person who pays it to someone else one must first understand how prices are determined. One determinant of prices, of course, is "demand." Demand is defined as the quantity of a product people will be willing to buy at all possible prices. In most instances, the lower the price the greater the quantity people will be willing to buy.

The other determinant of price is "supply." Supply is defined as the quantity of a product sellers will be willing to sell at all possible prices. The willingness to sell may be influenced by a number of factors but primarily by the costs associated with production. Thus, if the costs of producing each unit remain the same regardless of the quantity produced, the seller would logically be willing to supply an infinite quantity at the same price he received for a small quantity. Most costs of production, however, rise as the quantity produced increases, so it is necessary to increase the price in order to induce the seller to supply more of the product.

The relationship of this discussion to taxes and tax shifting becomes apparent when one realizes that a tax paid by a seller or producer is a cost. It is a cost of doing business just as is the rent he pays, or the wages, or the utility charges. An increase in a businessman's taxes, then, will alter his willingness to supply goods at various prices. Either he will insist upon an increase in the prevailing price or he will reduce the quantity he is willing to supply at the prevailing price.

The price which will prevail in the market, together with the quantity which will be exchanged, will be determined by both demand and supply and the point at which these two market forces are in agreement. This is shown graphically in Figure 1.

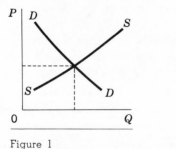

Figure 1

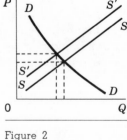

Figure 2

In response to a tax increase, the usual result is that the price increases (although not by the entire amount of the tax) and the quantity exchanged decreases, as is shown in Figure 2. It is assumed in Figure 2 that the tax is a constant levy on each unit produced, as is usually the case with respect to a sales or excise tax. If the tax is a fixed levy which does not vary in response to changes in output, such as is usually the case with a property tax, the change in price and quantity exchanged will be somewhat different; a typical pattern is shown in Figure 3.

Of course the relationship between the increase in price and the reduction in quantity exchanged will depend upon the attitude of the buyers. If it does not take a lower price to induce them to buy more of the product, that is, if the buyers will purchase substantially the same quantity regardless of the price, then the quantity exchanged will decline very little if at all. If customers will buy the same quantity regardless of the price, the results will be as shown in Figure 4.

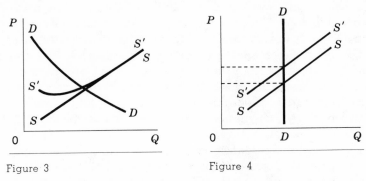

Figure 3   Figure 4

In any consideration of tax shifting, it must be remembered that an exchange is necessary. If there is no exchange, there is no opportunity to shift the tax, for the tax must be a part of those expenses which the taxpayer has an opportunity to recoup from those with whom he deals. It must also be remembered that for all goods for which the quantity demanded changes in response to a change in price (any situation other than is shown in Figure 4) it must be possible to reduce the quantity of the product available. If the quantity cannot be altered, there is no way that the price can be increased.

When one examines the various taxes, it is apparent that there is no uniformity with respect to shifting. Sales and excise taxes are assumed to be shifted. In fact, many state legislatures have required that a sales tax be added to the final price of the product at the time of sale, expecting in this manner to ensure shifting. However, shifting is an economic process rather than a legal one. The tax alters the final price of the product (that is, it shifts the supply schedule as in Figure 2). Unless the customers are willing to buy a constant amount regardless of the price, a higher price (but not by the full amount of the tax) and a reduction in the quantity exchanged will result. The relationship between the increase in price and the reduction in quantity exchanged will depend upon the willingness of the customers to buy at all possible prices. If a change in price will greatly alter the willingness to buy, then a large reduction in the quantity exchanged and a very small price rise will follow a tax increase. The probability is that sales and excise taxes will be shifted, but not so completely nor so automatically as is usually supposed.

The result is somewhat different with respect to income taxes. Seldom are the factors necessary for shifting the personal income tax present. It is true that the income is largely received in the form of wages and salaries and that there is an exchange of labor for the income. However, it must also be possible to reduce the supply to accomplish a shift, and it seldom can be verified that the quantity of labor available is reduced in response to an increase in the personal income tax. Only in very unusual circumstances will this tax be shifted.

The response is different, again, with respect to the corporate income tax. This is a tax paid on the profits of a business firm, profits earned in exchange for goods and services. The evidence seems to indicate that to a considerable extent this tax is treated as a cost of doing business by many firms, and so it is shifted in the form of higher prices for the output of the firm.

The property tax follows no single pattern. If the tax falls upon the real or personal property of a person who holds this property for his own use or consumption, it is extremely doubtful if it is shifted. There is no exchange to make this possible. If the tax falls upon the real or personal property owned by a business firm, the tax becomes another cost of doing business and will be shifted to the firm's customers through a reduction in the output of the firm and industry.

If the property taxed cannot be reduced in quantity, as is true in the case of land, there is no possibility of shifting the tax (barring an unvarying demand), and the value of the taxed good (land) is reduced by the capitalized amount of the tax. For example, if a piece of land is yielding an income of $1,000 per year and the accepted rate of return is 5 percent, the land is worth $20,000. If a tax of $100 per year is imposed on the land, the income is reduced to $900, and the value of the land now becomes $18,000. This is true only if the supply cannot be reduced. Some property, such as buildings, can be reduced in quantity only over a considerable period of time, so the tax may be capitalized at first, but later when the supply is reduced the tax may be shifted.

With no common pattern of shifting present for all taxes, it is important to understand this phenomenon in appraising the equity of any tax program. It is true that most taxes imposed by public school districts are in the form of levies on property, but to an increasing extent public school funds are provided through transfer payments from the state or federal governments. These transfer payments are usually not raised through the property tax.

The whole area of tax shifting also becomes more important to public school administrators when it is realized that school taxes are only a part of the whole system of taxes imposed by governments. Of prime importance is the equity of the whole system.

Case 29. Relating Ends and Means: A Consideration of the Nature of Taxes to Support Education

The State Education Association and its Legislation Committee had worked diligently for two years in organizing and conducting a grass roots approach in mobilizing popular support for modernizing and upgrading state aid for public schools in the state. Because of its effective work in selling the idea that education is the key to economic expansion ("Education is the State's *Best* Investment") and because of other external factors, legislators were now seriously listening to proposals for an increase in the state appropriation to the public school aid fund. The Governor had just assured the executive secretary of the association that both he and the majority leaders in the state assembly were willing to go along in principle with the association's proposal for the appropriation. However, the education appropriation along with increases in other key state functions would necessitate additional state tax revenues. The Governor indicated that his own and his party's support of the education bill would be contingent on the education association's support of the administration's proposal to increase the state sales tax in order to finance these additional expenditures.

Larry Goldham, the executive secretary of the association, consequently called in the latter body's legislative committee to consider the several aspects of the proposition. In outlining the situation as it had developed to date, Goldham pointed out that:

1. The campaign to depict education as a producer's good as well as a consumer's good was well accepted, and apparently education was recognized by the administration as being a public concern which could not be ignored. Also, the public had accepted the notion that additional taxes would be necessary to support the additional investment in education.

2. The Governor and his party's majority in the state assembly proposed a broadened general sales tax in the state. The present tax rate was to be increased from 4 to 5 percent on all sales starting at 11 cents rather than at 31 cents as it did formerly.

3. The education association became concerned when it was observed that if the proposed upgrading of the state aid to public schools program was to have maximum impact, the source of revenue and the incidence of the taxes used to collect the revenue would be of prime importance. For many years the association had maintained that public education as a social instrument was to be available to all the people in the state, was the responsibility of all the people of the state, and was to be supported by all the people, each person according to his own ability. Thus the question of the association's support of the Governor's "package" was indeed an open one.

Members of the Legislative Committee were not hesitant in plunging into the discussion of the Governor's proposal. Initial arguments were centered around the equity of the tax proposal. Many opinions were expressed—all pointing out alleged inequities. At first blush all seemed valid and little opposition developed until some conflicting evidence was presented. Then it appeared that the same tax could have almost opposite inequities built into it.

The seemingly contradictory points arose around the sales tax on foodstuffs, and more particularly garden truck. Joe Hermansen, a classroom teacher and Legislative Committee member who came from a rural background, maintained that a tax on these food items would fall heavily on the producer and would reduce to almost nothing his already narrow profit margin. Bertha Bethold, speaking from the posture of "a big city girl" and a secondary school civics teacher, took the position that the tax instead was inequitable in its effect on the consumer. This was evident since it was levied on a necessity which people consumed in roughly the same amounts regardless of the price. Furthermore, families of low income devoted a larger proportion of their income to these items than did families of high income.

After the presentation of the two basic arguments, the discussion began to deteriorate to an exchange of personal experiences or observations. The discussion turned when Goldham intervened and suggested that perhaps the basic problem was that of determining who would bear the burden of the increased tax. He pointed out that this is frequently a tricky business since tax shifting does take place. The incidence of a tax, or the identification of the person who actually suffers loss of income because of the tax increase, must be determined in order to assess the relative equity of a tax.

Following the careful questioning of Larry Goldham, the committee proceeded to analyze the Governor's proposal. It was concluded that in the matter of foodstuffs most of the tax would be shifted to the consumer. This would be especially true among low-income families since the increased price would not reduce the quantity produced because a given amount of food must be consumed. Thus, when an additional tax is levied and the price increases, the demand stays fairly constant, and the consumer, rather than the producer, pays the tax. However, in the case of certain segments of the population, e.g., the high-income families, some of the tax may not be shifted since a reduction in the amount of food consumed would not jeopardize life or health. Thus, the price goes up due to an increase in the tax, and the demand goes down. So the producer assumes some of the increased tax.

Several other classifications of goods included under the new sales tax program were also analyzed in the same fashion. In most instances it was observed that probably most of the tax burden was shifted to the consumer.

In generalizing on the phenomenon of tax shifting and the incidence of the proposed tax increase, the group agreed that by and large the broadened sales tax did shift the tax burden to the consumer. It was also observed that in the process of shifting, the heaviest burden was assumed by the lower-income families. Hence, the new tax was probably not equitable and thus it would not be appropriate for the education association to support that part of the "education package."

At this point, it became apparent that the Legislative Committee was forced, in good conscience, to rationalize its position in supporting the expenditure of more state money for public education and at the same time to oppose the Governor's proposal for raising the necessary money for the increased expenditures. The committee was forced to come up with an alternative which would meet the criteria which it had used to analyze the Governor's tax program.

In light of the history of the state revenue program and the fact that the Governor's proposal was already made public, it was conceded that some kind of a state sales tax was the only politically feasible alternative. Bertha Bethold suggested that perhaps the only real innovation that a Legislative Committee recommendation might contain would be a different way of analyzing the impact of a tax in the state.

Many specific suggestions were thrown out by members of the committee. There was consensus that the heaviest burden in the tax to be recommended by the committee should be borne by the higher-income group. It was also agreed that each component of the committee's recommended program should be carefully tested to determine the pattern of tax shifting and the incidence of the tax to assure compatability with the committee's implicit criterion of equalizing tax burden.

After several subcommittee and committee-of-the-whole sessions and consultation with public finance experts, the Legislative Committee's proposed sales tax program was decided upon. The committee's program incorporated the following features:

1. A 4 percent sales tax starting at 11 cents excluding sales of food, intermediate sales to business, housing, and household utilities

2. The 4 percent sales tax be extended to include the following selected services:
Personal services
Business services
Amusement group
Automobile services
Repair services

3. The 4 percent sales tax on the price of cigarettes, beer and malt liquors including the excise taxes

The committee was satisfied that their proposal was a good one. Members were convinced that the additional revenues could be raised by retaining the rate (at 4 percent) and extending the base (starting at 11 cents). At the same time hardships on low-income families would be minimized by making the tax selective by excluding food, housing, and household utilities. To somewhat offset these reductions in the tax collections, the tax was extended to include services and commodities which had not been taxed previously.

Questions for Discussion

1. What are the primary differences between the former sales tax and that proposed by the Governor? Between the Governor's proposal and the State Education Association committee's proposal?

2. What general differences in the pattern of tax shifting are probably present as you compare the several sales tax programs mentioned in the case?

3. Why might there be less shifting of the additional taxable items (personal services, business services, etc.) as compared to the sales of food, housing, and household utilities?

4. What do you think the pattern of shifting might be on the items of cigarettes, beer, and malt liquors? Why?

Case 30.   Perspectives on Shifting a Property Tax

Financial support of public education had been a major issue for the past three biennial sessions of the General Assembly of a relatively populous Eastern state. Six years ago the incumbent Governor was defeated for a second term—largely on the basis of his proposal for massive state aid for the public schools. The succeeding governor and legislative majorities emphasized the enactment of measures to promote efficiency in educational organization on both state and local levels, to stimulate local initiative and responsibility, and to evaluate and upgrade tax legislation.

The State Education Association had supported the original proposal for the massive state aid program and, as a result of its active involvement in the bitter gubernatorial campaign, lost all rapport with the newly elected governor and his legislative leaders. Consequently, the association's lobby was quite ineffective in directly influencing pro public school legislation. After four years of rebuffs, the association leadership was of the opinion it must either adopt new tactics to obtain more financial support for the public schools or jeopardize its leadership role with public school teachers, administrators, and patrons.

Under this kind of pressure, the association mobilized support of other public school related organizations, e.g., the School Boards Association, Public School Employees Association, the Parent-Teachers Association, and the School Administrators Association. By petition initiative this united group forced a statewide referendum on the issue to increase the state sales tax from 3 percent to 4 percent. Although the initiated measure did not earmark the additional revenue for public education, the implication was strong that this would be the case.

When the issue was placed on the November ballot, there appeared to be considerable support for it early in the campaign. The grass roots approach, the support of the petition by several influential newspapers, and little vocal and organized opposition all seemed to point to the enactment of the measure. In the last days of the campaign, however, several candidates issued statements questioning the wisdom of or actually opposing the sales tax increase. A supposedly "neutral" newspaper came out in opposition and prospects for its enactment dimmed.

When the vote was counted, the issue of the sales tax increase was defeated four to one. Again, the State Education Association was unable to effectuate substantial improvement in the state financing of public education.

The very severe rebuff did not, as some expected, lay the issue to rest once and for all. Instead it seemed to illustrate the necessity of using some other vehicle to influence the legislature in matters of education and its financial support. Clearly, the "educational establishment" was not adequate to the task.

It was in this kind of environment that representatives from nearly a dozen private philanthropic organizations from various cities in the state met to discuss the financial crisis of the public schools. It was agreed that as a wealthy state, financial support for the public schools had been steadily eroding for over a decade and this erosion was jeopardizing the state's economic future. Further, it was agreed that increased state financing must be provided to reverse the declining proportion of state support to that coming from the local school districts.

In order to effect these changes, it was decided that nationally recognized authorities from outside the state should be retained to conduct a study of the financing of the public schools. Consultants of national reputation in areas of economics, government and public administration as well as education were to be retained.

The combine of foundations formed a steering committee, employed a study director-coordinator, and charged the study team (1) to survey the state's financial support program for public education, (2) to analyze and evaluate it, and (3) to make recommendations for its improvement to the sponsoring philanthropic organizations.

During a short period of six months, the survey team gathered information. They interviewed and consulted with legislators, school administrators, industrial and community leaders, members of state and local governing boards, and members of educationally oriented organizations. Using national norms, they found that the state ranked in the upper 15 percent in overall wealth, but was in the average range in expenditure per pupil. The level of state support for public education was far below average and had been steadily decreasing. Increases in per pupil expenditures were largely accounted for by increasing the local proportion rather than that of the state. It was found that the present state aid formula tended to provide greater support for small and/or rural school districts than it did for the large urban districts. This was true despite the fact that the state was primarily metropolitan and industrial rather than rural and agricultural.

The recommendations of the study team were made to the sponsoring foundations, but even in such a sophisticated group, some surprise was registered. In essence, the team recommended changing the whole concept of state aid. Instead of an elaborate formula involving

(1) the development of a minimum educational program and its cost budget, (2) subtraction of the amount of a local effort factor and, (3) calculation of a net state support figure, the study team recommended flat amounts for elementary and secondary pupils. These amounts would be supplemented by grants to improve instruction in subject matter areas, equalized state sharing grants in capital improvements, and bonus grants for large city school districts.

A mandatory levy of 17.5 mills per dollar on the equalized value of real property in the school district would be gathered by the state and distributed by it to the local school districts.

A resource equalizer grant was also to be provided so as to assure average and poorer districts the same amount per pupil as the wealthier districts. The amount of the grant would be determined by the amount of local effort over the mandatory level.

Although the survey team's report was made to the philanthropic organizations, the report generated considerable interest among the general public. Shortly after its publication and distribution around the state, the report was the focus of study and discussion by several groups. One of these was initiated by Thomas Melbourne, a partner in one of the leading law firms in the state's largest city.

Melbourne saw the study team's recommendations as a lever to obtain a larger, badly needed, and more equitable amount of state resources for the city's public schools. Consequently, he organized an informal group of individuals who were interested in supporting the initiation of legislation along the lines suggested by the study team. This group included large city school administrators, school finance experts, university professors and state legislators. At the same time the "one man, one vote" ruling had forced a reapportionment of the state's legislature. The newly drawn state senatorial districts provided a more urban-oriented upper house. As a result, a more sympathetic legislature encouraged the Melbourne group to push for legislation similar to that recommended by the study team. The senator who was a part of the Melbourne group assumed the leadership in finding appropriate sponsors and in assisting in the actual drafting of the bill itself.

The "revised school aid bill" was referred to the Education Committee of the House, and hearings were scheduled. On the first day of hearings, most of the testimony dealt with the necessity of upgrading and/or improving the state aid legislation and a description of the proposed legislation. On the second day, primary attention was placed on the state-mandated 17.5-mill tax on real property and its impact. Various special interest groups had requested an opportunity to present testimony, and these were now being heard.

Alvin Lindell of the State Realtors Association applauded the basic purpose of the legislation stating that upgrading the school system was necessary both for the personal well-being of students and for the state's economic future as well. Lindell, however, did take exception to the 17.5-mill mandatory levy. His objection to this was based on the fact that the primary source of revenue for the program was the property tax. The tax, he argued, was already excessively burdensome statewide, and the mandatory level would increase property taxes in those few school districts which had to date escaped the nearly confiscatory level reached in most communities. The tax worked an especial hardship on the residential property owner. The elderly and retired, an ever-increasing segment of our population, he reasoned, are being asked to shoulder an even larger burden than they have consistently borne. These citizens do not derive any direct benefit and cannot pass on their property tax burden as can a manufacturer or merchant. Thus, argued Lindell, the new tax proposal compounds an already serious problem.

Mr. Lindell expressed his gratitude for being given a hearing and then excused himself.

The next witness to give testimony was Olen Fundy, executive secretary of the Retail Merchants Association. Mr. Fundy announced that his organization was composed of over 80 percent of the retail merchants (excluding the proprietorships) of the state and that his members were responsible for the annual retail sale of 92 percent of all retail-classified goods.

Mr. Fundy then proceeded to spell out a succession of federal and state actions which were progressively strangling the free enterprise system. He concluded by stating that the tax measure under consideration at this hearing was a continuation of this movement. The mandatory 17.5 mill property tax levy will, he suggested, increase the cost of doing business until it reaches the point that free enterprise will be profitless.

Fundy maintained that the real property necessary to conduct a retail merchandising establishment should not be under the same tax umbrella as other real property, for this level of taxation will reduce the already thin profit margins. This in turn would shrink the tax base and ultimately reduce the revenues collected on both the property tax base as well as the sales tax. This latter consequence would amount to killing the goose that has laid golden eggs for the state's general revenue fund for many years.

Fundy concluded his testimony by charging the legislators with the responsibility of deciding whether or not they would apply the coup de grace to free enterprise with this legislation.

Testimony was next taken from John C. Elliott, manager of the

Valley Electronics Division of Beauchamp Industries, Incorporated. Beauchamp was a large diversified corporation which included smelting and machine tool operations as well as electronics. It had nine primary plants in seven states ranging between the coasts. It also maintained sales offices in this country and in four overseas locations as well. After introducing himself, Mr. Elliott got right to the point.

"I would like to describe to the legislators who are hearing the proposed tax bill, the economic consequences of the measure to Valley Electronics.

"As you know, Valley Electronics produces components used in the many and varied electric and electronic mechanisms which appear on the market today. We compete in both the domestic and foreign markets. Therefore we must constantly be aware of our costs since competition forces us to accept a relatively low-profit margin. If we were required to increase property tax payments to the proposed 17.5-mill level for education, this would represent an increase of nearly 17 percent in such payments for us. Such an additional increase in the cost of doing business would of course be shifted to our customers. However, with the keen competition characteristic of our business, this would almost certainly reduce the demand of our product not only for Valley Electronics, but for the whole industry.

"The problem is acute, not only for Valley Electronics, but also for the state's economic well-being. You will recall that our company was attracted to its present location due to your state government's Economic and Industrial Development Division. Our parent company selected the site for Valley Electronics because of advantages to both the state and our organization. We have provided employment and have been a significant force in stabilizing the local economy. Some of these gains might be lost if we are forced to increase our costs of operation. We urge you give thoughtful consideration to these possibilities.

"Thank you, Mr. Chairman."

Mr. Charles A. Schneider, chairman of the board of governors of the State Agriculture Federation was the last witness to testify in this session of the hearings on the mandatory property tax bill. Mr. Schneider's organization was one of the most influential lobbies in the state legislature despite the state's relatively small percent of full-time farmers. This status was attained because of a long history of organized activity among farmers and very effective methods of influence outside the legislature as well as within it.

Mr. Schneider introduced himself and stated that he, as a representative of the agricultural interests as well as the family farmer, was much impressed with the previous testimony. Much of what was said about residential property, commercial property, and industrial property regarding increases in the local property tax for the state educational program applied to agricultural property as well. However, the problem with agricultural property was even more acute.

"It has been recognized for some time that the operation of a family farm requires tremendous amounts of capitalization today in order to derive a livelihood for its owner-operator.

"In our state the typical family farm of something under 200 acres represents a total investment of nearly a quarter million dollars. Much of this is in land which, under a higher rate of tax, produces less net income and hence is worth less. Suppose 200 acres of farm land was taxed at an additional $500 and thus its income was reduced from $10,000 to $9,500 annually. If we use 5 percent as a fair return, this means the land value is reduced by capitalizing the tax and so it is worth only $190,000 instead of the former $200,000. You can see the economic impact of any measure which would raise property taxes on agricultural lands. Any such measure could clearly become a confiscatory tax as it deprives the owner of the capital he has invested in his land."

Questions for Discussion

1. To what extent will shifting occur in the application of the 17.5-mill property tax levy on residential property? Why?

2. Describe the reasons and extent of property tax shifting on a retail merchant's establishment. Evaluate Olen Fundy's contention of the effect of the proposed tax.

3. To what extent may a property tax applied to Valley Electronics be shifted? What will determine the shifting phenomenon in this instance?

4. Which of the four types of real property discussed in the case (residential, retail merchandising, manufacturing, and agricultural) would likely shift the greatest amount of a property tax? The least?

Case 31. Legislators View Tax Shifting: Determining Who Should Bear the Tax

Although the General Assembly had been in session only three weeks, Peter Kloska and Ivan Bebar, chairman and vice-chairman, respectively, of the House Ways and Means Committee, were concerned with finding sufficient revenue to support the state's program for the upcoming fiscal period. Their state, located on the Eastern seaboard, was in reality a satellite of the adjacent metropolitan areas. The state was small, highly industrialized, and nearly completely urbanized.

Its industry was primarily that of large national and international corporations. These included heavy and fine tool machinery, chemical, petroleum, and electronics plants. The cities which accommodated these operations were largely middle- and lower-class communities in socioeconomic terms. Blue-collar workers and technicians were the predominant occupational types.

In recent years the state legislature, under severe pressure from both local and federal government levels, recognized the emergence of urban problems—especially those of the "inner city." Because of the homogeneity of the state and the spillover effects from city to city, state government was called on to mount programs to reduce urban decay and also provide a higher level of public services.

At an informal meeting, the two state congressmen tried to define the problem. With new and expanded programs bound to be enacted, Kloska and Bebar were of the opinion that some kind of a tax increase was a "given." The primary question was that of what kind of tax it should be. Having broached the question, Kloska continued by reviewing the major taxes in the present revenue program of the state.

"We have already pushed our sales and use tax to the limit. Four years ago we raised to 4½ percent, and two years ago we broadened the base and closed some of the loopholes—so there is no possibility of doing much there.

"The state income tax is not as high as some states, but I'm not willing even to open the question of an increase there. It's not a popular tax, and with possibilities of an increase in the federal level, we'll be lucky if we don't receive a lot of pressure to reduce this state tax.

"I don't believe we can do much with inheritance and estate taxes. Even a large increase in these will not give us the money we are going to need.

"It seems to me the only two real possibilities are excise taxes or possibly corporation income. We'll have problems with either one, but I don't see any other alternatives."

During Kloska's rundown of the major taxes in the state's revenue system, Ivan Bebar found himself nodding in agreement.

"Yes, for the kind of money we will need and in light of the development of the tax program, we can't touch either the sales or the personal income tax. We will need to raise significantly more revenues than we had to this last biennium but it also will have to be politically feasible and consistent with other elements of the legislative program.

"We know that much of the legislation will be oriented to the inner city. There will be efforts to upgrade public services in these areas, to provide better educational opportunities, to provide more and better jobs, and to provide better housing. But if we impose new taxes on the very people for whom the legislation is intended we will be defeating our own purpose. We will alienate the support we have mustered to pass the original legislation.

"We are going to have to look very carefully at the ultimate burden of the tax or the incidence as well as the initial money burden of the tax."

"Yes, I know" interrupted Kloska, "this is what I mean by not playing with the sales tax. It's probably already too high since most of it is shifted to the consumer—especially when it is coupled with the income tax. And this will also be true about the excise tax. I'm sure it is shifted to the consumer too. This would be a vulnerable point for us right now.

"What about the corporation income tax? The initial burden is on the corporation profits. But we have large companies who soon pass these taxes off to the buyers of their products, so the consumer still bears the ultimate burden," concluded Kloska.

"Yes, that is correct. However, there are several other aspects that we should consider. First, where are the consumers of the products of our corporations? Who are the ultimate bearers of our corporate profits tax burden? Most of these are outside the state, many are overseas. Thus, this form of income tax is shifted quite differently than our present personal income tax.

"Also, remember, not all the tax burden is shifted. Our industry is such that probably there will be some reduction in both demand and supply, and thus some burden will reside with the corporation. This will reduce dividends to stockholders who also are a largely nonresident group. Thus, from at least two perspectives, the corporate income tax has some advantage for us when analyzed in terms of shifting."

The chairman and vice-chairman of the state's House Ways and Means Committee concluded that even though much more investigation and study must be given to the question of the most appropriate tax, they agreed the consideration of shifting must be included in the deliberations.

Questions for Discussion

1. In the above case, Kloska and Bebar dismissed rather readily the possibility of a sales tax increase. What pattern of tax shifting might be assumed in this tax?

2. Before arriving at a firm conclusion on the shifting of a corporate profits tax, what other factors or data should be considered?

3. How would the pattern of shifting the corporate profits tax vary between the state described in the case and one which had corporations selling to a primarily in-state market?

4. Do you agree with the analysis of the shifting of the corporate profits tax as described in the case? Why or why not?

Suggested Readings

Concept K—Public Finance Theory: Shifting and Incidence

Battelle Memorial Institute: *Local Government Tax Revision in Ohio*, Columbus, Ohio: The Institute, 1968.

Burkhead, Jesse: *Public School Finance*, Syracuse, N.Y.: Syracuse University Press, 1964.

———: *State and Local Taxes for Public Education*, Syracuse, N.Y.: Syracuse University Press, 1963.

Committee for Economic Development: *Fiscal Issues in the Future of Federalism*, New York: The Committee, 1968.

———: *Modernizing Local Government*, New York: The Committee, 1966.

————: *Modernizing State Government*, New York: The Committee, 1967.

Freeman, Roger: *Taxes for the Schools*, Washington, D.C.: The Institute for Social Science Research, 1961.

McConnell, Campbell R.: *Economics*, 4th ed., New York: McGraw-Hill, 1969.

Musgrave, Richard A.: *The Theory of Public Finance*, New York: McGraw-Hill, 1959.

Samuelson, Paul A.: *Economics*, 7th ed., New York: McGraw-Hill, 1967, chap. 9, pp. 166–167, chap. 20, pp. 371–372.

Tax Foundation, Inc.: *State Tax Studies: 1959–1967*, New York: The Foundation, 1967.

Taylor, Philip E.: *The Economics of Public Finance*, New York: Macmillan, 1953.

Thatcher, George W.: *Tax Revision Alternatives for the Tax System of Ohio*, Columbus, Ohio: Ohio Tax Study Committee, 1962.

concept 1
Public Finance Theory:
Distributive Aspects

the problem

Through the study of the previous concept and its accompanying cases, it was established that taxes are shifted and that decisions must be made regarding who assumes what part of the burden for a given governmental service, such as public education. It now becomes important that some criteria be developed and justified which will provide a rational base for determining who bears what part of the burden.

Concept L explores the several bases for making this decision, i.e., how the tax burden should be distributed. Two major theories of distribution are presented: the principle of benefits received and the principle of ability to pay. In analyzing the two theories, it is obvious that the choice is not a simple one. Each principle carries with it many other economic ramifications. The cruciality of having a well-thought-out political and economic philosophy is demonstrated by an exploration of several varied and nearly opposite definitions of equality. Professional educators who are concerned with means as well as ends are obligated to understand the problem as well as to articulate and defend their position on the basic question, Who should provide support for public education and to what extent?

the concept

For the welfare of all citizens and for the benefit of all units of government, including the public schools, it is important to distribute the burdens of taxation as fairly as possible. Governments at all levels are calling upon the taxpayer for increased contributions to pay for the services those governments perform, and so any lack of equity in the distribution of the burden will favor some particular group over another and at the same time enhance the possibility of taxpayer unrest and protest.

An understanding of the pattern of tax shifting is necessary to any fair arrangement of the tax system, but this in itself is not enough. Decisions must also be made concerning the proper basis for distributing the costs of government services among the taxpayers. These decisions will greatly affect the taxpaying public and will have a significant influence on the equity of the entire tax system.

One group of tax theorists argues that in so far as possible taxes should be assessed in proportion to the amount of benefits received from the services which the taxes finance. This theory, called the "Principle of Benefits Received," holds that government should finance its operations as nearly like the private sector of the economy as possible. Direct charges and fees should be levied when feasible, and when taxes must be used they should be assessed against those who benefit from the service rendered.

There are many instances of government pricing according to this principle. Government fees and licenses are usually charged those who receive a specific benefit or service from the issuing government. We are used to the sewer fees which are assessed in proportion to the amount of water purchased. A third example which is familiar to all of us is the use of the gas tax to finance our street and highway system. It is believed that the benefit received from the highway system corresponds to a considerable degree with the amount of gasoline tax paid.

The benefit principle is also used to determine which set of taxpayers should pay for a particular service. For instance, the taxpayers of one municipality are not asked to pay for the street lights installed by another municipality. That citizens of the first community may receive much benefit from the street lights in the second without making any contribution for the service is ignored.

There are obvious faults as to the general application of the benefits principle. The most important, perhaps, is the inability to measure the benefits a particular taxpayer receives from each service of government. Even in those applications of the benefit principle which are considered most justified, the measurement is only partially accurate. As mentioned above, benefits from a particular local government service do not accrue only to the residents of that local government. Nor do the purchasers of gasoline receive all the benefits from our highway system. The owner of a motel or restaurant or for that matter a gasoline station located along a highway will probably receive benefits from the highway out of all proportion to the gasoline tax he pays.

Certainly benefits do emanate from the many services which are performed by government, and certainly these benefits are enjoyed by a great many different persons. To identify these persons and to measure the amount of benefits they receive with a sufficient accuracy to serve as a basis for charges, however, is impossible in most instances. The benefit principle will continue to be used where it can be applied, and it is probable that an expansion of this method of distributing the tax burden will be attempted. There are definite limits, however, to how far this principle can be extended and still maintain an equitable distribution.

The other theoretical basis for distributing the burden of taxes is the principle of ability to pay. The adherents to this principle maintain that since most government services are consumed in concert and since it is impossible to measure the extent of the benefits received by each taxpayer, these services should be paid for according to the ability to pay of the taxpayer. The difficulty of measurement is again immediately apparent. What shall be the basis of measurement? Shall it be income, or property, or expenditures, or still some other measure? There are advantages to each possible measure, as well as many disadvantages.

If an agreement can be reached as to the best measure of the ability to pay, the relationship between the possession of the measure and the ability to pay must be determined. For instance, if it is decided that the best measure is income, the question must also be answered, How does the ability to pay of the person with a small income compare with the ability to pay of a person with a large income?

In answering this question one must give serious consideration to the matter of utility or satisfaction. Does the first thousand dollars of income yield the same amount of utility as the tenth thousand? The answer to this question does much to determine the most equitable rate structure. If there is no change in the utility received from each succeeding unit of income, the ability to pay increases proportionately with the increase in income. However, if less utility is received from each succeeding unit of income, then the ability to pay increases faster than the income rises. The application of progressive rates—rates which increase as the base increases—can then be justified. Through the use of progressive rates, it is claimed, the burden can be equalized among taxpayers so that each will make the same sacrifice (in terms of utility) to the costs of government.

The inability to measure utility reduces the effectiveness of this approach. Utility is a personal matter, and the relationship between the growth of the base (income, property, etc.) and the amount of utility received from this increase will differ with each person. For this reason, opponents of progressive tax rates will argue that only proportional rates are justified.

The counter argument is that since proportional rates are in themselves inequitable (normally the person with a $10,000 income can afford to pay something more than ten times the tax paid by a person with a $1,000 income), it is better to introduce an element of progression into the rate structure and thus attain a higher degree of equity than to use no progression and remain clearly inequitable.

It is also pointed out that a proportional rate structure not only is inequitable with respect to the utility given up through the taxes paid, but the taxes paid, when related to income, often are not proportional. That is, one does not hold taxable property or spend for taxable items in proportion to one's income. Rather, the property held which is subject to the property tax or the purchases made which are subject to the sales tax become less and less a proportion of income as income increases. The property and sales taxes, then, are often described as being "regressive in effect."

Also important when considering the relative merits of proportional and progressive tax rates is the progressivity of the whole tax system. The federal personal income and inheritance taxes are highly progressive, while the corporate income tax is very slightly progressive and the excise taxes are proportional (and regressive in effect). The sales, excise, and property taxes used by state and local governments are proportional, although the effects are regressive. State income taxes are usually slightly progressive while local income taxes are usually proportional. The net effect of the entire system is probably very close to being proportional. Certainly there is no great degree of progressivity evident.

Public school officials can have only a limited influence on the distributive system selected to finance the public schools. Most school revenue raised at the local level is derived through the use of the property tax, a tax which is proportional in structure but regressive in effect. In a few localities school districts are permitted to use nonproperty taxes, but these are at best proportional in effect.

State taxes used to finance state aid to schools may be slightly progressive, as in the case of the income tax, or proportional, if the sales tax is used. Federal revenue transferred to local school districts is probably largely raised through the progressive personal income tax.

School officials can perform the greatest service in this area by being well informed concerning the distributional effects of the various taxes used for school purposes and by giving intelligent advice when called upon to exert an influence on the distributive system.

Case 32.   Bases for Local School Tax Burden: Tax According to Benefits or Ability?

The board of education of the Martin City school system and its superintendent had discussed both formally and informally, the necessity of a large-scale assessment and possible renovation of the total public school program. As in many medium-sized city school systems, the instructional program showed little penchant to change, the physical plant had been patched and added to with little real updating, and the administrative organization worked pretty much as it did in the late 1940s and early 1950s. It was agreed by both the superintendent and the board members that some kind of study should be conducted to determine emergent school system needs and cost estimates in providing for these needs. It was also recognized that in order to obtain the necessary citizen support for either or both of these activities, the lay public must be involved.

After considerable deliberation and the detailing and evaluating of several promising alternative plans, it was decided to conduct a series of neighborhood seminars. The city was divided into neighborhoods contiguous with the thirty-one elementary school attendance areas. Lay committees in each of the elementary areas, with the assistance of the central office administrators serving as resource personnel, were to provide leadership in conducting a series of seminars to review and evaluate the present program. On the basis of these findings, they were to recommend what should be done to improve the school system. Each seminar incorporated four sessions, i.e., considerations of curriculum, personnel, facilities, and financing. The present status of the given aspect of the school program was first studied and evaluated, then recommendations on that aspect were made. These reports from the thirty-one school neighborhoods were then to be collated by a Steering Committee and submitted as the committee's recommendations to the board of education.

At Valleydale Elementary School, Carl Reinke was appointed as discussion leader for the fourth and final seminar session on financing. Carl had lived in the Valleydale neighborhood for eight years. His older daughter had started kindergarten in the school and was now in a nearby junior high school. His younger daughter was in fourth grade and his son was a second grader. Despite his intense interest in the welfare of his children, Reinke was a somewhat less-than-active PTA member. Instead, Carl gave the impression of being a pleasant but rather matter-of-fact and realistic businessman. It was probably because of these characteristics that he was selected to chair the final seminar—especially since it dealt with school costs and taxes.

In exercising his prerogative as chairman of the session, Carl Reinke laid out the procedures and ground rules. The group was first to review the survey material in school finance as prepared and previously distributed by the Steering Committee. This was to be evaluated and questions or issues noted. The conclusions and recommendations which the group was to formulate were to be based on these questions or issues. Carl instructed the secretary to make note of these during the evaluation discussion. The recommendations were to be limited to these questions or issues.

When the review and evaluation phase of the session was completed the following questions were isolated:

1. What are the most important expenditures in the proposed program?

2. What are the available sources of revenue?

3. Will current revenue sources and amounts be sufficient to meet the future needs?

4. What are appropriate types and amounts of taxes needed?

The first three questions were disposed of with relative ease. The decisions previously reached and the data provided by the school administration made the conclusions and recommendations relatively obvious. It was on question four, however, that a clear issue was drawn.

Carl Reinke stated the question and requested discussion of it in order to derive a conclusion and a recommendation. The discussion of the appropriate types and amount of taxes needed was begun with very general statements. The positions of the first few speakers reflected the present taxation program. It was suggested that the local property taxes must probably be retained at the present level, but despite the need for more revenues, these levies should not be increased. There was nearly unanimous support for calling on the state to provide additional state aid to school districts but there was hesitation on supporting the proposition that state taxes be increased to accomplish this. Instead, it was agreed that a larger proportion of state revenues be channeled into public education. No specific recommendations were made as to which state function should be cut back in its appropriation. The issue was partially sidestepped by a recommendation that a study be made of the allocation of state revenues to determine if a greater proportion could be allocated to public education.

Chairman Reinke was not satisfied that the response was a clear position on the question. When faced with the issue, the seminar participants reluctantly recommended that state taxes be increased if sufficient revenue could not be obtained from present local and state sources.

The question of federal aid to education flowed naturally from the discussion concerned with the search for additional state and local revenue. The question of whether or not to use federal aid was soon turned to to what extent should federal monies be used. The initial discussion on this specific question prompted no strong feelings. This apparently moderate attitude was due not to a middle of the road political persuasion of the group but instead to a lack of understanding of the nature of the issue. The seminar participants seemed to reflect a negative attitude to federal aid in general. However, their prior decision to expand and improve the educational program and the decision to not increase local taxes along with the uneasy decision to increase state taxes "only if no other sources are available," implied that the federal aid question would have to be entertained. When Chairman Reinke pointed this out to the participants, several speakers from the floor warmed to the topic.

The first to speak on this point solemnly warned the group of the dangers of accepting, much less soliciting, federal aid to the schools. He cited the trend of centralizing educational authority in Washington, the bungling federal bureaucracy, and realizing only a small return of the millions of dollars sent to the federal government. He urged forgoing the "easy money" from Washington and instead retaining the quality and integrity of locally controlled education programs.

Several mild rejoinders were offered which reflected the notion that programs of the quality recommended earlier as good and reasonable would cost the local taxpayers from one-third to one-half again as much if there was not some method of defraying the additional expenses from either state and/or federal sources.

"Now just a minute, Mr. Chairman! I don't agree with that last statement," shouted a speaker who literally leaped from his seat near the rear of the auditorium. The speaker was recognized by Reinke and invited to explain his position on the statement.

"I am Paul Lansing, and I live on Elm Valley Road. I question the inevitability as well as the immediate necessity of looking to the federal government or even the state to support the Martin City schools. I agree we are facing a problem, and it is essentially a problem in the taxation system. And I further agree with the point that the present local property tax cannot be increased. However, I violently disagree with the conclusion that we must consider either raising state taxation levels or soliciting and accepting federal aid.

"The problem centers on the theory underlying the property tax. We, as well as many other cities, have experienced difficulty in raising local school taxes because of this theoretical flaw. We charge every property owner the same tax rate whether he has children in school or not. Now if the property tax for schools were based on the number of children eligible for the schools, people would be willing to tax themselves because they would know they were getting exactly what their taxes were buying. The people who benefit from public education would be paying for it. A pamphlet titled *Education Is Good Business*[1] points out that eighth-grade graduates typically earn an estimated $184,000 in a lifetime while the high school graduate earns $247,000 and the college student who graduates has lifetime earnings of $385,000. It is obvious that these differences in earnings are tied to the amount of education. Therefore, why not have those who benefit from public education pay for it? It should be clear to all they are the primary beneficiaries.

"Also, it seems to me that this kind of a local tax will stimulate the people to exercise their own authority in making the decision as to what kind of education they want and how they will assume the responsibility of paying for it. Those people who do not get benefits from the schools will not block the efforts of those who do receive the benefits and want to invest accordingly."

Nearly as abruptly as he began, Paul Lansing ended his comment and took his seat. After a moment or two of uneasy silence, James O'Connor pulled himself to his feet, cleared his throat, and began a low-key rebuttal of Lansing's views.

"I'm not sure whether one can so easily identify the recipient of the benefits of education. I agree that the youngster who gets the greater amount of schooling will tend to have the higher level of lifetime earnings, but precise measures of benefit are very difficult. How do you measure the benefit for the dropout, the slow student, the undermotivated?

"Also, is the student the single largest recipient of benefits from public education? When people are educated they tend to change their tastes, their levels of consumption, and many other behavior patterns. This opens the way for many others to benefit through the expenditure of their additional income.

"Consider too the wide range of social benefits. High levels of education are necessary for an enlightened electorate and forward-looking social legislation. The post World War II period of

---

[1] Charles S. Benson, *Education Is Good Business*, American Association of School Administrators, Association of School Business Officials of the United States and Canada, and the National School Boards Association, Washington, 1966.

economic affluence is due largely to the knowledge explosion and the advancement of education to utilize it. Everyone in the country has benefited from this, not just the individuals with the advanced education, but their employers, and the consumers of the better products which are now more available than before and, many times, less costly than before.

"These kinds of considerations make it impossible for me to think of financing public schools by using the benefit theory. It is not possible to measure benefits bestowed on those who are educated. Also, it is not possible to determine who receives the benefit since there are so many spillover benefits accruing to other individuals and society as a whole.

"Since I have deprecated the notion of raising local school taxes on the basis of benefits received, I should pose a positive alternative. Public education should be financed by means of using the ability theory. This suggests that, since the benefits of public education go not only to the individual who receives it but also to the society as a whole, everyone in the society should support public education according to his ability. In former years it was thought that the real property tax was a vehicle with this capacity: the individual with greater wealth possessed more property. With our current economic expansion and affluence, the forms of wealth have changed. Real property no longer adequately measures ability to pay. The problem is to find another means to adequately measure ability. Other tax possibilities are income or expenditures. In a dynamic society these 'true indicators' of economic ability are always changing. Consequently, we know of no single, definite answer. However, we can be comforted to know that our search is narrowed to that vehicle or blend of vehicles which, for the given time, best measures ability. Thus, we may never fully reach our goal; but we can be assured, through the process of tax reform, we are moving in the right direction."

Once again Chairman Reinke was aware of the fact that the clean-cut questions his seminar had generated would not necessarily have clean-cut answers.

Questions for Discussion

1. In what way did Paul Lansing articulate the benefit theory of taxation?

2. Are there other ways in this case to rationalize the application of the benefit theory in addition to the Lansing arguments? If so, what are they?

3. What specific kind of information would be needed to develop a rational local tax program in Martin City if one were to use the ability theory?

4. In what way might the ability theory be used and still retain the real property tax as a vehicle to provide local revenue for the public schools?

Case 33.   Increasing the State Sales Tax: Building on a Faulty Foundation?

The Council of City School Superintendents in one of the predominantly rural states in the South had long led the fight for larger state appropriations for the public schools. Although the council worked hard to increase taxes to provide larger appropriations, it enjoyed little success.

For the past decade or two, the state has faced the problem of severe economic dislocation. Recently it has enjoyed the dubious honor of being one of the leaders among the fifty states in terms of proportion of population which qualifies it for special federal assistance to combat poverty and unemployment. The state had, until a few years ago, a rather static, if not stagnant, economy. Agriculture was and still is the state's major industry. Lumbering and wood products industries are important also and have become more sophisticated in recent years. The state has modest mineral resources. After early and reckless exploitation, a carefully controlled expansion has taken place. Tourism, for some years a major industry, has likewise grown more sophisticated in recent years. The state's mountains and lakes provide excellent resort and vacation sites.

Poultry and garden truck industries have recently expanded as a result of urban development and increased efficiency in transportation of perishables from the farms to major cities in the state.

For several generations the state has been among those in the lowest quarter of states in income per capita, state and local revenues and expenditures per capita, and per pupil expenditures in the public elementary and secondary schools. In general, the state has enjoyed only limited resources, but more importantly, it has expended less than average effort in supporting state and local governments and their programs. Typical of these programs is that of public education. Despite the fact that the four other states among the nation's five lowest in wealth per pupil were investing a greater proportion of their wealth on public education than the United States average, this state spent a lesser percent. Thus the other four "poor" sister states were expending more effort than the national average with less than average ability, whereas this state was expending less effort than the national average with less than average ability. The end result, of course, was that the public schools were very poorly supported.

The tax structure in the state was such that property taxes were the primary source of local revenue. State revenues were obtained through sales taxes levied at a 3 percent level, along with excise taxes on cigarettes, alcoholic beverages and public utilities. Motor vehicle fuel and license taxes were used for developing and maintaining the state highway system. The state also used many of the other relatively common state taxes including levies on horse racing, corporation franchises, inheritances and estates, and intangible personal property.

With limited state revenues and extensive social needs on the state level, only a modest state aid program to public schools was in force. The primary function of the program was to assure a minimum program to all districts in the state. Because of severe economic depression in the mountainous area of the state, a substantial portion of revenues appropriated to the public school aid program went to these school systems. Consequently, the minimum level of support was extremely low, and it was a moot question as to whether the minimum program was not in reality subminimal.

When the massive federal programs were mounted in order to eliminate poverty, unemployment, substandard living conditions, and other attendant social ills, considerable attention was given to the state in its effort to upgrade its system of public education. It was at this juncture that the voice of the Council of City School Superintendents began to carry real weight. Because the federal government programs were almost entirely in the categorical aid model, most of them required the development of state and/or local proposals for implementing the guidelines in the federal legislation. Members of the council were clearly more sophisticated in these skills than superintendents in rural areas, and the federal money flowed faster and easier into the urban districts of the state than it did into the rural systems. Consequently, the set mind of the state legislature changed in regard to listening to the advice of the council on matters of financing education—especially when it came to strategies for attracting more federal dollars!

Recently a federal aid measure providing for aid to systems in regions of chronic unemployment and underemployment was introduced into the Congress. Considerable opposition was raised and several amendments were added to assure that the federal monies would not take the place of a minimum level of state and local monies. The most crucial such amendment was one which provided that all states qualifying for the aid must exert at least the national average of state and local effort in the support of the public schools. This effort was to be measured as per capita state and local public education expenditures as a percent of per capita personal income:

$$\frac{\text{state and local public education expenditures per capita}}{\text{state and local personal income per capita}}$$

It was clear to the state legislators that unless substantially more state and local money was pumped into the state's public schools, their state would be bypassed. It was at this juncture that the several legislative committees involved in reviewing school tax legislation began to again pay heed to the Council of City School Superintendents and their admonitions to increase state taxes for the support of the public schools.

Shortly after the intent of the proposed federal aid legislation pertaining to education in economically depressed regions was identified, several of the state's leading newspapers went on record favoring the immediate increase in state spending for public education. This position was supplemented by the recommendation that, in order to expedite this, state taxes be increased to cover the additional expenses. The *Post*, the largest daily newspaper published in the state capital (and the most influential journal in the state), supported these two points of view on the bases that:

1. Interparty haggling over the problems resulting from the low level of financing public education had gone on for more than ten years, and at present a state level solution of the problems was no closer than it was ten years ago.

2. The federal incentive provided an opportunity for the state not only to improve itself but also to demonstrate its commitment to invest its own resources in such improvement.

With the substantial grass roots support generated from the influential news media and with both parties finding an opportunity to take credit for significant improvements in public education with little real sacrifice and risk, the Governor and the majority party prepared a bill calling for a 1 percent increase in the sales tax and a supplementary appropriation to the school aid fund.

In one of the early hearings on the bill, William McCutlip, chairman of the Council of City School Superintendents, was scheduled to testify. The administration bill had been given a great deal of early press coverage as it represented something of a response to the program called for by the *Post*. The bill had been touted as an excellent piece of legislation since it only modified existing tax and state aid distribution machinery—it was not something totally new. It was also declared that the tax increase was fair to all since it was proportional. Those that had more to spend and did spend it were taxed more and hence contributed more to public education revenues. Thus the proportion of the tax burden was the same.

Superintendent McCutlip was introduced to the committee members present at the hearing. They were told he was chief school administrator of one of the largest yet one of the poorest school systems of the state. He was presented as a leader in long standing in the Council of City School Superintendents, one of the more influential educational groups in the state.

Mr. McCutlip thanked the chairman for the introduction and assured the committee he was pleased to have the opportunity to give testimony on the proposed supplementary appropriation and tax bill. He declared that the council had always stood ready to provide its help and counsel in considerations of educationally related legislation. He expressed hope that the committee's confidence would not be misplaced.

The school superintendent commended the legislature in general and the bill's sponsors in particular on their action to increase the educational appropriation and taxes to support it.

"These legislators demonstrated a great deal of foresight in relating the state to our national government and the nation as a whole. Neither man nor a state school system is an island. This kind of action to upgrade educational opportunity in our state will help immeasurably to get us back into the economically and socially productive mainstream of American living.

"I further commend and congratulate this body on its dynamic and decisive action. The proposal to increase the educational appropriation is important, but it is equally important that additional revenues will flow in from a greater tax effort from the people. It is vital that no other part of the state's program be cut back. However, since we are legitimately calling on the people of the state for additional tax effort, it is imperative that we carefully consider who is to make the effort and to what extent equitability of increased effort is assured. This brings me to a major reservation I have with the draft of this bill.

"The original sales tax structure in our state was designed over thirty years ago. It provides for a 3 percent levy on all taxable purchases. This type of tax is considered proportional as all taxpayers pay the same proportion but not necessarily the same amount. This pattern of taxation is equitable in one sense as those who purchase greater amounts pay a larger tax but in the same proportion as the purchases of lesser amounts.

"However, if we look at some statistics on the income of our people in this state and the tax burden they assume through the state and local tax programs, then we can get a different perspective on the equity of the tax program in general and the sales tax in particular."

Superintendent McCutlip then presented two tables of data which were developed in the Bureau of Research in the Commerce College of the state university. The first table, reproduced below, described the income of consumer units in the state.

Table 33.1   Income of Consumer Units in the State

Income Bracket	Number of Consumer Units	Average Personal Income	Total Personal Income
Under $ 2,000	296,556	$ 1,110	$ 329,177,160
2,000–2,999	110,925	2,440	270,257,000
3,000–3,999	124,110	3,422	428,704,420
4,000–4,999	167,285	4,216	705,273,560
5,000–5,999	188,436	5,002	942,556,872
6,000–7,499	232,387	6,208	1,442,658,496
7,500–9,999	229,729	8,111	1,863,331,919
10,000–14,999	197,642	11,021	2,178,212,482
15,000 and over	57,313	25,132	1,440,389,716
Total	1,505,383		

McCutlip paraphrased briefly the contents of the table and pointed out both the relatively low average personal income of the state as well as the heavy concentration of consumers at the lowest-income bracket. He indicated that he was sure the members of the committee conducting the hearing were aware of these data but he felt a base of understanding was necessary before presenting the next set of data.

The latter set, reproduced on p. 183, dealt with effective rates of state and local taxes as a percentage of money income.

Again the chairman of the Council of City School Superintendents paraphrased the contents of the table. He pointed out that the family

Table 33.2. *Effective Rates of State and Local Taxes as a Percentage of Money Income of State Residents*

Tax	Income bracket (in $ 000's)								
	Under 2	2–3	3–4	4–5	5–6	6–7.5	7.5–10	10 & over	Total
Retail sales	1.56	1.33	1.26	1.36	1.29	1.25	1.08	0.97	1.15
Cigarette	0.88	0.59	0.47	0.41	0.35	0.31	0.26	0.12	0.28
Horse racing	0.08	0.06	0.06	0.06	0.06	0.05	0.05	0.04	0.05
Alcoholic beverage	0.32	0.38	0.24	0.21	0.21	0.20	0.17	0.16	0.20
Motor vehicle fuel	2.88	1.98	1.68	1.29	1.33	1.20	1.00	0.65	1.10
Motor vehicle license	0.75	0.65	0.56	0.54	0.50	0.45	0.41	0.27	0.42
Corporation franchise	0.10	0.09	0.07	0.06	0.05	0.05	0.05	0.14	0.09
Public utilities excise	0.25	0.20	0.19	0.19	0.18	0.17	0.16	0.12	0.16
Inheritance and estate	0.23	0.22	0.12	0.07	0.05	0.05	0.06	0.22	0.13
Municipal income	0.44	0.60	0.53	0.42	0.31	0.28	0.25	0.20	0.29
Property: real and tangible	9.31	6.47	5.27	4.47	3.64	3.41	3.03	2.61	3.54
Property: intangible	0.46	0.40	0.28	0.22	0.19	0.18	0.17	0.37	0.27
Unemployment compensation	0.73	0.65	0.59	0.52	0.46	0.42	0.36	0.25	0.39
Total	18.21	13.86	11.62	10.09	8.83	8.20	7.18	6.26	8.21

with less than $2,000 income, and there are nearly 300,000 in the state, pays on the average of 1.56 percent of its income in retail sales taxes whereas the family unit with over $10,000 income pays only 0.97 percent. He pointed out also that this same phenomenon was apparent in nearly all the state and local taxes currently levied in the state.

He noted that the rates of the real property tax were likewise extremely regressive. Consequently, the effective rates of the total state and local tax burden are very regressive, e.g., families with incomes under $2,000 pay 18.21 percent of their income in state and local taxes whereas the family with over $10,000 annual income averages only 6.26 percent of its income for these tax payments.

"With these data, I believe you can see that the effective rates of the present tax program, and more specifically the 3 percent sales tax, are regressive rather than proportional. That is, the lower the income level, the greater the part of that income that is paid in taxes.

"The problem which the legislature faces today is that of designing an equitable tax program to increase the state public school revenues. It is the position of the Council of State School Superintendents and my own personal opinion that increasing the state sales tax to 4 percent will only compound the already acute problem of regressive taxes in our state. I urge that you not build a new tax structure on a faulty foundation.

"I wish to thank the committee for their kind attention. I will be happy to entertain any questions they have."

Questions for Discussion

1. How might one characterize the state and local tax program as described in Table 33.2 in terms of the type of taxes? In terms of the impact of the taxes?

2. Which taxes appear to be proportional-type taxes but are regressive in effect?

3. What might be some of the reasons that the municipal income tax shows such an erratic impact?

4. On the basis of McCutlip's analysis and criticism of the present state and local tax structure, what might be some alternatives that he would support?

Case 34.   Perspectives on Progressivity in the Personal Income Tax

At the last meeting of the Executive Committee of the National Association of Educational Administrators a report from the Program Commission recommended that during the next year key programs incorporate the theme "Public Education Two Decades Hence." The Executive Committee accepted the report and decided to assign it to the several standing committees so they in turn could study it and make recommendations regarding the feasibility of the proposal and ways the report could be implemented if it were thought to be an appropriate activity for the association's ongoing program.

The Committee on School Finance chaired by Lawrence Tingley was one of the standing committees charged with the responsibility of this kind of evaluation. Tingley was director of research for a state department of education located in the southeastern part of the nation. Other members of his committee included David Friedhan, a teacher in a suburban school system near a large Midwestern city; Peter Komarek, a school superintendent from a middle-sized city in the Pacific Northwest; Dorothea Pace, an elementary school principal from a plains state city school system; and Turner Barnard, a director of research from the education association of a small Eastern state. Neither Mrs. Pace nor Mr. Barnard were able to make the meeting of the School Finance Committee in the national association's headquarters building when it convened on a snowy Saturday morning in the nation's capital.

Tingley opened the informal meeting by reading the charge to the committee as it was spelled out in the memo from the association's executive secretary.

> "So, that's what we're to do—consider the feasibility of developing a program around this 'two-decade-ahead look' from the vantage points of its relevancy for matters of school finance.
>
> "I would suggest we kick around some ideas, then during the last hour we get a stenographer in here and have her take down some summary statements.
>
> "I guess the first question is whether there will be a problem which would necessitate a twenty-year look ahead. From our last meeting I'm sure we're all convinced we have real problems now in financing the schools and this will probably get worse before it gets better.
>
> "However, I think we will have to flesh out—at least in our own

thinking—what educational program demands will be before we can anticipate the kind of finance problems this will likely cause in twenty years."

"Yes, Larry, but I would like to push for a broader context," suggested David Friedhan.

"If we are looking twenty years ahead I think we can read some signs which will tell us in what direction the whole culture is moving.

"We recognize the nature of a dynamic society. We see the changes in technology, social organization, demographics, economics and all the rest. Nearly all these forces suggest a growing, changing, and emerging role for education. Old patterns of public education are no longer adequate. Education for literacy will no longer do. Education for vocational entry is passé also.

"I see an educational program that is intensive, comprehensive, and almost continuous."

Peter Komarek interrupted.

"Dave, I would surely hate to try to meet your implied current operations budget in my school system! But, seriously, I guess I don't disagree with you if we are considering a twenty-year look ahead. However, as a school finance committee, I don't think we are able or should try to spell out the program dimensions. At this stage I feel we can accept these as assumptions. We should go on from this point and explore the financing implication of these kinds of program demands.

"I think the twenty years view is good because I am certain we will need to change our basic pattern of financing the public schools. As Dave suggested the role of the school in society will change, so the support pattern must be overhauled.

"Assuming that education program dimensions are changing from a local orientation to a broader societal orientation because of the impingement of Dave's forces, it appears to me the financial burden of these educational decisions must be reconceived. I suggest that as a committee we zero in on the financial burden dimension of the question."

"Yes, Pete," nodded Larry Tingley, "I am sure we must do this—but the groundwork you and Dave developed should be identified as our 'jumping-off place.' I also agree that our consideration of the feasibility of the twenty-year look ahead can focus on the question of burden. For instance, given these changes in magnitude and direction of public education, who should assume the cost burden, and how should it be determined?"

"I think now we might have to look back before we can establish a forward direction in which to move," suggested Dave Friedhan.

"Up to the present time the burden for financing public schools was assumed by state and local government. But probably more important is the fact that the tax vehicles used by these units have been largely property taxes employed by local school districts and sales taxes used by state governments for state aid payments to local school districts. I'll grant there are some exceptions such as state income taxes supplying revenue for financing state programs of assisting local school districts. However, this accounts for well less than half of state aid payments.

"The important thing is that the producers of the majority of school monies are taxes which are regressive. Thus, the primary burden of supporting public schools has fallen on the lower-income group. Under these present conditions, educational programs will never be able to expand sufficiently to meet the needs of twenty years hence. In addition to being regressive, these taxes have low elasticity."

"I assume from your observation you see the necessity of moving to a more progressive tax with which schools can be supported," suggested Peter Komarek.

David Friedhan nodded and Komarek continued.

"Then I also assume that if you seek to attain a roughly proportional tax burden for public education, you would balance the regressivity of state and local taxes with progressive federal taxes. It is at this point that I think we run into trouble.

"All of us are aware of the relatively small percent of school support which is presently derived from federal sources. Think of the implications of increasing federal allocations so as to balance the regressivity of state and local contributions and at the same time increasing the total educational outlay for an intensive, comprehensive, and nearly continuous public education program. That will put quite a strain on the federal tax sources. How are we going to get this amount of federal dollars?"

"Education!" volunteered Friedhan.

"We know education increases productivity. The increases in productivity will boost the gross national product and this in turn will enable us to collect larger amounts of personal income tax."

Larry Tingley, who had sat back and enjoyed the earlier exchange of the classroom teacher and school superintendent, now entered the conversation.

"Certainly Dave has a good point, but I also can appreciate Pete's concern. The enlarged federal role in financing public education is predicated on a wholesome and growing national economy. The expanding economy will not happen unless there are rather immediate resources for capital expansion which in turn can accommodate a highly skilled labor force. This would suggest that we might sacrifice some of the progressivity of the federal income tax in order to stimulate economic growth which will return more dollars but on a less progressive scale."

"I can use your same point," interjected David Friedhan, "but at the other end of the progressivity continuum. Economic expansion is dependent on consumer demand. Let the income tax rates become even more progressive by cutting them for the lower-income group. Then there will be even greater consumer demand and this will provide a greater incentive for capital expansion. The lower-income households with lower income tax payments would spend a greater portion of the difference than would the higher-income group. This would pump in greater amounts of money for consumer goods."

Both points of view favored revision of the federal personal income tax in terms of progressivity in order to attain long-range economic growth but with nearly diametrically opposed methods. A committee member mused that even without the constraints of practicality answers to school finance questions do not come easily.

Questions for Discussion

1.   Why is it important to consider who provides support for public education as well as the amount of support needed or available?

2.   How valid is the committee's assumption that the existing tax structure would be inadequate with a rapidly expanding economy? What information would it need in order to arrive at this position?

3. Considering the proportions of the sources of school revenues from local, state, and federal sources in your state, how would you classify the overall tax structure—regressive, proportional, or progressive? Why?

4. The Friedhan-Komarek dialogue suggests that not only tax burdens for given functions (i.e., public education) must be considered but also the total program for all functions so financed. What roles are implied for public school officials in terms of fiscal planning?

Suggested Readings

Concept L—Public Finance Theory: Distributive Aspects

Burkhead, Jesse: *Public School Finance*, Syracuse, N.Y.: Syracuse University Press, 1964.

————: *State and Local Taxes for Public Education*, Syracuse, N.Y.: Syracuse University Press, 1963.

Committee for Economic Development: *Fiscal Issues in the Future of Federalism*, New York: The Committee, 1968.

————: *Modernizing Local Government*, New York: The Committee, 1966.

————: *Modernizing State Government*, New York: The Committee, 1967.

Freeman, Roger: *Taxes for the Schools*, Washington, D.C.: The Institute for Social Science Research, 1961.

McConnell, Campbell R.: *Economics*, 4th ed., New York: McGraw-Hill, 1969, chap. 9, p. 146.

Musgrave, Richard A.: *The Theory of Public Finance*, New York: McGraw-Hill, 1959.

Ohio Tax Study Commission: *1967 Ohio Tax Study Commission Report*, Columbus, Ohio: The Commission, 1967.

Samuelson, Paul A.: *Economics*, 7th ed., New York: McGraw-Hill, 1967, chap. 9, pp. 154–157.

Tax Foundation, Inc.: *State Tax Studies: 1959–1967*, New York: The Foundation, 1967.

Taylor, Philip E.: *The Economics of Public Finance*, New York: Macmillan, 1953.

Thatcher, George W.: *Tax Revision Alternatives for the Tax System of Ohio*, Columbus, Ohio: Ohio Tax Study Committee, 1962.

Transfer Payments:
State and Federal

the problem

It has been well established that all three levels of government have some interest and responsibility for public education. There is considerable evidence of this in both educational policy making and in the financing of the schools.

Since local school systems are the basic operating units (relatively few schools are operated directly by the state or federal government), the fiscal responsibility of state and federal governments is carried out in the form of monies channeled directly or indirectly from these units to the local school system. These grants, known as "transfer payments," have in the last several decades, become extremely important in the operation of the public schools. For the last few years in nearly half of the states, revenue from transfer payments from state and federal governments exceeded that raised locally.

The basic functions, character, and effects of transfer payments are of growing import to the educator. Any rational public education policy must consider the impact of transfer payments at both the state and federal levels. This is especially true as new policy is molded to meet the interacting needs of growing educational demands, the dynamic character of an increasingly sophisticated economy, and the changing roles of government at all three levels.

the concept

The largest part of the funds spent by governments is raised internally, most of it through taxation and a lesser amount through fees and charges. To an increasing extent, however, state and local governments are receiving their revenue through transfer payments. A transfer payment is defined as a payment for which there is no direct and immediate exchange of a good or service at the time of the transfer. We are all familiar with many examples of transfer payments. A father sends money to his son or daughter at college; a foundation grants an art association money to purchase a painting; or a local welfare office makes a relief payment to an indigent citizen. In this same category must also be included those payments made by the federal government to a state or local government or by a state government to a local unit. These payments may be designated for some particular purpose, such as highways, or welfare, or education. Conceivably, they could also be undesignated, and available for any use the receiving government might wish. In most instances, the granting government will prescribe certain standards which the receiving government must follow in spending the money, but there is a growing interest in the establishment of unrestricted transfer programs. The outstanding characteristic of the government transfer program has been its rapid growth in the recent past and the very great certainty of even more rapid growth in the future. The historical developments of these programs are shown in Table M. on p. 192.

Transfer payments from one government to another in the beginning were usually designed to establish standards throughout the area covered by the granting government. Thus the federal government inaugurated the highway grant-in-aid program in 1916 to establish a nationwide network of highways which would meet a uniform standard of construction and specifications. So also have most of the states established aid programs for the public schools in an effort to guarantee an acceptable minimum level of education for all children in the state. The establishment of standards of performance is still an important goal of most transfer programs, but in recent years another important purpose has developed. It has become increasingly apparent that some governments, particularly those at the local level, are not so able to finance their activities as are others. The resources available to them and the tax system which they must use are not adequate for the task. For this reason, the federal as well as many of the state governments have undertaken transfer programs designed to help those governments which cannot help themselves.

In a few of the programs the state government merely acts as a tax collector for the local governments. Such programs include the local sales taxes in California and Illinois. These are called "local taxes," but they are collected by the state and returned to the city or county in which they are collected. Most transfer programs, however, whether they are designed to establish certain standards or merely to ease the fiscal plight of disadvantaged governments, do not distribute the payments according to the pattern in which the money is collected. The program inevitably has a redistributional effect and results in the citizens of one community financing, to some extent, an activity which has usually been considered a responsibility of the government in which the activity is being performed. Thus the taxpayers in one community may pay in part for the street lights, or the highways, or the educational system in another community.

The redistributional aspects of transfer programs require a re-

Table M.1.   Federal Aid to State and Local Governments (selected years, $ millions)

Year	Amount	Percentage Yearly Increase or Decrease
1902	7	
1913	12	6.5
1922	108	88.9
1927	116	21.5
1932	242	160.0
1934	1,016	−9.0
1936	948	−3.4
1938	800	7.8
1940	945	9.0
1942	858	4.5
1944	954	5.0
1946	855	−5.0
1948	1,861	58.8
1950	2,486	16.8
1952	2,566	1.6
1953	2,870	11.8
1954	2,966	3.3
1955	3,131	5.6
1956	3,347	6.9
1957	3,893	16.3
1958	4,835	24.2
1959	6,355	31.4
1960	6,994	10.1
1961	7,011	0.2
1962	7,735	10.3
1963	8,663	12.0
1964	10,002	15.5
1965	11,029	10.3
1966	13,214	19.8
1967	15,505	14.8

Source: *Facts and Figures on Government Finance*, 15th ed., Tax Foundation, Inc., New York, 1969, p. 137.

examination of the programs and a determination of the desirability of financing activities which have usually been considered a responsibility of the government in which the activity is performed. What justification, particularly what economic justification, can be given for requiring the taxpayers in one part of the state or nation to pay for governmental services performed in another part of the state or nation? A justification often advanced in defense of the redistribution resulting from most transfer programs is that this is a method of equalizing the tax burden throughout a state or the nation. This is a result of the program, and it does permit citizens in the poorer sections to enjoy government services comparable with those enjoyed by the citizens in the wealthier districts. Such a justification is usually not appreciated by the taxpayers in the wealthy areas, but another aspect of the program often does justify to them the redistribution involved. This aspect deals with the effects in one district of programs carried out in another district.[1] With most programs, particularly with education and highways and economic development, there is an economic effect which carries far beyond the boundaries of the governmental unit instituting the activity. For example, most children will migrate from the district in which they receive their public school education so that an employer located elsewhere will receive the benefits of their basic training and education. Even for those who do not migrate, a higher level of education will inevitably lead to a higher level of income and an increased standard of living. This higher level of income will result in a larger market for goods produced in some other part of the country. The spillover effects of local government activity are many and far-reaching, and cannot be overlooked when considering the appropriate methods of financing these activities.

Another effect of those transfer programs which stipulate the conditions for spending the transfer is the increased control which is acquired by the transferring government over the activities of the receiving government. There is a very real potential for such increased control, and this aspect has been used repeatedly as an argument against the transfer programs instituted by the federal government. This can only be an objection to the federal programs, for the states already have a complete power over the local governments within their borders. All local units of government have been created by and derive all their powers from the state. There are no inherent powers of local government.

With respect to the increased power placed in the hands of the federal government through the use of transfer programs, it should be remembered that this power is not always exercised. Furthermore, when it is exercised it usually takes the form of prescribing minimum standards of performance for the protection of the citizens within the district as well as those living elsewhere. The unjustified use of this power seldom can be demonstrated.

Whatever the individual's opinion regarding the desirability of transfer and grant-in-aid programs, it seems inevitable that they will

[1] This problem was also discussed in concept H.

grow in number and in magnitude, both at the state and the federal levels. As our nation grows in population, the effects of the government programs (or lack of programs) in one section will be spread to a greater extent throughout the rest of the country. The increasing inability of the local units to finance their activities will require an increasing interest in the financing programs of these local units. One of the surest public finance developments of the future is the increase in state and federal transfer programs.

Case 35. Updating Guidelines for State Transfer Payments for Public Education

Public education has always been taken seriously in most of the Great Lakes states. However, in recent years one of these states in the old Northwest Territory has shown an extraordinary concern for the status of its public schools.

For over a century this state demonstrated considerable national leadership in initiating and developing educational innovations. The state's fortunate circumstances have, to a considerable degree, made this possible. It is a relatively wealthy state with a per capita income well over the national average. It has a remarkably heterogeneous character embracing an urban, cosmopolitan population; rich farm-lands which not only produce agricultural wealth but also support small and medium-sized manufacturing cities; and large areas of non-glaciated and submarginal agricultural lands with occasional concentrations of rich fields of oil, natural gas, and coal.

The structure for public education carries many of the features so clearly characteristic of the New England origin of the state's founders. The concept of local control of public education is manifest in both education programs and financing dimensions. The state spells out few specific mandates for local school districts in terms of curriculum. Only skeletal requirements have been developed in areas of school calendar, teacher certification, mandatory local property taxes for public school support, and school district operation.

The state aid program has been characterized as a "weak district" aid program. The formula is based on a $360 per pupil calculation from which the local school district substracts the sum of 12 mills on its real property valuation based on true market value. To the remaining amount, all school districts add a flat grant of $45 per pupil. Thus even the wealthy districts (which receive no aid on the $360 per pupil calculation because the mandatory local effort exceeds the calculation) can be assured of this minimum flat grant. Additional reimbursable programs include special education, pupil transportation, and special subjects, e.g., vocational education.

The strong feeling for local control with its concomitant of little state financial support and much local support has resulted in total local and state educational costs being shared on an 80 percent to 20 percent basis. With the relatively heavy demand for educational services, the state has recently expended $540 per pupil with $432 coming from local sources and $108 from state and federal revenues.

The source of local revenue for the public schools is constitutionally limited to the local real property tax. This tax is determined by the local board of education's budgetary demands, but in conformation with a patterned set of tax ceilings. The tax ceiling is set by referendum of voters in the district. If the board-proposed ceiling is approved, it remains in force until either it is raised by the referendum process or lowered by a voter-initiated remonstrance procedure. Naturally the tax levy may be set at any figure at or below the ceiling. Thus, a given tax rate may be well below the voted ceiling.

The real property tax is levied on the real property supposedly assessed at full market value as determined by the county assessor. In this state, there has been considerable concern regarding uniformity of real property assessments both within and among the several counties.

State funds for the public school aid program are drawn from the general revenue fund and thus are an admixture of many kinds of revenues. However, the major source of such revenues is the state sales tax. Other taxes include sales taxes on motor fuels, tobacco, alcoholic beverages, and corporate profits taxes along with various licenses.

During the past few years, increasing public concern has been expressed in matters pertaining to the state's public schools. These concerns seemed to focus in four major areas: program, costs, taxes, and professional negotiation or teacher militancy.

Since the state incorporates two major metropolitan centers, it is not surprising that the problems of urban education would be manifested. The general problems of providing for the unique demands of urban education were felt as well as the overt crises of racial unrest in the city ghettos. The schools and their education programs were looked to in order to resolve much of the problem.

The education program was viewed as being inadequate in suburbia as well. Considerable pressure has been exerted on school boards, administrators, and teachers to provide "quality education." Parents in middle- and upper-class neighborhoods have been demanding the "new" curricula as well as updated methods, materials, and equipment to assure better academic performance of their youngsters.

Residents in the rural areas of the state have been less aggressive in making program demands, but there are recognized needs for program expansion, a more functional curriculum, and upgraded vocational education subject offerings.

As program demands have been both met and increased, problems of rising costs have become very visible. These costs have seemingly increased in geometric proportions. Personnel costs have increased markedly without changing the quantity and quality of personnel. Thus, when even more personnel are needed, the costs of these have fairly leaped up. Urban education, with upgrading in both quantity and quality, has demanded a startling increase in costs. The maturing suburbs have experienced sharp cost increases as the fast initial growth is over and a full range of public services is now being demanded.

It has naturally followed that the increasing costs for public education in the state have caused problems in raising sufficient revenues. Incidents of "taxpayers' revolts" at the polls have been frequent. Numerous referenda to raise tax ceilings have failed despite the demand for program improvements. The issues seem to revolve around the questions of who should pay the taxes for the schools and what are appropriate tax vehicles. Many groups have taken the position that more state aid is needed and that local property taxes have reached their upper limit.

The relatively recent advent of teacher militancy, a two-week teacher strike in one of the major cities, and numerous short "professional study day" sessions in both rural and urban school systems around the state precipitated another major problem. Teacher salary demands in nearly all these instances were met by the boards of education. However, in several communities the voters defeated the referendum to raise the tax ceiling to obtain the additional revenues for the salary increases. This has in turn precipitated many other problems involving program cutbacks, deficit financing, and other costly stopgaps.

With the high degree of citizen interest in these problems and with the splintering of opinion as to how they might best be resolved, the state legislature authorized an assessment of public education within the state. A team of out-of-state consultants was employed under the direction of an educational specialist in a nationally known private university. After a year-long study, the study team's report was submitted and accepted.

The major findings of the study included the following:

1. The quality of the public school program varied considerably throughout the state. Programs of the quality suggested by several authoritative and nationally recognized groups were found only in a few suburban school systems where there was a very high local property tax base and also a tax which exceeded the statewide average among local school districts. Many substandard programs were found. The majority of these were in the rural areas of the state where there was a relatively low local property tax rate. The educational programs in the large cities of the state were deemed to be clearly inadequate in terms of contemporary needs.

2. Many school districts in the state were found to be so small that adequate educational programs could not be offered except at prohibitive costs. To a large extent these very small districts were those which demonstrated exceedingly high or low per pupil measures of wealth as well as the same radical measures of per pupil costs and tax rates.

3. There were wide variations of financial ability throughout the school districts of the state. Despite the fact that the state as a whole ranked among the five most wealthy states, many school systems even with state assistance and relatively high local tax rates could not provide adequate programs.

4. Measures of local effort, as measured by tax rates and per pupil expenditure figures, indicated that there was no clear pattern in the ability-effort relationship. Many low-ability districts exerted great effort, but at the same time other poor school systems exerted little effort. The same condition was found among high ability or wealthy systems.

5. The state-mandated program standards and financial support system were inadequate in providing a justifiable program base for all school systems in the state. This was demonstrated in instances where local districts did not exercise their option to provide a broad curriculum or to utilize local taxes to finance a program exceeding the state minima.

Because of the nature of the charge given to the team of consultants, the report of the study concluded with general guidelines which could be used to attack the problems the consultants identified. The guidelines suggested by the team included:

1. The fiscal policies which the state uses in supporting public education should be predicated upon the principle of state and local sharing of total financial needs instead of those reflected only in the foundation program. The state should share with the local district a given proportion of the total school district budget rather than just that portion spelled out in the foundation program. Thus, within reasonable upper limits, the state aid program would be "open ended" in that the local district could count on the same proportion of state assistance if the local district mounted an "excellent" (and costly) program or a "minimal" (and inexpensive) program.

2. A minimal program for the next fiscal year should be set at $14,000 per teacher unit in order to meet realistic education needs. This would provide an average teacher's salary ($7,800) and $6,200 for all other operating costs. This figure should be recalculated annually in order to keep the minimal program realistic. In order to have the program, which changes in thrust as well as item costs, keep pace, operating costs should be updated in nature of costs as well as amounts. The program costs thus projected should be used to determine the amount of current expenditures required to expedite state budgeting.

3. The measure of financial need should be determined on a valid measure of cost. Thus the financial needs should be computed on the bases of:

a. Number of teachers for pupils in various classes (regular, special, elementary, secondary, etc.)
b. Average teacher salary
c. Nonteaching professional personnel
d. Proportion of staff for replacement due to absence, leaves, in-service education, etc.
e. Retirement payments
f. Other current operating expenses (materials, equipment, auxiliary services, operation and maintenance of school plant, fixed charges, etc.)
g. Extended programs beyond required school year

4. The determination of the ability of the local school district to share the financial burden of the educational program should be conditioned to some extent by the burden placed on the property tax by other local government agencies. Throughout the state there will be much variation in this regard. Several of the largest cities will have a high "municipal overburden" as they are called on to provide considerably more services, e.g., police and fire protection, local welfare payments, social worker services, and health services. High nonschool property taxes invariably depress school taxes.

5. The problem of providing adequate school plants to house adequate educational programs must be resolved by joint state-local effort. With constitutional as well as realistic financial burden limits, many school systems throughout the state are not providing and will never be able to provide adequate buildings. The costs of such provisions should be shared on the same basis as the instructional program as they are both integral parts of an adequate educational program.

Questions for Discussion

1. Using the several characteristics or features of state transfer payments to local governmental units as described in the concept statement, what are the characteristics or features of each major component of the original state transfer system to local school districts? What are the characteristics or features of each major component of the proposed state transfer system?

2. How would the proposed state transfer payment to local school districts influence the performance standards of the schools?

3. What redistributional effects would likely take place under the proposed programs?

4. How could the neighborhood effect be used as a rationale to support the proposed transfer program?

Case 36.   The "Have-nots" Design a State Foundation Program

To the people who knew Carl Joseff, it came as no surprise when the "Joseff ruckus" hit the headlines in most of the daily newspapers throughout the state. Some recalled that Carl was an independent and even rebellious youngster. He was born to a hardworking, and God-fearing couple living in a shantytown near a large sulfur mining and refining center in one of the Gulf Coast cities.

Others remembered Carl as a crusading student editor of a high school newspaper, who refused to participate in the graduation ceremonies when the principal mercilessly censored his speech on "A Citizen's Responsibility for the Political Renaissance."

Still others remembered the myriad of scrapes Carl got into as a state university student. When issues of free speech, administration domination of the campus newspaper, and student evaluation of professors were considered, Carl seemed omnipresent.

Even after his graduation from the university and his entry into a teaching career, Carl's crusading spirit was much in evidence. He challenged the status quo in terms of criticizing the social studies curriculum in the junior high school where he taught. This particular joust with the "authorities" yielded considerably more than did his previous confrontations, however. Carl succeeded in bringing about a major change in this program, but only after he learned he had to propose viable alternatives and mobilize the support necessary to work on the project and thus bring the new program into being.

Probably as a result of this experience and his hounding of the superintendent of schools and the junior and senior high school principals on the matter of junior-senior high school articulation, Carl Joseff was appointed to a junior high school principalship. In this new role Carl continued to question, challenge, and attack. However, maturation and the experience of suffering the consequences of a few ill-conceived campaigns with the attendant defeats, Joseff tempered his crusading tendencies. At the same time, however, he recognized that the "establishment" was not always impenetrable and could be forced to accommodate change.

With this motivation, Carl Joseff left his principalship after three, often stormy but generally productive years and started work on his Ed.D. degree at the state university. At the end of two years of resident study he had completed all the requirements for the degree except his research project. Rather than extend his period of study, Joseff elected to seek an administrative position and finish his degree while on the job.

Carl was interested in a superintendency, but he was not highly salable since he was young and had only a short period of principalship experience. It was quite late in the hiring season when the superintendent of schools resigned in Joseff's hometown, Canaan City. The board of education was in a hurry to hire a replacement and was not greatly bothered by Joseff's lack of experience. The image of a "clever hometown boy" also appealed to them, and Carl was hired as superintendent.

Canaan City was actually a new incorporation since Carl Joseff graduated from high school. At the latter time it was an unincorporated area in Canaan County. The community was predominantly a shanty-town in the county adjacent to Harminton County which had several sulfur mines, refineries, and processing and manufacturing plants. Canaan County was the residence of the employees of industry-rich Harminton County. Ironically, the state's richest and poorest school districts were adjacent—Canaan City on one side of the county line and Ellisville on the other side in Harminton County. The wealth disparity between the two school districts had not changed since Carl Joseff left high school twelve years earlier. Despite the fact that the shantytown in Canaan County has now incorporated as Canaan City, it still is largely composed of laborers employed in the mines and plants in Ellisville. The community is made up of marginal housing for these workers and little else. When school finance is discussed in Canaan City, one invariably hears, "Ellisville's got the money and we've got the kids." Statistics from the State Department of Education bear out both generalizations. The Canaan City school district enrolls 7,032 pupils from a total population of approximately 30,000. The per pupil assessed valuation of the district (based on 50 percent of market value) is $3,462. In Ellisville, the school district enrolls 2,002 pupils from a total population of 12,000 or thereabouts. The per pupil assessed valuation of the Ellisville district is $87,607.

The state aid formula is designed to equalize educational opportunity and to some extent equalize the burden for supporting a minimal educational program guaranteed to each school district. However, this is a traditional-type state aid plan calling for a minimum program based on allotments per teacher units. These are calculated; then a minimum local property tax based on assessed valuation is charged off against the teacher unit allotment. The difference between the required local tax effort and the allotment constitutes the state aid.

Under this plan last year Canaan City received $347.20 per pupil or nearly 80 percent of the $435.70 it spent for current operation per pupil. Ellisville, on the other hand, did not qualify for any state assistance as it did not levy the minimum local property tax. It, however, expended $797 per pupil from its own local sources.

It was this situation in which Carl Joseff found himself as superintendent. By reacquainting himself with his home community after more than a decade, Joseff became more appreciative of the complexity of the educational problems of Canaan City. He recognized the limited expectations he must hold for a school system which had only a marginal teaching staff, a clearly inadequate school plant, and both inadequate and inferior materials, equipment, and supplies. He recognized that calling on increased local effort would show little improvement. Even if the local property tax were doubled from 20 mills to 40 mills, it would only provide an additional $69.24 per pupil!

So. it was that Carl Joseff set about to bring major change in state financing of public education. His initial activities were not entirely motivated by the prospect of hatching a new finance scheme. Because of his ability and initiative he was elected to the Delegate Assembly of the State Education Association. At the same time he was appointed as an educational consultant to a council of labor unions in this end of the state. From these rostrums Joseff recognized his opportunity to mount a campaign to mobilize a confederation of economic, educational, and political have-nots. Many weak, loosely organized, and/or politically impotent groups were co-opted by Joseff in an effort to reformulate the state foundation program. Each of the separate groups saw promise in enhancing its own power through support of Joseff.

The Joseff proposal for a state foundation program was composed of four major features:

1. A foundation program should be set up in the amount of $600 per elementary pupil and $775 per secondary pupil.

2. A statewide mandatory property tax of 19 mills should be levied on equalized valuation. The property should be assessed by a single state assessing agency. Monies collected from this tax should be distributed by the state to the local school districts.

3. A "resources equalizer" grant should be set up so that school districts of average or below average wealth (in equalized assessed valuation) would receive the same amount as the wealthier districts if they levied the same millage in excess of the mandatory 19 mills. Thus, a poor district levying additional millage on a low assessed valuation would receive proceeds as large from this levy as would a district with average wealth.

4. A "percentage equalizing" plan should be set up to provide for state sharing of the cost of capital improvements with the local district on an equalized basis. School districts with low assessed valuations would obtain proportionately more state assistance than would wealthy school districts. The formula would be:

$$1 - 0.5 \frac{\text{District assessed valuation per pupil}}{\text{State average of assessed valuation per pupil}}$$
$$= \text{state share of approved capital outlay}$$

Because of his membership in the Delegate Assembly of the State's Education Association, Joseff was able to introduce his proposal for a new state financing plan for public education.

The bylaws of the State's Education Association provided the right of any delegate to submit a proposal directly to the Association's Legislative Committee for study without preliminary review and approval by a subunit of that committee. When the Legislative Committee did review this proposal, all the organizations in Joseff's confederation literally flooded the news media with supporting resolutions, supplementary data, and other statements. Pressure was also applied to other organizations and their leaders, and to the legislators and the Governor. Thus it was that the State Education Association was forced to act on the proposal. It would have been in a very uncomfortable position if it sought to reject it or to change many of the features of the proposal. Under the leadership of Carl Joseff, the have-nots were having their hearing, and it was one which could not easily be ignored.

Questions for Discussion

1. The wealth differential between Canaan City and the state in general and Ellisville in particular appears to be significant in this case. What rationale could this condition provide for the Joseff proposal?

2. Transfer payments are made by states to school districts in order to set performance standards and/or enable local districts to finance their programs more adequately. To what extent are these two purposes met in the proposal?

3. The Joseff proposal clearly is a redistributional transfer. How may this program be justified on the basis of equalization of tax burden?

4. How may the Joseff program be justified in terms of the economic phenomenon described in the concept statement as the effect "which carries far beyond the boundaries of the governmental unit instituting the activity? For example, most children will migrate from the district in which they receive their public school education so that an employer located elsewhere will receive the benefits of their basic training and education."

Case 37.   Examining Purposes of Federal Transfer Payments to Public Education

Kenneth Pavlovick and John Unger had much in common and so developed an ease in intercommunication while they were undergraduate students in a small liberal arts college in a lower Great Plains area state. Both were bright, articulate, and socially motivated. Each assumed leadership in his own professional interest group—Kenneth in politics and John in education. In these capacities they more frequently tended to reinforce each other than to compete with each other. During their senior year they ran successfully on a joint ticket of class president and student senate moderator.

After graduation, Pavlovick went to law school and Unger started a career in public education. However, they maintained contacts—mostly on a social basis—for the next several years.

Pavlovick completed law school and joined a law firm in the state capital. While in the firm he started "moving through the political chairs." He was elected to the post of city solicitor, member of the State Board of Education, state assemblyman, and recently he was elected to the United States House of Representatives from a newly created congressional district in his state.

John Unger "moved through the chairs" that led to one of the most prestigious administrative positions in the state's public school system. Unger entered the teaching profession in a fine city school system, completed a master's degree in four summers at a large private university, and was appointed as a principal of a junior high in the same school system. After two years in that job, John took a competitive examination for and was named to an assistant principalship of the largest senior high school in the capital city. He served in that capacity for three years.

At this point, the superintendent requested that Unger be named to a newly created post, assistant to the superintendent. In this position he worked "across the board" with the several central office specialists, the school principals, and the community leaders. The position, as well as John Unger, grew in stature, and after two years he became the "number two man" with the title assistant superintendent for administration.

Unger worked in this capacity for six years, with the exception of a one year's leave of absence to complete his doctoral residence period at the state university. Shortly after he was awarded the Ed.D. degree, the superintendent of schools retired and Unger was named to that post.

This was the setting in which Congressman Pavlovick telephoned Superintendent Unger to arrange an informal meeting in order "to exchange a few ideas for some proposed education legislation." The conference was set for Pavlovick's congressional office suite. It was scheduled right after Unger completed a conference with officials of the Department of Health, Education, and Welfare regarding the funding of a Title III project, Elementary and Secondary Education Act.

After brief greetings, inquiries as to the health of their families, and how the new jobs were going, discussion centered on federal legislation for public schools. Pavlovick broached the subject:

"John, I have been mighty concerned about where we should go, or where we may go on the federal aid to schools question. This

is a major program now and many people around here are
looking at it very critically.

"You know I'm on the House Education Committee—and that's
probably why I feel that I need to get many different points of
view about the various programs. It seems to me that many
people are questioning the programs and the purposes they
serve. As a schoolman, you can give me some insight in analyzing
these programs and suggesting what they should be. Sometime
soon, I will have to decide what should be retained, what should
be thrown out, and what should be added. Then whatever seems
desirable will have to be equated with all kinds of proposals
from other committees. Real hard looks are going to be taken at
all these programs, and only the ones for which a good case
can be made will stand a chance of being fully funded."

John Unger had leaned back in his chair, rubbed his temples and
gazed at the congressman's ceiling as Kenneth Pavlovick expressed his
concern about the assessment of education legislation. When Pavlovick
finished, Unger started his response.

"Educators in the field are as concerned as the Congress about
what we have already done in federal support and in evaluating
it.

"But their overriding concern is that it be evaluated for what it
is. You know, Ken, that the vast majority of the so-called federal
aid to education that has been provided is not just that. In fact,
it has been an aid to accomplish something *through* education.
Prior to World War II, public education had been used as a
vehicle to stimulate agricultural and industrial production, to
keep youth off the labor market, to provide employment during
depressions; and right after the war, to consume surplus agricultural commodities.

"In more recent years federal aids have been provided for public
education to contribute to the resolution of such problems as
developing space scientists for our national defense, reducing
technological unemployment, upgrading the economy in
depressed regions, and providing weapons for a war on poverty.

"School people are leery about having these costs charged up
to public education when the schools were used, and not
unwillingly mind you, for larger social purposes. This is why it
is difficult to evaluate the programs—the purposes are not
altogether clear on this kind of legislation.

"Also, and you know this better than I, the political processes in our legislative machinery are such that motivations for enacting a given program vary with the congressman and his constituents."

"Yes, John, I agree. But what does this mean? What does this have to do with reevaluating the program? It sounds like the general aid-categorical aid differentiation," observed Pavlovick.

"It's more than that," responded Superintendent Unger, "but that's a good starting point for an assessment. First of all, any program should be evaluated in terms of purpose. The purpose must be identified and judged in terms of its appropriateness. Two major purposes of federal aid are suggested by the general-categorical differentiation: Should it provide assistance to the state and local school districts in mounting specific programs as defined in federal guidelines for purposes which are not solely educational or should the federal government provide assistance to the individual states and/or school districts for them to expand or better implement their own locally defined programs?

"The first basic purpose—that associated with categorical aids—is the purpose we are currently meeting. There are several arguments which support the categorical aid position.

"First, it provides a careful check on the expenditure. It can be controlled and the taxpayer is assured that generally the aid is used in the designated ways. Therefore, reasonable efficiency is being maintained.

"Secondly, categorical aid provides some assurance that federal dollars are being used for the accomplishment of national purposes. No school system is given the opportunity to use the monies for its own narrow purposes.

"A third argument is that general aid provides a means of making a uniform and concentrated attack on a given problem on a nationwide basis.

"A fourth argument suggests that categorical aid programs permit the primary control to remain at the local level since categorical programs are designed to supplement and stimulate development of the locally defined programs.

"Now let's look at the other purpose—that suggested by general aid programs. General aid has been conceived as a flat grant or 'no strings attached' type of aid. Probably the purest form of this type aid was the Murray-Metcalf bill of the 1950s which proposed flat grants of initially $25 per pupil to the several states.

"Arguments used to support the purposes of general aid go something like this:

"1.   The most adequate way to solve the problem of the wide range of per pupil expenditures among the states and the consequent differential in educational opportunity is to have the federal government provide a federal equalization program among the states. Thus, educational opportunities would be equalized, and since wealthier states require less assistance, the tax burden is equalized at the same time.

"2.   Because public education dollars are invested in people and people are mobile, educational benefits created in one state are frequently enjoyed in another. At the same time, educational deficiencies created in one state cause problems in others. This spillover effect suggests that all states are affected by the quality of education in the others.

"3.   General aid proposals can be effectively used to stimulate state and/or local educational expenditures where this kind of effort is below a minimal level. Thus, before a state could qualify for general aid it could be required to expend a given proportion of its per capita income for public education. This would equalize, at least on a foundation level, the minimal effort throughout the nation.

"4.   General aid grants can be used to enhance and augment the decision-making role of states and school districts since they are given the means of broadening and deepening the educational programs to meet the unique needs of their own localities."

"That's an interesting rundown on purposes, and I'm impressed with the arguments supporting each. It would be difficult to discount any of them. And in thinking about them, I believe this is why we have this current problem of appraising the program of federal aids to education—we are being pressured to do a job that heretofore has not been done, that is, facing up to the question of the primary purposes of federal aid to education."

Ken Pavlovick paused to contemplate the problem he just identified. He resumed the conversation in a "thinking out loud" fashion.

"It seems to me at least part of our trouble comes from trying to look at purposes of federal aid from only the educationist's or politician's point of view—you know, the vested interest orientation. Could we look at this from the public administration perspective? What we are talking about is a transfer payment from the federal government to the state and thence to the schools.

"Transfer payments have multiple purposes. The first is that of the establishment of standards of performance. In federal transfers to support public education, this purpose is met by the categorical aid programs. The Smith-Hughes Vocational Education Act, the National Defense Education Act, and the Elementary and Secondary Educational Act are all examples of the federal government's having certain program standards established, usually by the separate states within federal guidelines, and then funding these specific programs.

"A second type of transfer is that of one governmental agency transferring funds to another which cannot finance its own unique activities. The general aid to education programs will illustrate this type. The old Murray-Metcalf proposal we talked about earlier was this type of aid.

"The last kind of transfer is not really a transfer in one sense. The collecting of the taxes of one unit (usually a smaller one) by another (usually a larger one) is an example of this third kind of tax. In the area of federal transfers to local and state units for educational purposes, the proposal to return a given proportion of a state's federal income tax payments to that state would be an example of this type transfer.

"Through this kind of analysis, we would classify purposes of federal aid to education, then ask the question, What is the basic purpose of the aid? Should it set up and implement uniform standards of performance, or provide general support for state or local educational enterprise, or assist the state or school system to collect its taxes to operate the school program?

"We have extensively used the categorical or uniform standards of performance model; we have only proposed the general aid model; and we have really just begun to think about the federal collection of state or local tax model. I believe our first step should be to fully investigate all alternate purposes before we accept any given one. This gives us a taxonomy of purposes, and now perhaps we can find ways to determine the extent to which these purposes have been met."

Questions for Discussion

1. In terms of federal transfer payments in education, how do categorical aids establish performance standards? Cite some specific examples.

2. If one designed a general aid to education bill for the purpose of guaranteeing a minimum level of educational expenditures for all states, what are some of the key features one would incorporate in the bill?

3. How would the redistribution effect take place, and to what extent would it occur in the three federal transfer models—categorical aid, general aid, tax return—suggested in the case study?

4. Which of the three federal transfer models might best resolve problems related to spillover? Why?

Case 38.   Federal Grants-in-aid to Promote Local Autonomy

For the past three years Libertyville State College has sponsored a superintendent's seminar on school finance. The department of educational administration in the college has provided leadership in organizing these meetings to promote its work in field service activities and in continuing education of school administrators. Members of the department staff, professors from other academic areas, practicing school administrators, and prominent laymen have prepared and presented papers, served on panels, or reported on pertinent research. With severe fiscal problems being always present in this Southern state, the seminar has become very popular.

Braxton B. Claypool, the superintendent of one of the more populous county school systems was one of the speakers on a three-man panel assigned the topic, "Prospects for Financing Public Schools: Local, State, and Federal Sources." Members of the panel decided to have each member present a position on one of the sources. It was agreed that Claypool should speak to the federal sources segment.

The panel was presented at the second general session of the seminar. The first two speakers presented their ideas as to prospects for local and state revenues in the immediate future. Both suggested some of the problems attendant to these projections.

Braxton Claypool, however, changed the approach in his presentation.

"People of our state have had a long and proud tradition of independence and self-determination. We have developed a rich heritage. Many elements in our culture today reflect the contributions of this tradition.

"Our heritage has not only served us well in the past but even today, independence and self-determination are as viable as ever. The opportunity to speak on the topic of prospects for federal aid to public education will allow me to demonstrate this in dramatic terms.

"School administrators in our state always have been dedicated to providing the best possible education for our youth. At the same time they have been dedicated to doing so in an environment characterized by independence and self-determination. However, in recent years men holding both of these values have seemingly been placed firmly on the horns of a dilemma. We have recognized the opportunities to upgrade our educational programs by taking advantage of federal aid programs. We have been concerned that our state gets and uses all the federal aid it can. However, when the money is to be used in the local school systems, we become concerned with how we, as local school system administrators, can meet the requirements set by the state programs designed to implement the federal acts. This is especially true of those requiring local matching monies.

"We find our needs are so severe that we must look to federal programs to provide additional revenue, but in order to obtain it we must divert monies used in vital program areas to provide the matching monies necessary to obtain additional federal monies for the federally supported program. Both kinds of programs are necessary—but we must choose between them.

"Some years ago many of us chose not to participate in such federal programs, and even today many in good conscience still do not. This thinking suggests that the federal government is not a legitimate revenue source. I submit, however, that it is not the source to be held in question; it is the design of the device that is faulty.

"Federal aid is clearly needed in our state. Educational demands are as great here as they are throughout the nation. Our wealth to support educational programs is significantly less than that of the rest of the country. While nationally the personal income per pupil of school age is $10,820, this figure in our state is only

$5,980. It is because of inadequate wealth that expenditures
in our state are below those of the nation as a whole in terms of
per pupil outlays. The nation as a whole expends $580 per
pupil while we spend only $341.

"Some are tempted to believe that good educational programs
are not necessarily the ones which cost the most. It is difficult to
find precise measures of quality to challenge this position,
however I am persuaded that there is a significant relationship
between measures like illiteracy rates, selective service rejections
for educational reasons, and proportions of National Merit
Scholarships; and indicators of our per pupil wealth and
expenditures. In the matter of illiteracy, our proportion of
illiterates who are fourteen years old and older is 6.1 percent of
that population while the national average is 2.4 percent. In our
state we have 54.1 percent of eighteen-year-old youth rejected
for military service for mental reasons while the national
average is 28 percent. The proportion of our state's youth who
score in the top 6 percent of the National Merit Scholarship
Tests is 0.48 percent while the national average is 1.69 percent.

"It is clear to me that given our present ability to support
education, it is unrealistic to expect much more state and local
effort to increase per pupil expenditures. With present levels of
such expenditures I cannot foresee any significant change in
quality of educational programs in our state.

"It is also obvious that despite more than a decade of substantial
federal aid being made available, we have not improved our
position very much. To a considerable extent we have not been
able to utilize fully even the inadequate amount of federal aid
available. It can be concluded that we need financial support
beyond the state and local levels, but we cannot fully utilize the
federal aid programs as presently constituted. The present
categorical aid programs are inadequate in several ways, but a
change in character of these programs offers some promise.

"In looking to the future of federal support for public schools,
let me suggest a program that will meet the needs of the whole
nation. This is not an original idea with me, but it fits into the
context of my concern for an appropriate form of federal aid to
education. The idea was articulated in the *Institute for
Administrative Research Bulletin*[1] several years ago.

[1] William S. Vincent, "The Shared Cost Plan as a Method of Federal Support for
Education," *IAR Research Bulletin*, vol. 4, no. 1, November, 1963, pp. 1–6.

"The heart of the plan is the 'shared cost' feature wherein the federal government shares the costs of education with state and local education units. On the basis of the local school district budget, the federal government shares all legal expenditures. These would include all current operating expenditures as well as capital outlay and debt service costs.

"The federal government's share would be determined by the relative ability of each state to support its schools. This ability would be measured in terms of personal income per child of school age.

"The process of calculating federal support in this program requires several steps. First, we must decide what proportion of the nation's total school expenditures the federal government will assume. This can be set at any figure—10 percent, 20 percent, or even 60 percent. For the sake of illustration let us take 10 percent. The combined local and state share would then be calculated by using the formula $S/N \times 0.90$. In the formula S represents the state's personal income per child of school age, while N represents the national personal income per child of school age. This formula will yield the 10 percent federal share which is adjusted according to the wealth of each state considered.

"When applied to the local school district budget, the proportion of federal aid provided for each dollar budgeted locally is expressed by the formula: Federal support $= 1.00 - (S/N \times 0.90)$.

"Thus in our state where the state personal income per pupil of school age is $5,980 and the national is $10,820, the ratio of S/N is 0.5527. This multiplied by 90 percent equals 0.4973. Thus the proportion of federal support to be given to each school district will be $1.00 - 0.4973$ or 50.27 percent of the local budget.

"It naturally follows that in a state of average wealth, as measured in personal income per pupil, the percent of local budgets supported by the federal funds would be substantially smaller, i.e., 10 percent.

"In a relatively wealthy state like one of the industrial Northeastern states, the formula would provide no aid at all since the state personal income figure far exceeds that of the nation as a whole. Using such a state the formula would be:

$$1.00 - \frac{(\$14,302}{(\ 10,802} \times 0.90) \text{ or } 1.00 - 1.19$$

"On a 10-percent federal sharing level, ten states would receive no assistance. If the sharing level were raised to 30 percent, all states would share. However, if it was desirable to have all states share and still maintain a lower level of, say 10 percent or 20 percent, a lower limit on the ratio could be arbitrarily set. Thus all states would be guaranteed some federal assistance in this plan.

"This plan not only is sound educationally but also is sound in terms of public finance. It includes several features that are recognized as being desirable by experts in this field.

"1.   There is a growing interest in general aid or block grants-in-aid rather than categorical aid or conditional grants.

"2. The plan moves from a standard setting function to one which provides for equalization of resources.

"3.   Redistribution of income is present in both the gathering of the revenues and the allocating of the grants-in-aid.

"4.   The plan establishes a new role for the federal government, i.e., the responsibility of assuring a minimum level of resources for a state's school systems while not calling for an excessive and/or unreasonable effort on the part of poor states.

"5.   It promotes a wholesome spillover. In states receiving substantial support, the youth who migrate to other states will present themselves more educable and more employable. Therefore the relatively wealthy states which contribute more to the sharing than they receive from it might gain from a better educated in-migration.

"6.   Upgraded educational systems in the states receiving substantial aid will provide better income, standards of living, and the like. Therefore, these states will provide better markets for the nation's productive capacity.

"7.   The plan will increase the capability, autonomy, and fiscal responsibility of the states. They will be actually strengthened to balance the growing strength of the federal government.

"Gentlemen, I urge you to reconsider massive federal aid to education in this new context. I am convinced it can resolve one of our severe problems and at the same time retain and strengthen one of the most prized and distinctive elements in our heritage—our independence and self-determination."

Questions for Discussion

1. What redistribution effects might be expected from the Claypool proposal?

2. How would this federal transfer formula tend to equalize the educational tax burden?

3. What performance standards would be assured by the proposal? What standards would *not* be guaranteed?

4. How would the Claypool proposal influence the spillover effects of public education throughout the nation?

Suggested Readings

Concept M—Transfer Payments: State and Federal

Allen, Hollis P.: *The Federal Government and Education*, New York: McGraw-Hill, 1950.

American Association of School Administrators: *The Federal Government and the Public Schools*, Washington, D.C.: The Association, 1965.

Bailey, Stephen, et al.: *Schoolmen and Politics*, Syracuse, N.Y.: Syracuse University Press, 1962.

Burkhead, Jesse: *Public School Finance*, Syracuse N.Y.: Syracuse University Press, 1964.

Committee for Economic Development: *Fiscal Issues in the Future of Federalism*, New York: The Committee, 1968.

————: *A Fiscal Program for a Balanced Federalism*, New York: The Committee, 1967.

————*Modernizing Local Government*, New York: The Committee, 1966.

————: *Modernizing State Government*, New York: The Committee 1967.

Heilbroner, Robert L., and Peter L. Bernstein: *A Primer on Government Spending*, New York: Vintage Books, 1963.

McConnell, Campbell R.: *Economics*, 4th ed., New York: McGraw-Hill, 1969, chap. 9, pp. 137–138, 253, 262.

Meranto, Philip: *The Politics of Federal Aid to Education in 1965: A Study in Political Innovation*, Syracuse, N.Y.: Syracuse University Press, 1967.

Munger, Frank J., and Richard F. Fenno, Jr.: *National Politics and Federal Aid to Education*, Syracuse, N.Y.: Syracuse University Press, 1962.

Musgrave, Richard A.: *The Theory of Public Finance*, New York: McGraw-Hill, 1959.

Samuelson, Paul A.: *Economics*, 7th ed., New York: McGraw-Hill, 1967, chap. 8, pp. 145–147, chap. 9, 165–166.

Sufrin, Sidney C.: *Issues in Federal Aid to Education*, Syracuse, N.Y.: Syracuse University Press, 1962.

Tax Foundation, Inc.: *State Tax Studies: 1959–1967*, New York: The Foundation, 1967.

The Federal Tax System

the problem

In previous sections the role alternatives for the federal government in relationship to public education have been explored. Likewise, the nature and impact of federal transfer programs have been examined. It is now appropriate to assess the federal tax system in order to develop a clear concept of the operational implications of a fiscal role of the federal government in public education.

When public demand for federal participation in education has been voiced, professional educators have usually sought to provide leadership in articulating these concerns. In many instances the educator has felt that in order to be professionally responsible he must not only spell out clearly the nature of educational needs to be met at the federal level, but must also take a position on how the necessary revenue should be obtained at the federal level. In order to establish a firm base for his position it is necessary to have a working knowledge of the character and operation of the federal tax system. Clearly, an investigation of potential revenue for public education at the federal level must consider those revenues available at the state and local levels. Only through such an analysis will the most appropriate mix of federal, state, and local dollars be raised and expended to bring the maximum benefits to the citizen's investment in public education.

the concept

The Constitution of the United States, which provides the authority for the present federal tax system, was designed to overcome the many failures of the Articles of Confederation under which this country was previously governed. One of the most glaring failures of these articles was in the area of taxation, and this particular fault was one of the specific points which the Constitution was designed to correct. The fault of the Articles of Confederation in the field of taxation lay in the lack of power vested in the central government. The central government had been created by the states, and it derived all its power from the states. It could collect no taxes directly from the people; all its revenue was collected by the states and paid by the states to the central government. The result was that the states forced their will upon the central government by refusing or agreeing to collect the needed revenues. All too often this resulted in the states turning over no money to the national government, so that the bills were unpaid, the interest on the national debt which had been created during the revolution was in default, and the general credit of the United States was in widespread disrepute.

The Constitution provided that the national government could collect taxes directly from the people and limited this power in only three ways. It provided that all tax rates should be uniform throughout the country, that no duty should be placed upon exports, and that no direct tax should be levied unless it should be apportioned among the states according to population. Only with the latter has there been difficulty, and this difficulty has been due to different interpretations of the term "direct." Since the Constitution does not define the term, this task was left to the courts, who first defined it in 1796. The particular case (*Hylton v. United States*, 3 Dall. 171) involved a tax on carriages, and the tax was challenged by Mr. Hylton on the grounds that this was a direct tax and therefore must be apportioned according to population. The Supreme Court, however, ruled that it was not a direct tax, for it was a tax on the privilege of owning a carriage rather than on the carriage itself. The Court further pointed out that there was not the same proportion of carriages to population in all states, and that any apportionment of the tax among the states on the basis of population would place higher levies on the carriage owners in some states than in others. Since the tax could not be apportioned fairly, the Court concluded that the tax must be indirect.

In the *Hylton v. United States* decision the Supreme Court did define a direct tax as a head tax or a tax on land, and this definition prevailed for almost 100 years. It was not until 1895 in the case challenging the income tax passed by Congress in 1894[1] that the Court altered the definition. At that time the income tax was declared unconstitutional because it did not distinguish income from land and income from other sources. Taxing the income from land, the Court held, was the same as taxing the land itself.[2] It is interesting to note that in 1909 Congress adopted a corporation income tax which the Supreme Court ruled constitutional, even though corporate income inevitably includes some income from land. Any further consideration of whether the income tax is direct or indirect was avoided with the adoption of the Sixteenth Amendment to the Constitution in 1913.

With the question of the validity of the income tax finally settled,

[1] *Pollack v. Farmers Loan and Trust Company*, 158 U.S. 601 (1895).
[2] The 1894 income tax was almost identical with the income tax adopted by Congress during the Civil War, which the Supreme Court held to be an indirect tax.

the only major tax the federal government cannot collect directly from the people is the property tax. This would have to be apportioned among the states according to population. Because of the inherent difficulties of collecting revenues from the states, the property tax has been used by the federal government only three times. In 1798 and in 1812 a tax was placed on slaves, land, and dwellings and apportioned among the states, and during the Civil War a 20 million dollar levy was divided among the states to help defray the costs of the war. Of the 20 million dollars, only two-thirds was ever collected in the thirty years following the levying of the tax.

A large portion of the costs of the federal government during the early years of its history was derived from the sale of land. Tax revenues before the Civil War were largely confined to import duties, although there was some experimentation with excise taxes.[3] Liquor and tobacco excises became a permanent part of the revenue structure during the Civil War, and additional excises were added during World War I, the depression of the 1930s, and World War II, so that today the federal government applies excise taxes to a wide variety of goods, services, and occupations. The Excise Tax Reduction Act of 1965 eliminated the tax on many items and reduced it on others, but it is still expected that excises will account for approximately 10 percent of the total federal tax revenue. Excises long have been criticized on the grounds that they are regressive in effect and that they place an undue hardship on the producers of the taxed items. It is hard to imagine a modern government, however, which does not make substantial use of excise taxes, and it is probable that these levies will continue to maintain their present relative importance in our federal tax structure.

Although tariffs and excises were for the most part adequate to meet the needs of the federal government during the nineteenth century, the great push toward industrialization and urbanization which has taken place during the past sixty years has made the use of the income tax mandatory. As indicated above, the income tax was used during the Civil War and was attempted during the 1890s, but the structure of the tax and the methods of administration used made it a very unpopular levy. The tax structure adopted in 1914, following the ratification of the Sixteenth Amendment, recognized the inherent differences between the income tax and other levies, and adopted the self-reporting, audited system we know today.[4]

---

[3] The adoption of a liquor tax in 1791 required the use of militia as tax collectors, and led to what history calls the "Whiskey Rebellion."
[4] The income tax as structured in 1914 was patterned very closely after the Wisconsin state income tax adopted in 1911.

Perhaps the most important change in the federal income tax since its inception was the adoption of withholding in 1947. The provision that most of the personal income tax liability shall be deducted from the wages and salaries of the taxpayers before it is received by them has had the effect of eliminating the burden of the tax. Of real importance to the taxpayer today is the amount of his take-home pay. Labor unions bargain on the basis of the wage after withholding, and opponents of the income tax and government spending complain that the withholding provision makes the taxpayer indifferent to the size of the federal budget. Certainly withholding has taken most of the "pain" out of paying the income tax; that this is undesirable would probably be disputed by the great majority of taxpayers and certainly by the government which has enjoyed the greater revenues resulting from the increased efficiency and reduced evasion which has been the result.

The modern federal corporate income tax, as noted above, was adopted in 1909 and was absorbed into the 1914 income tax structure. Since that time, it has contributed annually from one-sixth to one-half of the federal tax revenue and is now second only to the personal income tax in revenue importance in the federal system.

Although the corporate income tax does produce such substantial revenue and the administrative costs are so low due to the relatively small number of corporations, it is often charged that this tax is an undesirable influence on the economy of the country. One claim is that since most of the corporate profits are distributed as dividends, and so taxed as a part of personal income, distributed corporate profits are subjected to double taxation by the federal system. This criticism overlooks the fact that many corporations shift the corporate tax to their customers and that the price paid for common stock is usually based upon after-tax earnings, so that no corporate tax burden is borne by the stockholders.

Another criticism is that the tax reduces corporate savings and so impedes business investment. A reduction of the corporation income tax rate, it is claimed, would increase the retained earnings of business and this increase would induce businesses to increase their capital expenditures. This argument overlooks the fact that business investment usually occurs when there is believed to be an opportunity for profit, and not just because the company has idle funds on hand. The opportunity for profit will probably be the greatest when consumers are spending at a high level, and the collection of a large portion of the federal tax receipts from corporations, rather than through higher personal tax rates, will probably enhance consumer spending.

In favor of the corporation income tax it must be recognized that there is relatively very little cost involved in the collection of the tax, on the part of either the government or the taxpayer. Furthermore, because corporations control the use of such a substantial portion of the economy's resources, corporate profits are necessarily an important subject of income taxation. It is certain that this tax will continue to provide important revenues to the federal government.

The limitations of the Constitution and the needs of the federal government for such large sums of money have dictated the present pattern of federal taxes. It is probable that the three types of taxes discussed above will continue to maintain their present importance. A minor amount of revenue is received from the federal estate tax, but no great expansion in this area is considered possible. The adoption of a general federal sales tax, probably applied at the manufacturer's level, has been proposed at various times; but the adoption of such a tax, particularly in view of the heavy reliance upon sales taxation by state governments, is highly unlikely. The distribution of federal receipts among the various tax sources is shown in the accompanying table.

Table N.1.   Federal Tax Collections (by source)

	1965	1966	1967
Individual income tax	47%	48%	45%
Corporate income tax	23	24	25
Total income tax	70	72	70
Excise taxes	13	10	10
Estate and gift taxes	2	2	2
Employment taxes	15	16	18
	100%	100%	100%

Source: Department of Commerce, Bureau of the Census.

A very reliable prediction is that the role of the federal government will remain large and will very probably grow in importance in the future. Thus the revenue needs of the national government will remain large and the taxes described here will continue to play a very important role in the lives of the American taxpayers. Because of the domination of those tax sources now used by the federal government, financing of the public schools will need to be accomplished to a large extent through the use of taxes not used as a federal source. There is the strong probability, however, that increased aid to education by the federal government will result in a considerable financing of public education by and through the taxes imposed at the federal level of government and discussed in this chapter.

Case 39.   Federal Taxes for Public
Education in the 1980s

The National Society for the Study of Educational Administration was formed to provide an inquiry base in order that educational administrators could be apprised of social movements that affect education and thus best determine the appropriate direction for their actions. The basic purpose of the society stemmed from the concern of many professional educational administrators that by and large most of them tended to be predominantly reactive rather than pro-active. It was the opinion of the society's founders that the schools and the people who administer them were constantly reacting to the larger environment. They observed that there was little planned and aggressive action on the part of the schools or the administrators to exert substantial influence on the environment to promote needed changes in the purpose or operation of the schools.

The society was formed to promote a pro-active behavior, and this was to be stimulated by the inquiry conducted by the society. In the few years of its existence, studies were conducted in areas of community attitudes in regard to educational purposes, the locus of educational decision making, analyses of teacher concerns, and bases of educational policy making at the state level. Without exception, these reports were well received, and the society grew in prestige.

However, one concern or reservation expressed toward all the studies was that of the current orientation. Many of the practitioners and professors of educational administration who were members felt that these studies were based on conditions present today. As such the studies were helpful in the analysis of past or immediate problems but were not futuristic so as to suggest the pro-active behavior which was the major objective of the society.

As a result of this concern, the Steering Committee, which had the responsibility for study design and supervision, approved a "crystal ball" study devoted to the topic "Administration of Education in the 1980s." After nearly a year of work, a design was approved, a study team was assembled, and specific assignments were made. The major study components included community and professional demands; teachers, professional, and service personnel; curriculum and instruction; pupil personnel and services; administration and organization; and economic and financial support systems. Each of these study components was to identify the major forces that would affect it through the 1980s, how these forces would influence education, and the implication of the forces and their effects for educational administration. An intricate sequence of priorities was set up among the component groups along with communications procedures so members of each study component were aware of the progress of all others. Initially, each group was to "brainstorm" a major question or assignment and then develop working papers to be used as a beginning document for review and analysis by the whole study team.

It was agreed, and subsequently scheduled, that the economic and financial support system component have the working papers and preliminary data from the other committees regarding projected needs before it in turn projected a financial structure for administering the public education system of the 1980s.

Titus Cartwright, chairman of the committee dealing with the economic and financial support system, was superintendent of schools in one of the largest cities in New England. As he and the committee looked at the preliminary data from the other study components, several generalizations were made:

1. The population to be served by public education will be substantially increased in both number and proportion of the population.

2. Educational programs will be perceived as an investment so educational experiences will be continuous as economic and technological advances are made and labor forces will need to be trained and retrained.

3. Most of the presently constituted educational programs will be broadened and deepened.

4. New programs will be instituted which will require unique personnel and material resources.

5. Educational program emphases will include both individual and social benefits.

6. Education in the 1980s will require a substantially larger expenditure than it did in the 1970s in terms of total dollars, per pupil expenditure, proportion of public sector expenditures, and proportion of the gross national product.

In reviewing these observations, Cartwright and his committee developed certain assumptions about the economic base from which a financial plan must be developed to meet the program needs as suggested by the other study component groups. Among these assumptions were:

1. The economy will undergo a marked expansion, and its character will change also. The public sector will expand significantly; however,

the proportion of gross national product derived from the public sector will expand only slightly.

2. In all sectors of the economy the demand for services will expand much faster than the demand for products.

3. A substantial part of the manufacturing process will be highly automated.

4. Public services will still be provided and financed on federal, state, and local levels. However, the nature and scope of these services will change markedly.

5. The proportion of revenues drawn from federal, state, and local levels will change also with the greatest amount coming from federal revenues and the least amount coming from local sources.

6. Public schools will continue to be financed through taxes derived from all three major sources. However, the amount of revenue raised for schools will increase along with educational expenditures in proportion to other governmental expenditures.

After the committee ascertained the basic program needs, these needs were "priced out" to determine the financial needs. From the latter type of data, the committee then considered the vehicles necessary to provide financing for the program. Chairman Cartwright set the tone for the session devoted to the above concern with this question: What are the appropriate tax sources and tax vehicles, and to what extent should they be used to finance the educational program as projected?

The initial discussion following his question ranged over many varied suggestions without specific reference to each other. Finally Lawrence Lauton, a superintendent of public instruction from a Pacific Coast state, suggested the necessity for considering some of the committee's own projections regarding the nature of the economy as a basis for finding appropriate tax vehicles to tap the nation's wealth in order to support the program.

"That's an excellent suggestion, Larry, but remember we are assuming support from all three levels—federal, state, and local. We'll have to consider each separately or we'll get all fouled up."

Joe Carmichael, the speaker, was an aggressive young superintendent from a rapidly growing area in the nation's Southwest. This concern was consistent with that which he displayed throughout his service on the committee. Carmichael was very vocal in advocating a clear role delineation among levels of government and their functions in supporting education. Without it, he maintained, there will be confusion, buck-passing, and abdication of responsibility.

Carmichael continued:

"The working papers we developed on the nature of the economy in the 1980s pointed out very clearly the necessity for considering a system that gives meaning to discrete roles for federal, state, and local financing. We cannot suggest a specific tax without reference to the function to be performed. We agreed that the state is plenary and its role should reflect this. We further agreed there is evidence that states are retrieving much of their authority—and fiscal responsibility—which they perhaps unwisely delegated to local school districts. We projected the local responsibility to be that of a minor partner with the state in providing the basic program, but with considerable authority and responsibility to supplement and augment the basic program according to the local district's own unique needs.

"You remember our projection for the role of the federal government in public education changed more than any other level when compared to the current scene. We saw the federal government expenditures increased by 400 to 500 percent. Its projected functions were those of stimulating the development of specific programs through categorical grants-in-aid and the providing of general aid to all the states on a variable grant according to ability.

"The specific question, as Titus Cartwright indicated, is *how* to provide the necessary support—but within our own agreements as to role.

"So, then, let's zero in on types of taxes appropriate for each of the governmental levels. Could we start with federal taxes since we said these would probably show more change than the others?"

Douglas Jorgensen, superintendent of a large rural school district in the Great Plains region, asked to be recognized.

"I appreciate Joe's concern for ordering our discussion. As I prepared for our brainstorming today, I found that specific suggestions for federal taxes were related to three considerations:

1. Consideration of the nature of the economy

2. Consideration of the relationship of education of the economy

3. Consideration of the nature of the educational program.

"I believe it would be helpful if we could use a similar scheme to keep our thinking straight."

A brief discussion ensued on the viability of Jorgensen's classification of considerations. With an apparent consensus and some signs of impatience among several members of the group, Chairman Cartwright suggested that the committee try to begin the process using Jorgensen's considerations in making suggestions for federal taxes to accommodate educational expenditures in the 1980s.

"Let us start with your first consideration, Douglas. I believe it was that of the nature of the economy. In considering what the nation's economy will be like in the 1980s, what will this imply for federal taxes in light of our projected educational needs?"

"Well," responded Douglas Jorgensen, "I believe we have to start with our assumption that public schools will continue to be supported by taxes, and these taxes are largely derived from current income. Income in turn is derived from productive capacity. Thus the changing economy will necessitate a different tax structure.

"In the 1980s our American economy will be highly automated. The cybernetic revolution will be felt on the production line where machines will not only make the products but the machines. Thus, the most important source of productive capacity will be know-how rather than things. An expanded economy will place much more emphasis on services instead of products. A smaller proportion of national income will be spent on consumer goods.

"Industry in the 1980s will have a national base rather than a local one. Thus, extensive spillover effects must be considered when a tax program is designed."

After a brief pause, Joe Carmichael picked up the conversation.

"If what you describe as the American economy of the 1980s is reasonably accurate—and I have no major argument with it—it's pretty clear we'll need major changes in the nation's tax structure. It also demonstrates the superiority of the federal tax machinery over that of state and local government."

"But Joe," interrupted David Lefkowicz, an Eastern city superintendent, "with expanded needs for federal support to public education of the magnitude we've spelled out, this committee must recognize that the present federal tax program must be expanded as well."

"Not necessarily," responded Carmichael. "This is one of the unique features of the federal tax system. The present federal tax system places a heavy reliance on the personal income tax and this tax is quite elastic and progressive. Thus, when our economy grows in terms of gross national product and the major segment of growth within it is services, wages, and the know-how kinds of things, the revenues collected by this tax might be sufficient. At least, the basic features of the tax are compatible with the social needs and the economy of the 1980s.

"However, since it is not the only federal tax, it must be considered in relationship to the others. Excise taxes probably should not be increased since they are regressive and not as compatible with the economy of the 1980s.

"The corporation income tax has possibility of expansion, especially in light of projections of nationally and internationally based big industry. But, this will have to be watched closely in expansion."

Carmichael's analysis immediately stimulated both questions and comments among the committee. There was general agreement as to the necessity of obtaining data to verify Carmichael's generalization as to the productivity of the personal income tax in an expanding economy.

Chairman Titus Cartwright used this moment of consensus to shift the discussion to Douglas Jorgensen's second consideration: the relationship of education to the economy. He asked Jorgensen to initiate the discussion.

"Well, Mr. Chairman, I am of the opinion that in the decade of the 1980s there will be widespread recognition of the notion that education is a producer's good in addition to a consumer's good. In the past few years we have just begun to realize this and it has only started to be reflected in our political and social decisions and programs. In the decade of the 1980s, we will have already demonstrated this principle, and education will be widely used as a governmental tool to stimulate economic development. It will be employed to maximize our utilization of technology and cybernetics. It will be a major input in economic expansion, for already there is evidence that as an investment education yields an 8 to 20 percent return.

"Another factor of a different order is that of education being necessary to implement the social functions of technological advances. Technology by itself is useless if not actually dangerous unless we are able to live with it. Some social scientists are of the opinion that we are experiencing a widening cultural gap when technological sophistication is outstripping social maturity. To make economic expansion meaningful, we must provide the social context to have it implement social purpose.

"A third factor which relates the economy to education is that of the function of education in providing equilibrium, balance, stability, and an even, orderly growth in the economy. This is done by governmental intervention in providing education and training in "soft spots" in the labor force, by providing education which in turn stimulates production and spending, and by providing education to eliminate unemployment and under-employment."

"That's a big order," volunteered Lawrence Lauton. It was apparent that few on the committee had conceived such an inclusive role for public education in the 1980s.

"I guess the implications for a federal tax program are quite clear, though. If we buy your notion, it will be necessary for the federal government to mount a tremendous program. The crucial factor, as I see it, is not the amount of dollars but the flexibility and responsiveness of the tax system to provide the right amount of resources at the crucial moment of need—say, during a recession or in a period of technological unemployment. It seems to me we shall need not only highly productive and predictable tax sources but also a system which provides the confidence necessary to engage in deficit financing when huge outlays are necessary during periods of low tax collection. As of now, it appears to me that our personal income tax does this. It is another question whether it will be able to do this in the kind of future we anticipate between now and 1990."

A lively discussion ensued on both the validity of Jorgensen's original considerations and the implications of his and Lauton's statements. After nearly thirty minutes of disjointed discussion the chairman of the Committee on Administration of Education in the 1980s called for order.

"I realize one of our charges as a committee was to brainstorm various ideas, but it appears we are beginning to emphasize the latter half of the word brainstorm to the detriment of the first half. Let us move on to Mr. Jorgensen's third consideration.

"Douglas, could you spell out this one for us, please?"

"The third consideration is the all-inclusive concern for the nature of the educational program. We have drafts of the working papers from other committees on what they foresee in the 1980s. So, in light of my first two considerations—those of the nature of the economy and the relationship of education to the economy—we can now look at educational needs in this context."

Chairman Cartwright reviewed the generalizations the committee derived from the other committees' drafts. He than asked what kinds of federal taxes these needs seemed to suggest.

David Lefkowicz started the discussion.

"On the basis of these needs, our federal financial support system must have the capability to expand rapidly, and not necessarily with economic expansion.

"Since we are anticipating this basic shift into an automated or cybernetic economy, it is obvious to me there will continue to be a wide gulf between the country's haves and have-nots. This suggests the necessity for a progressive federal tax program to augment the effective redistribution of wealth coming through the broadened educational programs. The haves will benefit immediately and most from this 'new economy.' Therefore we would complicate the problem if we used a federal tax which would have a heavy burden on the poor. On this basis, I favor expanding the progressive federal personal income tax, reducing federal excise taxes, and modifying the corporation income tax to reduce the possibility of it being shifted to customers."

Titus Cartwright intervened as Lefkowicz finished.

"With that pronouncement, Dave, I think we have some specifics to which we can react. So I suggest we adjourn for the day. Tomorrow we can pick up the discussion at this point and hopefully identify several topics or questions for intensive study."

Questions for Discussion

1. What is your opinion on the validity of the notion that tax programs must be related to the nature of the economy? What past events support or reject this idea?

2. If the committee's projections are accurate and the economy becomes less goods-oriented and more services-oriented, what is your opinion as to the appropriateness of applying the present structure and rate of federal taxes on excise items? Why? On personal income? Why? On corporate income? Why?

Case 40.   A Federal Tax Policy to Revitalize State and Local Tax Structure

Anthony Cardi had done a superlative job in chairing the discussion "Are Local School Boards Obsolete?" at his State School Board Association Conference. The question was clearly posed; it was carefully analyzed; the subissues were logically derived; and the evidence for the pro and con positions was convincingly presented. Despite the sincere congratulations by panelists, audience, and other conferees, Cardi was troubled. He was convinced of the necessity to alert his fellow school board members to the changing role of the local board of education. However, he was even more certain that only dramatic action taken very soon could prevent not only obsolescence but actual disappearance of the local school board. Cardi's discomfort was centered on the observation that people interested in school affairs were still debating whether or not local school boards were in fact obsolescent rather than moving on a conclusion based on the overwhelming evidence. There was very little predisposition to investigate the basic causes for this dysfunctionality and what might be done to modify the concept of educational governance on the local level to make it viable.

Because of the absence of any organizational or mass support for rethinking the nature of local educational governance, Anthony Cardi was forced into the role of the initiator. This was not, however, an unreasonable part for him to play since by virtue of a gubernatorial appointment he was a member of his state's Commission on Educational Problems. This group was designed to provide liaison between public education bodies and the state legislature. The Governor appointed all five members: one from each of the state's two legislative chambers, and one each from the State Teachers Association, the State School Board Association, and the State School Administrator's Organization. Cardi was serving his third three-year appointment as the school board representative.

The Commission on Educational Problems operated informally. Quite often position papers prepared by one of the educational organizations would be presented, and considered in free and open discussion. On occasion a legislator would transmit a paper or statement from a constituent or interest group which he thought was relevant.

Although ideas were solicited from all interested parties, the commission was a free and independent body. Only after long, intensive, and wide-ranging study would recommendations be submitted to the legislature by the commission.

Many of the key problems examined by the commission came from the often general but vaguely defined concerns expressed by all members of the commission. Usually it took a keen analytical description of the problem to place it in the context of other problems in order to mobilize the efforts and insights of commission members. It was this tactic that Cardi used to bring the issue of local school governance to the attention of the commission and hence to the appropriate initiators of policy.

It was during the winter meeting of the commission following the November elections when Cecil Goodwin, chairman of the commission solicited "suggestions of problems to which the commission should address itself." Several papers were presented and discussed briefly as to relevancy and then temporarily put aside so as to consider other problems for the "agenda."

John Kesserling, a veteran state senator and a long-time member of the commission as well as the Senate Education Committee, proposed a study of the problem of state administration of federal grants, especially in terms of the influence of federal monies in local budgets and how this affects local claims for state aid. Kesserling maintained that the federal money flowing into local school district budgets distorted the intended pattern of state aid to local school districts. After a brief but spirited discussion there was consensus that this problem was indeed worthy of future consideration.

At this point, Anthony Cardi indicated support for studying the problem John Kesserling described. In stating this support, Cardi went on to describe what he saw as the larger, or root problem—that of the dysfunctionality of the present concept of local educational governance.

On obtaining the chairman's approval for developing the background for his point, Cardi related his concern for the lack of public interest in examining the conditions which are moving local school boards toward obsolescence. He summarized the evidence which suggested that local boards now exercised little real authority. He pointed out instances of major educational decisions moving to the locus of state and federal levels. He also cited the dramatic influences of the private sector on public education decision making.

The upshot of all this, Cardi proposed, is that local boards of education have lost much of their power, authority, responsibility, and influence. Several reasons are apparent:

1. The nature of public education has changed from a local function

to a national concern and interest. Thus, it is natural that as it has expanded over local district boundaries, authority for these additional concerns be lodged outside of the local district.

2. A second major reason is that even with its original or resident authority, the local school district has lost power. In some ways it has abdicated its responsibility for certain functions, for example, supplementary programs to meet unique educational demands. At the state level and especially at the school district level, the American educational philosophy has maintained that local people are best able to determine these needs. However, local districts and states have been rather ineffective in agreeing on these needs and even less effective in meeting them.

3. The proximate cause for the above reason is not the innate inefficiency of a democracy. It is instead the incongruity between ends and means. State and local districts have limited their educational ends because of inadequate means. In a few words, local governance of education—and perhaps even state governance—is obsolete because the tax system to support it is obsolete. The taxes used for educational purposes on these levels are largely sales and property taxes. They are regressive in nature and generally unpopular. They are vulnerable to popular disapproval—especially the local property tax. Renewal or additional rates are voted down at the slightest provocation. Almost never are they adequate to do the job. The educational burden which cannot or will not be assumed at the local or state level is shifted to the next higher level. The higher levels have more adequate means of implementing educational decisions, so power flows to them.

The nature of the federal tax machinery very naturally causes this flow of authority. In the contemporary American economy our major federal tax, the personal income tax, is highly productive and efficient, it is relatively painless to extract, it is progressive, and it is very responsive to economic growth. It has the feature of automatic expansibility which has enabled it to grow faster than increases in national governmental expenditures for domestic civilian services. It has been predicted that this differential between federal income tax revenues and normal domestic civilian services will amount to 11 billion dollars annually by 1975.[1]

Thus, with means of assuming educational responsibility readily at hand, the federal government has been wooed and has responded to become a partner in providing public education.

[1] Committee for Economic Development, *A Fiscal Program for a Balanced Federalism*, The Committee, New York, 1967, p. 43.

Another concomitant effect has also been felt on the state and local level. Because of the character of the federal personal income tax, many states have avoided the adoption of a similar progressive tax. In the interest of "tax balance," states have allowed the federal government the de facto preemption of this tax. Thus, states and localities have largely been left with types of regressive taxes.

As the federal personal income tax has become more potent, the total tax burden has tended to become more progressive and the states and localities have moved to more of the regressive and popularly controlled taxes which grow more and more unpopular. This in turn precipitates taxpayers' revolts and opens the door to further upper-level government intervention and consequent loss of authority by the lower-level unit.

After spelling out the three major reasons for loss of authority by local school boards, Cardi tried to put the problem into perspective. He suggested that there is a legitimate and expanding role for the state and federal government in public education. This expansion is both necessary and desirable as the growing comprehensiveness and complexity in public education requires both support and control from these higher levels. At the same time there is a vital function of local governance—it should not be ignored or deprecated simply because of the expansion of state and federal authority. Instead it should be maintained and probably expanded. More effective means of raising public school revenues on these levels will expedite the expansion of local governance. This will call for a modification in the present role of state and federal governments in the area of public education. Instead of subsuming the educational authority of lower levels of government, the state and federal governments should use their powers to complement the authority of the lower-level units.

Anthony Cardi continued to isolate the proximate cause of the problem by suggesting that the key action must be taken at the federal level. The federal government must expand the capability of the state to support public education. Since the state is plenary in matters of education and has the original responsibility for providing education, the state with federal assistance can command means to accomplish this purpose. By expanding the program in the states, the states in turn will be able to delegate more responsibility and to channel more resources to the local school districts, thereby expanding the local governance of public education.

Anthony Cardi's proposal for modifying the federal tax system to accomplish these ends was essentially that described by the Committee for Economic Development in 1967.[2]

[2] *Ibid.*, pp. 43–49.

In anticipation of personal income tax revenues increasing faster than expenditures for domestic civilian services at the national level, it is desirable to take some action to prevent fiscal drag (revenue surpluses which act to retard economic growth). This action could be federal income tax reduction, debt reduction, or increased spending for appropriate public needs. However, a fourth alternate appears to have the most salutary effects, i.e., federal support of state and local government. Anthony Cardi indicated that the business-oriented Committee for Economic Development proposed that the federal government share the personal income tax with state and local governments. This would ease the danger of fiscal drag, would assist the state and local government units, and would provide an incentive for those states with no or very weak state personal income taxes to use this tax source.

The Committee for Economic Development considered two major plans to reduce federal surpluses. The first was a general grant-in-aid which only transfers funds from the federal government to the state. The second plan, and the one ultimately recommended by the committee, called for a reduction in the federal income tax by providing a partial tax credit. This would enable individual taxpayers to receive a credit on their federal income tax equal to a given proportion of their state income tax. The proposal would encourage states to increase state income tax levels and would at the same time reduce the federal income tax revenues to the federal government.

Cardi terminated his remarks by indicating there are many possible refinements, but the basic concept should be considered.

Cecil Goodwin, chairman of the Commission on Educational Problems, expressed his thanks to Cardi for a new perspective on an old problem. Goodwin noted that the type of action suggested by Cardi might very well occupy more time of the commission since remedial legislation has been almost the only concern of the group. It might be quite appropriate for the commission to exert influence beyond the state capital and into the federal legislature.

Questions for Discussion

1. Anthony Cardi observed the movement of educational decision making from local and state levels to the federal level. In what ways might the nature of the federal tax system contribute to this movement?

2. If the proposal for the federal government to share personal income tax receipts with state and local governments is enacted, what

are some changes that one could expect in the pattern of public school financing?

3. Assuming that the national Congress enacted the proposal for giving partial credit on federal personal income taxes for payment of state personal income taxes:

    a. What would be the likely effect on the progressivity of the school tax structure?

    b. Would it increase or decrease tax shifting in the school tax structure?

    c. How would it change the location of the school tax burden?

Suggested Readings

Concept N—The Federal Tax System

American Association of School Administrators: *The Federal Government and the Public Schools*, Washington, D.C.: The Association, 1965.

————: *Federal Policy and the Public Schools*, Washington, D.C.: The Association, 1967.

Galbraith, John K.: *The Affluent Society*, Boston: Houghton Mifflin, 1958.

McConnell, Campbell R.: *Economics*, 4th ed., New York: McGraw-Hill, 1969, chap. 9, pp. 143–144.

Meranto, Philip: *The Politics of Federal Aid to Education in 1965: A Study in Political Innovation*, Syracuse, N.Y.: Syracuse University Press, 1967.

Munger, Frank J., and Richard F. Fenno, Jr.: *National Politics and Federal Aid to Education*, Syracuse, N.Y.: Syracuse University Press, 1962.

Ott, David J., and Attiat F. Ott: *Federal Budget Policy*, Washington, D.C.: The Brookings Institution, 1965.

Samuelson, Paul A.: *Economics*, 7th ed., New York: McGraw-Hill, 1967, chap. 9, pp. 163–165.

Seidner, F. J.: *Federal Support for Education*, Washington, D.C.: The Public Affairs Institute, 1959.

Sufrin, Sidney C.: *Issues in Federal Aid to Education*, Syracuse, N.Y.: Syracuse University Press, 1962.

concept o
State Tax Systems

the problem

In terms of proportions of the total revenue provided for public education, the states' share of the total has increased more than either the local or federal share during the past 12 years. The local share has dropped from 54 to 42 percent while the federal has increased from 10 percent in 1955 to 15 percent in 1967. It is clear that the state tax systems have been under severe pressure during these years. However, in light of their plenary power in matters of public education, this movement is seen by many as not being inappropriate.

With no reversal visible or predicted in the immediate future, it is imperative that the nature, operation, and impact of state tax systems be carefully assessed in order to determine how the state can best meet its obligation in public education.

As state officials, members of the governing bodies of local school systems have a vital interest in developing state policy in matters of this kind. The administrators of the local schools, as professional advisors to their individual governing bodies, need to thoroughly understand the structure and function of the state tax system so they in turn may provide the best possible advice to their boards.

the concept

State tax systems have been shaped and influenced by the limitations imposed on the states by the federal Constitution, the competition of the federal tax system, and the attitudes and desires of the voters in each state. The constitutional limitations are few. The states, as is the federal government, are expressly prohibited from imposing a tax on exports. Also, the commerce clause of the Constitution, which vests jurisdiction over interstate commerce in the national government, by implication denies to the states the right to levy a tax against such commerce. It should be added, however, that there has been considerable disagreement in the past as to the definition of interstate commerce, and in recent years the Supreme Court has permitted the states to exercise a much greater taxing authority in this area. A third limitation, which is implied by the wording of the Constitution and enforced by the Supreme Court, concerns the taxing of the property of another government. The rule is that states may not tax such property.[1]

[1] First stated in the case of *McCulloch v. Maryland*, 4 Wheat. 316 (1819).

Effective as these constitutional limitations are, it is probable that an even greater influence on the tax systems of the states is the existence of and the effective competition provided by the federal system. For many years the states were able to finance their needs adequately through the use of the property tax. When this source became inadequate, the states turned to consumption taxes, particularly to the sales tax, at least partially because of the heavy federal reliance on the personal income tax. Today, sales taxes provide approximately 28 percent of the state tax revenues.

The usual state sales tax is placed upon the final or retail sale of goods. The exact list varies from state to state, with the most noticeable difference being the inclusion or exclusion of food for home consumption as a taxable item. The usual intent is to exclude the sale of capital goods as well as those items which are intended to become an integral part of another product. However, the tax is sometimes applied against these items. In most instances, services are excluded from the list of taxable items, although there is little theoretical or practical justification for such exclusion.

The state retail sales tax laws usually specify that the tax shall be added to the final price of the good at the time of the sale. This provision is apparently included in the belief that it will make more certain that the sales tax will be shifted to the customer. Most legislators are apparently unaware that shifting depends upon the ability to reduce the quantity of the taxed good which is available in the market and the willingness of customers to buy the good at higher prices. The retail sales tax is not always shifted to the customer, even though the tax is added to the final purchase price at the time of the sale.

Accompanying most retail sales taxes is the use tax, which is levied against those goods exchanged outside the taxing jurisdiction, in a state which does not levy a sales tax, and which are brought into the taxing jurisdiction for use or consumption. The purpose of the use tax is to prevent an avoidance of the sales tax through the purchase of the taxed goods outside of the taxing state. As a practical matter, enforcement of the use tax is very difficult except for those goods for which a title must be recorded, such as automobiles.

A common criticism of the retail sales tax is that it is regressive in effect and so bears more heavily on the lower-income groups. This criticism is based on the belief that a greater proportion of the income of the lower-income taxpayer is spent for taxable items than is true for the upper-income taxpayer. That the retail sales tax, as well as most other consumption taxes, displays some element of regressivity cannot be denied. However, empirical studies indicate that the degree of regression is much less than is popularly supposed. As a practical matter, this is not a valid criticism.

It is also charged that sales tax collections, since they vary proportionately with sales, do not have a built-in ability to combat extremes in the business cycle as does a progressive tax such as the federal personal income tax. A change in taxable income will result in a proportionately greater change in federal income tax collections, so that the effects of the change on disposable income will be reduced. The retail sales tax does not have the ability to blunt the effects of a change in the business cycle as does the federal personal income tax. However, it can hardly be said that this inability is a fault so far as the states are concerned. States levy taxes in order to finance government programs, and not with the purpose of influencing the business cycle. This particular criticism may be valid with respect to the federal excises; it is not valid when applied to the state consumption taxes.

State sales taxes have proved to be a reliable source of large amounts of revenue which are collected at very reasonable costs. None of the sales taxes as now used by the states is theoretically or practically perfect. However, the imperfections have not been so serious as to prevent this tax from becoming the most important source of state tax revenue. There is every indication that this importance will continue.

States also receive substantial revenue from excise taxes. Revenue from the gasoline tax is second in importance only to the general sales tax, and taxes on liquor and tobacco are also important. Some excises, such as the tax on gasoline, are sometimes earmarked for specific purposes; others provide additional general fund revenues. During 1965, states received 25.4 percent of their tax revenue from excise taxes.

Although the income tax field is dominated by the federal government, states still receive an important share of their revenue from this source. The first successful state income tax was adopted by Wisconsin in 1911, two years before the Sixteenth Amendment was ratified, and by the end of World War I four more states had adopted levies on income. Today, approximately two-thirds of the states collect some of their revenue from a tax on personal or corporate income.

Most of the state personal income taxes are slightly progressive, and the rates, at least in comparison with the federal tax, are quite moderate. Taxes on corporate income are usually proportional and these rates are also very modest. In spite of the relatively low rates, state governments collected $5,586,000,000 in 1965. This represented 21.4 percent of all state tax receipts. Although the dominant position of the federal government in the income tax field may prevent the states from collecting a greater proportion of their revenues from these sources, it is also highly probable that the present relative position will be maintained.

For the public school administrator, the source of state tax revenues is important because of the increasing reliance of the public schools on state financing. State foundation programs are common throughout the country, and the number of states underwriting a portion of school financing costs is growing. The acquaintance of school administrators with the state tax systems which finance these foundation programs is most important.

Case 41. The Comparative Consideration in Determining New State Taxes

When Gerald Lafferty was sworn in as state superintendent of public education in a Northeastern industrial state, his inaugural statement characterized the forthcoming term of office as ". . . a time of awesome problems but magnificent opportunity." If his audience did not recognize this as an apt description of the times at his swearing in, they became convinced of the validity of the statement shortly after.

In this state, public education was seemingly always under financed. Educational costs were high. Demands for more state aid were perennially made to the state executive and legislature by many education agencies. However, the state maintained the same relatively small proportion of contribution to public school revenues. On an average, the local school districts provided over 80 percent of total revenues for public school expenditures. The local property tax was the almost exclusive vehicle for raising these revenues. In the big industrial cities the high valuation of plants, warehouses, machines, and the like along with the relatively modest educational programs demanded by the blue-collar residents placed a relatively light burden on the local property tax. This, in turn, was quite acceptable to the business leaders.

The suburban school districts were largely peopled by upper middle-class executives and managers who were upward mobile and thus very education-minded. As long as high property taxes went for "quality education" which enhanced the chances for their youngsters to go to a "good college," the suburban taxpayers groused about taxes, but usually supported school levies.

The relatively large but often ignored rural region of the state had long ago reconciled itself to the heavy dependence on the local property tax to provide the majority of revenue for public education. In this section, such taxes were recognized as the price of local autonomy in educational affairs. The state provided little in financing education and expected little beyond conformation to a few basic program standards.

In recent years these comfortable circumstances began to deteriorate. Many difficult conditions stimulated by a variety of factors began to develop into a series of awesome problems. Educational costs, reflecting the jumps in the consumer price index, fairly leaped when new and additional programs were demanded by the citizens of the state as well as those throughout the nation. Although local property taxes did rise, this tax could not expand fast enough. Taxpayers' revolts became prevalent throughout the state. Even in the lighthouse districts, innovative and education-minded patrons staged dramatic opposition to further local school taxes.

Agitation for local property tax relief brought a modest increase in state aid drawn from the general fund which had a moderate state sales tax as principle source of revenue. An increase in this tax was thus necessitated since education was a major expenditure, and providing state aid to local school districts would be a continuous obligation.

In April, only four months after enactment of the increased state sales tax, the teachers in the state's largest city went out on strike. The city board of education broke off negotiations with the teachers when it was concluded that salary demands of teachers would exceed the amount the board could raise for this purpose from existing local levies plus monies from the recently increased state aid. After seventeen days, eleven of which were days of impasse with no negotiations whatsoever, the Governor intervened. He conferred briefly with the president of the city board of education and then announced the intention to update the state aid formula which would provide considerably more revenue for the city schools. He implied, when interviewed by the press, that the net increase to the city school district would not by itself be sufficient to meet the original demand from the union. The salary dispute, he stated, must be finally settled by the teachers and the board.

Two days later, a settlement was reached and the city schools were in operation again. However, a rash of strikes, "professional study days," and threats of these spread throughout the state. As a result, local boards of education were quick to recognize teachers' demands for higher salaries on the basis of the expected additional revenue to be provided in the new state aid formula.

At this same time, another side of the problem of providing revenue for the public schools of the state became visible. This was caused not only by the Governor's largesse in increasing state aid to local school districts but also by the fact that the federal government was expanding legislation to combat poverty. This federal legislation called for increasing state and local expenditures for public education in deprived neighborhoods. In order to qualify, this state (with a level of personal income higher than the national average) would have to increase its state and local expenditure. Without the additional state aid, the state would not have been eligible for considerable federal monies.

The second half of the theme of Gerald Lafferty's inaugural statement—a time of magnificent opportunity—was recognized by Lafferty and many of his brothers of the educational fraternity. The significant opportunities appeared to be six in number:

1. An infusion of considerable amounts of money into state and local agencies to expand educational expenditures.

2. Provisions in the state aid formula which would benefit school districts in particular need of program modification, i.e., large cities with high proportions of economically and educationally handicapped, and rural areas with inadequate and/or obsolete programs and organization.

3. New relations with the federal government which the state had previously avoided and even resisted.

4. The emergence and mobilization of significant, substantial, and influential support groups interested in identifying and better meeting public education needs. Based on models of organizations of national scope and visibility, local and state units adopted the point of view of the national organizations and initiated local studies on topics such as "Education for Low-income Groups," "Full Employment and Economic Growth," and "Modernizing State and Local Government." These reports, prepared and funded by prominent business and professional leaders, were lodged with the Governor and the state legislature and then subsequently published. The reports contained an assessment of the problems, analyses of them, and recommendations for their resolution.

5. A new readiness in the formerly "intellectually defunct" professional organizations to examine and possibly adopt new approaches to these problems.

6. A public attitude that "something must happen," a general acceptance that change is inevitable, and that the "good old days" must make way for a new era.

It was in this context that Gerald Lafferty was preparing himself for a meeting of the Governor's cabinet. This was the first formal meeting since the surprise announcement of a new state aid formula.

Lafferty was certain that questions of not only the components and design of the formula would be raised, but also the means of raising the necessary revenue. Consequently, Lafferty had called David Soloman, the department of education finance director to check out the latter's thinking on the tax implications of a substantial increase in the state's aid to local schools.

The two members of the State Department of Education team worked very informally. Lafferty suggested an exchange of perceptions regarding the whole system of financing public education. General agreement was reached on the nature of the system's character and the problems inherent in it. It was also agreed that it was a time for bold leadership in education. Both men felt that the State Department of Education, and the state superintendent as its chief executive, did not have in the past an appropriate amount of influence on educational decisions made at the state level.

Aggressive action seemed to be in order. However, the thrust of educational leaders must be practical as well as theoretically sound. Lafferty and his finance director decided that they must work within several "givens." These were:

1. Additional taxes must be levied in order to provide for the expansion of public school expenditures.

2. The additional taxes must be levied at the state level.

3. Any modified tax structure must fit the state in terms of its economic base, need, competition with other states, and the like.

4. Any new or additional taxes must be integrated into the total tax structure. Thus, all elements of the structure must be viewed in relationship to each other.

5. The modified tax structure must be acceptable by influentials in the state. Since industrial interests were most potent, the modified structure must be predicated on the ability of the state's industry to compete with the several other states having a comparable economic base.

Lafferty summed up his concern for acceptability for any modified tax system:

> "We could talk to educators and drum up support for a state personal income tax or a corporate income tax. We would have endorsements from all the education interests, but we would be dead when and if it got to a vote in the legislature. We have to find a tax or a combination of taxes which will provide the

additional resources but not increase our tax level so it exceeds tax levels in states which are our industrial competitors."

Soloman agreed with a nod, and picked up the dialogue.

"In the past I can recall that our people have gone into the tax revision game and tried to make their point only on the theoretical bases of taxes, the criteria of good taxes, and the relation of education and economic productivity. These are appropriate, but the 'real world' must be considered also.

"If we are going to the legislature with a proposal for raising more state money for education, I want to be able to defend it on the basis of what this will do to our state as it competes with other states."

"Yes," Lafferty interjected, "I think there are a couple of approaches that can do this for us. Our state is way behind in *state* effort—this suggests additional taxes. Some of our tax rates and levels are well below others around here. We don't levy any personal income tax."

Lafferty paused to think, then continued.

"I believe what we need is some comparative data on the performance of several major state taxes in our state and similar states. Then we can see where we can increase a tax which will still keep us competitive. Do you have anything like that, David?"

"Yes, Jerry, the *Compendium of State Government Finances* and *Governmental Finances* carry these data. I could have preliminary figures for you tomorrow. These would tell us if we're going in the right direction."

The next day finance director Soloman called Gerald Lafferty to tell him he had some general information on comparative state and local tax distribution for the state and its six competitive counterparts. He indicated he also came upon another interesting comparative device and would have additional data ready for a meeting scheduled in two days.

At the latter meeting, Soloman first presented the material found in Table 41.1 and commented on it.

"These data show our state and the six states comparable to us in economic base and general character. The table shows the

Table 41.1. Percentage Distribution of State and Local Revenue (percentage of total tax revenue)

State	All Taxes	General Property	Sales and Gross Receipts		Income	Other Tax Revenue
			General	Selective		
A	100%	54.2	19.3	16.0		10.5
B	100	48.9	20.8	16.1		14.2
C	100	44.7	10.7	14.5	21.7	8.4
Our state	100	62.6		21.9		15.5
D	100	50.8	13.0	22.5		13.7
E	100	33.2	17.2	19.4	6.9	23.3
F	100	48.7		26.4		24.9
All Fifty States	100	48.4	13.8	17.8	9.3	10.7

proportions of the major taxes. Local government in our state depends heavily on general property taxes—and this is levied at the local level. The selective sales tax is levied at the state level. We have no general sales tax or income tax. Two of our competing states do levy income taxes.

"When I started scouting around for some way to interpret better the differentiated tax distribution among several states, I remembered that some years ago the Committee on Educational Finance of the National Education Association published a study dealing with the determination of revenue potentials of the states.[1] Well, I used the format that was employed in the study, applied it to the most recent data available, and have in this table a rough measure of what potential revenue we have in the major tax sources.

"The concept of tax potential is essentially the amount of tax we raise compared with a standard rate applied to the actual tax base. If the standard rate multiplied by the actual base yields more than that which is collected, then we have an unused tax potential. If we collect as much or more than the standard rate times the actual base, then we have no unused tax potential.

"The second table shows the tax potential of the seven states including our state. From the table we can conclude that we have

[1] National Education Association: *Revenue Potentials of the States*, Washington, D.C.: The Association, 1964.

Table 41.2. Potential Tax Revenue in Excess of Amount Actually Collected (in thousands)

State	General Sales and Gross Receipts Taxes	Individual Income Taxes	Corporate Income Taxes	Death and Gift Taxes	Personal Income
A	$ 9,300	$273,826	$122,523		$27,410,000
B		180,359	80,701	$ 7,585	18,054,000
C	253,698				48,504,000
Our state	275,066	169,311	49,408		16,948,000
D	119,210	229,900	102,868	15,942	23,013,000
E	33,959	259,071			25,933,000
F	316,534	194,835	87,178	10,632	19,503,000

tax potential in three of these four taxes. The relative ability of the seven states may be deduced from the personal income."

"Yes, David, this is what we need. Now, what taxes are the best bets for raising?"

Questions for Discussion

1. What generalizations can be made from Table 41.1 regarding the tax structure of "our state"?

2. How does the tax structure in the state described in this case study reflect the three influences mentioned in the concept statement:

   a.   Limitations imposed by the federal Constitution
   b.   Competition of the federal tax system
   c.   Attitudes and desires of the voters in each state

3. What are the most logical sources (disregarding "political" considerations) of additional revenue? Why?

4. What recommendations are Lafferty and Soloman likely to make? How might they rationalize or justify this (these) recommendation(s)?

Case 42.   Alternatives in Redesigning a State Tax Program

The newly elected Governor of a state in the south central part of the nation realized that he would be obliged to take positive action to fulfill his campaign promises. His state was one of those which was rapidly changing from a somewhat insular, tradition-dominated character to a growing, dynamic, and outward-looking state.

During the previous Governor's administration, there were many demands for state services which had not been previously provided. Often programs to meet these demands were initiated, then curtailed or dropped as it became apparent that sufficient revenue would not be available to fully finance them.

As a candidate, the new Governor put two planks in his platform to respond to this situation:

1. A special commission would mobilize the best thinking of lay representatives throughout the state to identify the pattern of the most necessary state government services. Consultants expert in each of these service fields would be called on to develop an integrated program of services to promote maximum efficiency and cooperation among fields.

2. A special commission was to be appointed to study the tax structure of the state. This group would employ scholars in public finance and experts knowledgeable in business, agriculture, and industry. The commission was to be charged with the responsibility of recommending changes to streamline and upgrade the tax structure.

Shortly after taking office, the Governor's recommendations, based on his platform planks, were accepted by the state legislature. Both commissions were appointed, and each began to work. The Special Tax Study Commission employed its consultants and started to design the study. It was agreed that the commission's report should have three components:

1. A statement of principles of taxation

2. A survey of the present tax structure of the state, as compared with the principles set forth

3. Recommended changes in the state tax structure which would cause the overall structure to conform more nearly to the basic principles of taxation and which would also increase the revenue available for the support of needed state services

The statement of principles of taxation as approved by the commission pointed out three bases of taxes—wealth, income, and expenditures.

The commission's statement also included basic criteria for "good" taxes. Such a tax should be:

1. Conducive to economic growth

2. Neutral

3. Equal or fair

4. Administratively feasible

5. Inexpensive in compliance costs

6. Responsive to the contemporary economy

After assessing the present tax structure of the state, the commission concluded that the structure was based on a turn-of-the-century concept which was modified during the Depression of the 1930s. The most salient features of the structure were found to be:

1. Heavy reliance on local property taxation sharing the financial burden of state programs

2. Heavy reliance on sales taxation

3. Very little income-based taxation

A comparison of the state's level of taxation with other states and the national average revealed that:

1. The state level of taxation was in the lower quarter of the fifty states.

2. The percent of personal income paid for state taxes was in the lowest quarter of the fifty states.

3. The percent of increase in per capita state taxes during the past ten years was in the lowest quarter of the fifty states.

4. The state sales tax produced less revenue than all the states with a comparable sales tax rate because of numerous exemptions.

5. In toto, the state's tax structure was slightly regressive which made it less regressive than that of the median state among the fifty states.

The commission reviewed the specific state taxes. Generalizations derived from an intensive study of each tax were as follows:

1. Sales tax—the retail sales tax was the predominant state tax. The 3 percent rate was below average among states with this type. However, because of the many exemptions, the per capita yield was far below that in comparable states. During the last fiscal year 292 million dollars was produced by this tax.

2. Excise taxes—as a group, excise taxes were relatively low. The rates on gasoline and cigarettes were significantly lower than similar taxes in other states. Other excise rates were at or above the national average. These taxes produced 107 million dollars for the last fiscal year.

3. Corporation franchise tax—corporations paid this tax for the privilege of doing business in the state. The tax was levied on the proportion of the value of the capital stock which corresponds to the portion of property owned or used and of the business transacted in the state. The rate was fixed at 3 percent and the yield was 49 million dollars as collected during the last fiscal year.

4. Insurance company taxes—the state levied a gross premium tax of 2½ percent on both foreign and domestic companies. Domestic companies were also taxed under the intangible personal property tax. These combined taxes produced during the last fiscal year a yield of 24.7 million dollars.

5. Other taxes—a group of other state levied taxes was reviewed by the commission and treated somewhat differently than the four major taxes listed above. These other taxes (including levies on public utilities, financial institutions, intangible personal property, and inheritances and gifts) had features which made them unique. Some were shared with local governments, others were relatively small producers, and still others were earmarked for funds other than the general revenue fund. Consequently, the commission gave them only passing consideration and proposed no changes in them.

A second phase of the work of the Special Tax Study Commission began after it completed the analysis of the present tax structure of the state and after it received a preliminary report from the commission which studied state services. From this report it was obvious that the Special Tax Study Commission would be called on not only to streamline the existing structure to make it more efficient but also to change the structure to provide substantially more revenues to support expanded state services.

Members of the commission and their consultants quite readily agreed that their first attention should be devoted to considerations of taxes to provide additional revenues. On the basis of the comparison of the tax structures of the other forty-nine states with their own, there was consensus among the consultants that substantial amounts of additional revenue could best be derived from either or both of two taxes: the state sales tax or a state personal income tax.

With the issue so stated, lines of difference among the consultants were quickly drawn. Nearly half of the consultants were of the opinion that a state income tax should be levied. However, within this group there was no agreement as to what the key features of the tax should be.

The other group of consultants, who were in the majority, favored the expansion of the state sales tax. Here again, there was disagreement among the supporters of the idea. Some favored retaining the 3 percent rate while eliminating nearly all the exemptions. Others advocated an increase in the rate. Still others favored lowering the starting price of the lowest taxing bracket and thereby taxing a greater proportion of purchases in the taxable commodities.

After considerable discussion within and between the two "camps," it was agreed that both pros and cons of the sales tax and the income tax should be explored in the context of the present conditions found in the state.

The supporters of a plan to expand or extend the state sales tax made their case first. The major advantages of the sales tax were pointed out as follows.

1. The sales tax as an expenditure-based tax is superior to an income-based tax from the standpoint of incentive, economic expansion, and inflationary effects.

2. The sales tax is superior to the income tax from an administrative point of view.

3. The state sales tax is needed by the state government to develop an autonomous revenue source in a federal system.

4. State sales taxes can be designed to be generally proportional, which will offset the progressivity of the federal tax system.

In the discussion of the general disadvantages of the sales tax, the following points were cited:

1. Sales taxes tend to place a relatively heavy burden on persons whose expenditures on taxable goods constitute a large proportion of their income.

2. Sales taxes penalize groups which are compelled to spend greater proportions of their income to attain a given standard of living.

3. Sales taxes are not always confined to consumption goods, thus shifting becomes a problem.

4. Sales taxes provide some slight incentive to spend less and save more.

5. Exemptions from the sales tax tend to increase the relative consumptions of the exempt commodities. Unless this is appropriate on the basis of general economic or social policy, it is contrary to economic welfare.

The proponents of the personal income tax presented eight major advantages:

1. The personal income tax provides the most rational means for the state to measure and tax the capacity of citizens to contribute to the cost of public services.

2. The personal income tax is more equitable than most taxes if an individual accepts the ability-to-pay theory as a basis for the equitable distribution of the tax burden.

3. The personal income tax is subject to less shifting than other state taxes and thus provides a relatively accurate measurement of burden.

4. The personal income tax as a progressive tax will promote economic stability.

5. The personal income tax can be used to reduce inequalities in the distribution of income and wealth.

6. The personal income tax is more versatile than most other taxes.

7. The personal income tax creates tax consciousness.

8. The personal income tax may be structured to require low costs of collection and compliance.

It was recognized by the consultants that a personal income tax levied by a state has some inherent disadvantages. Among these are the following:

1. The federal government has preempted the income tax.

2. The personal income tax may adversely affect the economic growth of the state and/or nation.

3. The personal income tax at the federal level is progressive so the addition of progressivity at the state level may not be necessary or desirable.

4. The personal income tax has the inherent problem of determining whether to tax on the basis of the residence of the taxpayer or tax on the basis of the place where the income is earned.

5. The personal income tax does not provide a stable yield of revenue.

Having broached the pros and cons of the two major tax alternatives, the group of consultants attempted to move toward consensus on the most appropriate alternative. However, after a series of spirited but rather disintegrated debates, it was recognized that generalizations regarding tax programs would not provide an adequate basis for decision. Instead, it was agreed that specific programs must be assessed. The suggestion was made and accepted to set up two "task forces." One would develop a series of different approaches to a viable state sales tax, while the other would develop a similar group of approaches to a state income tax. It was also agreed that each proposed program should be based on the principles and criteria for "good taxes" identified in the initial phase of the study. It was assumed that the application of these approaches to the state's economic and needs structure would provide the specifics so the best alternative could be identified.

The task force assigned to developing sales tax alternatives prefaced its report by stating that many factors must be considered in the development of a sales tax program. Among these factors are rate, level of taxable sales, and classes of taxable items in the tax base; thus, a series of sales tax alternatives must include all these factors.

In order to provide perspective, the proposed sales tax alternatives were stated in comparative terms using the last fiscal year as a base for projecting potential yield of each tax alternative. The major alternatives suggested by the sales tax task force were:

1. *Extending the present sales taxes to include all sales on the existing tax base.* This alternative would make all sales subject to the sales tax rather than only those of 30 cents or more as required under the present law. If this alternative were to be employed, approximately 12.6 million dollars would be added to sales tax revenues.

2. *Broadening the sales tax to include selected services in the tax base.* The present sales tax base is very narrow as it excludes foods, household utilities, and services. If selected services were included, the increases in sales tax yields would be increased in the following amounts:

    a. Personal services (including laundries, cleaning and dying, beauty and barber shops, funeral services, and miscellaneous)

                                                                       $11 million

    b. Business services (advertising, business consultants, credit bureaus, detective and protective agencies, duplication and stenographer services, employment services, interior decoration, maintenance and repair services, news services, and others)

                                                                    $16.3 million

    c. Amusement (theaters, dance halls, sports promotions, bowling and billiards, race tracks, golf courses, and others) $ 4.8 million

    d. Auto services (repair, parking, and others) $ 7.4 million

    e. Repair services (electrical, watches and clocks, jewelry, furniture, and others) $ 4.7 million

3. *Increasing the nominal rate from 3 to 4 percent on the existing base.* This alternative would apply a 4 percent nominal rate to the present base. It would yield approximately 373 million dollars, an increase of 70 million dollars over the present yield.

4. *Increasing the nominal rate from 3 to 5 percent on the existing base.* This alternative would increase the rate and produce 487 million dollars, an increase of 184 million dollars over the present yield.

5. *Broadening the sales tax to include selected services and setting the nominal rate at 4 percent.* If a 4 percent rate is applied on the selected services listed in Alternative 2, the increased yields would be:

    a. Personal services — $14.6 million
    b. Business services — 22.3 million
    c. Amusements   —   7.4 million
    d. Auto services   — 10.0 million
    e. Repair services   —   6.2 million

6. *Broadening the sales tax to include selected services and setting the nominal rate at 5 percent.* If a 5 percent rate is applied to these selected services, the increased yields would be:

    a. Personal services — $18.4 million
    b. Business services — 28.4 million
    c. Amusements   —   9.2 million
    d. Auto services   — 12.4 million
    e. Repair services   —   7.8 million

The sales tax task force concluded its statement on alternatives by indicating that a viable sales tax program could be developed by carefully selecting a pattern of alternates from those just presented. Such a pattern would surely conform to the principles of and criteria for a "good" tax program as articulated earlier by the Special Tax Study Commission.

The task force concerned with the development of state income tax alternatives took an approach similar to that used by the sales tax group. It was pointed out that in designing a state personal income tax several factors must be considered, i.e., the tax base, exemptions, and rates. In one sense, these factors can be thought of as variables in a state personal income tax.

The task force on the state personal income tax program presented three basic alternative proposals:

1. *A state personal income tax as a supplement to the federal income tax.* This tax would be levied on each resident of the state who pays the federal personal income tax. The state merely levies a tax equal to a given percent of the personal income tax paid to the federal government. Although the rate of the state tax is a flat proportional rate, the effect is progressive, as it is based on a highly progressive federal tax. At the present level of personal incomes in the state, a 10-percent state tax on federal income taxes paid by residents would yield approximately 254 million dollars.

2. *A state personal income tax with a proportional rate.* A tax of this nature should be levied on the taxable income as reported on the federal income tax, thus including gross income less exemptions and deductions. At a rate of 3 percent with exemptions for dependents, this tax would yield 286 million dollars.

3. *A state personal income tax with a progressive rate.* The base of this type tax should be the taxable income as reported on the federal income tax form. One form of this type of tax incorporates the following rates on various income classes:

1 percent on taxable incomes under $2,000
2 percent on taxable incomes $2,000 to $5,000
3 percent on taxable incomes $5,000 to $10,000
4 percent on taxable incomes over $10,000

This type of personal income tax for the state would yield approximately 302 million dollars.

Members of the state personal income tax task force pointed out that the models were illustrative only and that by modifying any of the variables the yields could be changed. The question of the degree of predominance of a personal income tax in the total revenue program of the state must be answered as well; e.g., what kind of a sales tax–personal income tax mix should there be if both taxes are to be used?

Members of the consultant group of the Special Tax Study Commission recognized the complexity of their task. They were, however, more confident that they had some "hard data" with which they could test the viability of their proposals.

Questions for Discussion

1. In the case study, it was concluded that the state's tax structure was slightly regressive but that there was heavy reliance on local property taxes to share the financial burden of state programs. What kind of questions would you ask and what kinds of data would you look at in order to determine the degree of regressivity or progressivity of the total tax structure used to support state programs?

2. Give some examples of how local property taxes might be used to share the burden of state programs.

3. How could one account for the fact that the sales tax was the predominant state tax and yet the state's total tax structure was less regressive than most of the fifty states?

4. In considering only the pro and con arguments of the supporters of the sales tax as opposed to those of the income tax, which tax would you favor? Why?

5. Assuming that *additional* revenues in the amount of 250 million dollars to 300 million dollars are needed in this state, what pattern of state tax increase (from among the alternatives supplied in the case study) would you favor? Why?

Suggested Readings

Concept O—State Tax Systems

Advisory Commission on Intergovernmental Relations: *Measures of State and Local Fiscal Capacity and Tax Effort*, Washington, D.C.: The Commission, 1962.

Bailey, Stephen, et al.: *Schoolmen and Politics*, Syracuse, N.Y.: Syracuse University Press, 1962.

Burkhead, Jesse: *State and Local Taxes for Public Education*, Syracuse, N.Y.: Syracuse University Press, 1963.

Committee for Economic Development: *Modernizing State Government*, New York: The Committee, 1967.

McConnell, Campbell, R.: *Economics*, 4th ed., New York: McGraw-Hill, 1969, chap. 9, pp. 142–144.

McLoone, Eugene P., Gabrielle C. Lupo, and Selma J. Mushkin: *Long-range Revenue Estimation*, Washington, D.C.: The George Washington University, 1967.

National Education Association: *Revenue Potentials of the States*, Washington, D.C.: The Association, 1964.

Ohio Tax Study Commission: *1967 Ohio Tax Study Commission Report*, Columbus, Ohio: The Commission, 1967.

Samuelson, Paul A.: *Economics*, 7th ed., New York: McGraw-Hill, 1967, chap. 9, pp. 163–165.

Tax Foundation, Inc.: *State Tax Studies: 1959–1967*, New York: The Foundation, 1967.

Thatcher, George W.: *Tax Revision Alternatives for the Tax System of Ohio*, Columbus, Ohio: Ohio Tax Study Committee, 1962.

concept p
Local Tax Systems

the problem

It is a fact that the proportion of local taxes is decreasing while the proportions of state and federal taxes are increasing for the support of public education. However, it is also significant to note that more changes are taking place within the local tax structure than in the structure of either state or federal tax systems. This is due to the changing educational roles of the three levels of government, the increased competition for local resources among local governmental units, and the tremendous changes that have taken place in the economic base of the predominant local tax systems.

A rationale for the professional educator's study of the local tax system can be developed on several points. The authors suggest that the major points include the general issues of taxation at any level; e.g., what are appropriate tax vehicles to support the activities of this level of government in terms of its appropriate role in public education. Other issues unique to considering local tax systems today include:

1. To what extent is the local property tax obsolete?

2. Should the local property tax be improved or discarded?

3. Is the local taxing unit viable or should it be scrapped in favor of a regional or state unit?

Because of these and many more questions and issues being raised about local tax systems, it is incumbent upon professional educators to obtain a rudimentary knowledge of local tax systems.

the concept

The most important legal characteristic of local governments and the one which has had the greatest influence on the development of local tax systems, is the dependence of local governments on the state. Local governments are created by the states and receive all their rights and privileges from the state.

The Property Tax

One observes that in most instances the rights, privileges, and responsibilities of local governments are supervised in great detail by the respective state governments. This supervision usually takes the form of limitations, and so the local government officials find that their activities are limited by the federal Constitution (to the same extent as are the state governments), the state constitution, and the laws and statutes which the state legislature has passed.

These legal limitations, together with the relatively small size of most local units of government, have determined the tax structure adopted for the support of these local governments. The result, except in very recent years, has been an almost complete reliance upon the property tax. The importance of the property tax to local governments is shown in the accompanying table.

It is sometimes said that there are only two things wrong with the property tax. First, it is not theoretically sound, and second, it does not work in practice. Such an indictment is too severe, and it is certainly true that, under certain times and circumstances, a levy on property is a very satisfactory source of government revenue. A property tax is most successful when it is applied in a rural community, for in such an environment ownership of property is usually the best measurement of wealth and the ability to pay taxes. It is also usually true that the smaller the governmental unit, the greater the reliance upon the property tax. Small governments cannot as economically administer nonproperty taxes as can larger governments.

For government, the property tax offers several advantages. It yields a large, stable, and very predictable revenue; and the costs of collection and administration are relatively very low (particularly if the tax is confined to real property). For the taxpayer, however, the property tax offers few advantages. In most sections of our country, we no longer have a rural economy in which property ownership is closely correlated with wealth.

In our modern urban society, an increasing proportion of a person's wealth is held in the form of intangible property (stocks, bonds, and similar claims on real property held by others). There is usually a very low correlation between the value of the real and personal property held and the holder's equity in this property. The result is that the taxpayer is asked to pay a property tax which bears little relationship to his ability to pay the tax.

There are other disadvantages of using the property tax in our modern society. Farmland is no longer the largest part of taxable property. Instead there are large amounts of commercial and industrial property which is harder to value than is farmland. The major determinate of taxable value is the selling price, and there are usually an insufficient number of sales of industrial and commercial property to enable the tax administrator to fix a value. These developments re-

Table P.1.   Local Government Revenue by Taxation (selected years, $ millions)

Years	Total Revenue (own sources)	Total Tax Receipts	Property Tax	Property Tax as a Percent of Total Revenue	Property Tax as a Percent of Total Tax Receipt
1902	858	704	624	72.7	88.7
1913	1,658	1,308	1,192	71.9	91.2
1922	3,827	3,545	2,973	77.7	83.9
1932	5,381	4,879	4,159	77.3	85.3
1940	5,792	5,007	4,170	72.0	83.3
1950	11,673	9,586	7,042	60.3	73.5
1954	16,468	13,629	9,577	58.2	70.3
1957	21,357	17,866	12,385	58.0	69.3
1960	27,209	22,912	15,798	58.1	70.0
1962	31,506	26,705	18,414	58.4	69.0
1963	33,846	28,530	19,401	57.3	68.0
1964	35,749	30,256	20,519	57.4	67.8
1965	38,583	32,703	22,152	57.4	67.7

Source: *Facts and Figures on Government Finance*, 15th ed., Tax Foundation, Inc., New York, 1969, p. 233.

quire the use of new and modern assessment techniques, but in too many instances the property tax administrator follows the same procedures and uses the same methods which were developed in the rural economy.

In many parts of the country, improvements are being made in the property tax. These improvements include the professionalization of the assessing staff, the adoption of electronic data processing equipment and the perfection of statistical techniques so that commercial and industrial property may be more equitably assessed, and the adoption of administrative procedures designed to fit our modern society. In spite of these improvements, however, some of the inherent faults of the property tax remain, and for at least a partial replacement of the property levy, many local governments are turning to some form of nonproperty taxes.

Nonproperty Taxes

There is no chance that our present society will abandon the property tax. That levy yields such a large amount of revenue that it would be impractical to substitute nonproperty taxes completely. Certain other taxes, however, can be used to supplement the property tax, and in those areas where it is believed that the property levy has become too large, a nonproperty tax may be the desirable solution to the governmental financing problems.

CONSUMPTION TAXES. There are many kinds of consumption taxes and it is probable that local governments use them all to some extent. Most prominent are the retail sales tax, the use tax, the motor fuels tax, admissions taxes, and other special excise levies. Whether or not these taxes can be successfully used by local governments will depend upon the size of the local government, the size of the tax levy, and the number of other governmental units in the area which are using the same tax. These factors will determine the tendency for the taxpayer to migrate to another tax jurisdiction to consume or acquire the taxed good. Thus, if the governmental unit is too small, the tax too high and if other nontaxing areas are easily accessible, there will be a considerable attempt to avoid the tax.

One solution to this problem has been particularly successful in the state of California. There a 1 percent sales tax levy is collected throughout California by the state collection agency, and this is remitted to the local government (either the city or the county) in which it is collected. Thus, one must go out of the state to avoid paying local sales tax in California. A system of municipal sales taxes almost as universal as in California exists in Illinois, and very recently many municipalities in the states of Oklahoma and Texas have been enacting local sales tax ordinances. In these states also, the state tax agency collects the levy and remits it to the government unit of origin.

LOCAL INCOME TAXES. The local income tax is also used extensively in certain states. A common type of local income tax is a low, nonprogressive rate confined to wages, salaries, and the net profits of unincorporated businesses and professional activities. Occasionally, the profits of corporations will also be included. The first successful local income tax of our modern society was adopted by the city of Philadelphia in 1939 and was of the type described. Since World War II there has been a wave of adoptions, particularly by cities in the states of Pennsylvania and Ohio. The primary disagreement concerning the application of the local income tax is whether it should be applied on the basis of residence or income source. Some cities, such as Philadelphia, tax both, so a resident will pay a tax on all his income irrespective of where it is earned, and a nonresident will pay a tax on the income which he earns within that jurisdiction. The justification for taxing nonresidents on the income which they earn in the taxing city is that services must be provided for their use while they are at their place of employment. There is always the danger unless reciprocity agreements exist that a taxpayer's income could be subjected to a local income tax at his place of employment and his place of residence. In those areas where such agreements have been concluded this problem is usually solved by each jurisdiction reducing the rate which is applied to nonresident taxpayers.

The local income tax is well adapted for use by many local governmental units; however it is doubtful if the tax will ever be used universally, because the federal government, as do most states, levies a high personal income tax. It should not be overlooked, however, as a possible source of nonproperty revenue.

OTHER NONPROPERTY LEVIES. Other nonproperty levies such as motor fuel tax, amusement taxes, and a number of special excises can be important to the areas in which they are applied, but there are so few governments using these levies that they are of minor importance nationally. They should seriously be considered, however, by those local governments seeking to reduce the importance of the property tax.

IMPORTANCE TO OTHER GOVERNMENTS. It must be kept in mind that the use of a nonproperty tax by one government will benefit all governments serving the same area. Thus, if a city levies a local income tax, the school district in that city will benefit because it is now able to make a greater use of the property tax. The city's use of the property tax will decline, but the school district's use of that levy will increase. The total tax burden will probably be greater than if only the property tax levy were used by both governments. Those persons who wish to keep government activity and tax burdens as low as possible, irrespective of the need for the services which government provides, will therefore usually oppose the adoption of a nonproperty levy. It is important in these instances to demonstrate the need for the increased governmental services and the benefits which these services will provide.

Transfer Payments

Another source of local governmental revenue which is growing in importance is transfer payments. These payments to local governmental units by the federal and state governments have grown rapidly in recent years, primarily because of the recognized inabilities of local governments to raise their needed revenue through taxation. Transfer payments have been discussed in detail in Concept M, and so it is sufficient at this point merely to point out the growing importance of transfer payments as a source of local government revenue and to forecast that this growth will continue, probably at an accelerated rate, in the foreseeable future.

Conclusions

It is not anticipated that the property tax will be replaced as the most important source of local government revenue. The inadequacies of this levy in our modern society, however, make it mandatory that an increasing proportion of local government revenue be obtained from other sources. The use of local sales and income taxes will probably increase throughout the country, and the accelerated use of government transfer payments to local units can be anticipated.

Case 43.   Considerations in Modernizing Local Tax Structures

Jess Claymoore had deep roots in the Great Plains soil. His great-grandfather, Aaron Claymoore, was a minor land baron in this region after the Civil War, and had literally wrested a living from this wilderness. He not only secured and settled the land, he also devoted most of his adult life to personal and community improvement. Aaron Claymoore recognized the potential of the region and developed many diversified interests—cattle raising and marketing, irrigated agriculture, and soil and water conservation.

The two generations which followed Aaron Claymoore saw and accepted their elder's contributions and continued to innovate. With oil and mineral discoveries being made in the territory, the Claymoore family organized local landholders to maintain control of drilling and mining operations. This resulted not only in increasing the Claymoore holdings but in increasing the wealth of the inhabitants of the whole territory. Community stability and local authority and responsibility were well established, and statehood was expedited by this responsible local leadership.

Following statehood there was a marked population influx, especially in this region where the Claymoores were active. Under the leadership of Jess's father and four uncles, Claymoore money had penetrated the commercial banking and real estate fields along with some oil rigging enterprises. If, in this land of rugged individualists, there was a power structure, Jess Claymoore, as the fourth generation of a powerful family, must clearly be counted as a part.

Jess was reared on the family ranch near a small town which in turn was 60 miles from the state capital. Consistent with the family tradition, the youngest Claymoore was, as a boy, expected to pitch in at the workaday activity on the ranch. He attended local public schools, went to the state university, and thence to the university's law school. He was the first member of his family to complete college.

All during his college career, Jess was never completely relieved of duties pertaining to the family business interests. In fact, these tended (through his own interests as well as family expectations) to increase steadily. As a consequence, Jess moved directly into one of the family banks after completing the law degree and being admitted to the bar.

With the family's diversified economic interests as well as the tradition and reputation of being concerned with larger community welfare, it was quite natural that Jess Claymoore became active in the statewide issue of the property tax reform. The state, since its admission to the union, had been heavily dependent on the real property tax. In the early days this tax seemed to be ideal. Land and real property were rather accurate measures of one's wealth. It was an easy tax to administer in the then sparsely populated state. As the state developed and matured, special interest groups grew up and influenced the legislature to enact laws which accommodated the newly emerging industries and economic powers. Although making minor modification in the property tax, the amendments tended to institutionalize it and other legislation which supported it. This institutionalization was further strengthened by a generally faster acceleration in the rate of personal income than the increase in the rate of necessary government revenue.

However, during the past several years there has been considerable agitation in the state for major tax reform at the local level. It has been observed that local governmental units have ignored many of their responsibilities. The state's minority groups in the past were very passive, even resistive, to community efforts to provide them with public education. Consequently public education was relieved of a considerable financial burden. In the past there was little pressure on local communities to provide for the disabled, needy, or indigent among these groups. In more recent years in this state as well as the rest of the nation, the urbanization acceleration has increased the magnitude and visibility of the problem. The increasingly sophisticated economy has reduced the market for the unskilled. The unacculturated no longer can be hidden out on the prairies. Instead they have gathered in urban ghettos with other minority group migrants. Here the cycle of inadequate education–unemployment–poverty–alienation–inadequate education is very apparent.

The issue was joined when a neighboring state to the east (with only general similarities in environmental, economic, and demographic characteristics) enacted a local property tax reform measure. The measure provided for an immediate and substantial reduction in local property taxes and substituted for it a county income tax with revenues derived from it to be prorated among local taxing units. The measure was eagerly seized upon by some groups in Jess Claymoore's state as a panacea for the recently identified problems in local government. Other groups, especially those representing the old line vested interests of the state, branded such legislation as "harebrained," shortsighted, or even socialistic. In the first encounters, the discussion of the relative merits of the applicability of this plan to the state soon broke down into emotional shouting matches and personal vendettas rather than reasoned debates. It was at this time that Jess Claymoore became active in the issue.

Although for several years he had expressed his concern for the inadequate funding for vital local services, Jess had limited these observations to his immediate business associates and his personal friends. However, when he observed the almost irrational confrontation of the opposing groups on the neighboring state's property tax reform bill, Jess Claymoore was convinced he must articulate his concerns regarding the problem of financing vital local services lest they be completely ignored in an emotional side issue.

Jess chose as his platform, the report of his Economic Development Committee at the Great Plains Banking and Investment League. The league is an organization of the state's leaders and executives in financial institutions in the region. Jess, as chairman of the Economic Development Committee, was charged with reporting the recommendations of the committee on policy matters pertaining to the long-term economic growth of the region. Typically the committee met three or four times a year to discuss existing proposals or formulate new ideas relevant for economic development. The committee worked to formulate a proposed resolution, and it in turn would be submitted to the membership for approval. Usually these took the form of policy proposals or study and research proposals. Study teams would be established and staffed by members of the committee and assistants from the league's resident research bureau.

In the committee's initial session for the current year, Chairman Claymoore broached the subject of the tax reform issue. In his presentation he developed a rationale for the committee to entertain the possibility of proposing a resolution to the league regarding a tax reform proposal. The rationale was predicated on two major points: (1) it was vital that the public have a clear, well-reasoned statement of the issue which heretofore had not been presented by either the proponents or opponents of a tax reform bill, and (2) that future economic development of the state was highly dependent on the effective and efficient provision of vital local governmental services.

Consensus within the committee was easily reached in regard to the relevancy of this issue. However, when the discussion moved to what kind of study or research proposal should be drafted for submission to league membership, there was a considerable range of opinion. The term "vital local governmental services" opened an extended discussion of priorities, ways to identify future needs, jurisdictional boundaries of state versus local services, and the like. Committee members readily saw the problems related to providing operational definitions for "effective and efficient" in the context of local governmental services. After considerable discussion, it was decided that since the original issue turned on the property tax, that tax itself should be the focal point of the study. It was further agreed that three implicit subissues or questions should be answered:

1. Should the present local property tax be retained?

2. Should the present local property tax be abandoned?

3. Should the present local property tax be substantially modified, and if so, how?

With this general direction established, the committee engaged in a wide-ranging discussion about what the study group should consider in its deliberations. Chairman Claymoore initiated this phase of the dialogue.

"It seems to me the study team must address itself to the problem of finding or designing a local tax source that can perform adequately in a changed and changing economic system. Many years ago land and real property were the basic sources of wealth. Ranching, farming, mining, and pumping oil constituted our means of creating income. Now these have changed. We have moved into exotic and "know-how" industries. Even the basic industries have changed to the extent that more wealth or income is created in related businesses and industries than in the actual extraction of the commodity itself. Agribusiness gross receipts are nearly as large as basic agriculture. The allied fields of the petroleum industry generate nearly as much wealth as the oil pumping operation. The mere fact we're sitting around this table suggests that the intangibles of stocks, bonds, mortgages, credit instruments, and all are important creators of wealth. I know I would like to feel just as productive as my great-grandfather who built up a range of cattle. Much of this new productive capacity is not reflected in the present local tax base, and as a result the basic services are not being provided."

Durwood Adams, a close friend as well as business associate of Claymoore, felt he could take reasoned exception to some of the implications in his friend's statement.

"But Jess, we must recognize that much of the real property base of wealth still exists—and this is the very heart of our economy. We must be careful not to throw the baby out with the bath. Granted there are changes in the means of production of wealth, but it is still generated from much the same base. And as a base, it represents a basic and stable source of revenue. The use of this base has been responsible for much of our state's steady and enviable development."

"Yes," seconded Tyler Whitcomb, the very vocal president of the only bank in a small prairie town. "We must be sure that the study team is aware of the confidence that the people have in the property tax. To them, this is familiar. It is known; it is visible. And most important, the people realize that it is their means of directly effecting local government policy. The locally voted property tax gives them the authority to expand or contract many local government programs. It is the very heart of local control. It provides the best means of real citizen involvement in our town's government. It assures local control of schools."

John Eboch, a major executive in a building and loan association, crushed out his cigarette and began to speak.

"I have to take some exception to the somewhat glowing endorsements of the property tax. I think our study team should carefully consider just what control should be tied to a local school district's property tax. It seems to me that often this is an inappropriate exercise of power. Often this kind of control deters rather than encourages progress in public education. If we are concerned with economic development, we might appropriately begin in the school system. We need a tax for education that will stimulate educational expansion and improvement, and we need a tax that will not incorporate the repressive controls of localism.

"In this state most public school revenue is derived from local sources. Thus, educational needs are primarily defined by what local taxpayers see or want to see. Today this is very frequently inadequate. Because of technological advancement, population growth and shifts, urbanization, and all the rest, our needs are different than those identified by the local citizenry."

"Before we get too far down the road, I want to point out another weakness in the property tax that Jess only alluded to." The speaker was Carl Allegeyer, a loan officer in one of the largest banks in the state capital.

"The value of property held today is not a very accurate measure of a man's ability to pay taxes. Residential property, for example, is not closely related to the income of the owner—or at least the man paying the mortgage, interest, and taxes on it. If any group should be aware of this, we in banking should!"

William B. Morse was the next committee member to speak. Morse was president of a mortgage company which specialized in financing petroleum outfitters. He also was active in the state's school boards organization.

"John Eboch mentioned property taxes as a source of public school support. Since the schools take the largest part of the local property tax dollar, the relationship between school finance and the local property tax deserves special attention.

"Property tax practices in this state are particularly questionable as they apply to schools. It is true that most of a school system's operating funds come from the local property tax, but a significant proportion—about 30 percent—does come from state sources. The real problem lies, however, in the state formula for allocating revenue among the school districts. As many of you know, in our state a variable formula is used to provide relatively more aid to poor systems and less to wealthy systems. This is calculated on the cost of a basic program. Each system contributes to the cost of that program in an amount which is the sum of a mandated millage (currently 10 mills) times the real property valuation of the district. The state pays the difference (if any) between the cost of the basic program and the local contribution. Thus a poor school district with low property valuation will contribute little to the basic program and receive much from the state. Contrariwise, a richer district will contribute more to the basic program and receive less from the state.

"Now, with our pattern of locally elected county tax assessors and only very general state guidelines for assessment processes, there is considerable variation both in and among counties in the state. The statewide variations among counties range from averages of 34 to 62 percent of market value. In our own county on individual parcels of property we recently found the variation to range from 37 to 58 percent of market value.

"In addition to inequity among neighbors, we have the problem of some school systems being underassessed and thus qualifying for more state aid than they actually deserve. This weakness in the property tax results in inequity in the distribution of other tax monies."

"Yes," reflected John Eboch, "that is a real problem. If we require comprehensive and frequent assessments by professionals in order to make these valuations equitable, we significantly increase the administrative costs of the tax. There is no doubt that it is a very difficult tax to administer fairly and efficiently."

"Just a minute now," exploded Tyler Whitcomb, "you guys sound like you're ready to throw the whole thing overboard. But that's not practical! The people in this state are not about to revolutionize the tax system. They know it. They like it—or at least they tolerate it more than any other tax we could have. Remember, if our committee, or even the league, recommends we do away with it—that wouldn't make it so. The people are going to decide that."

Sensing that the committee might fall into the same emotional trap that claimed the laymen engaged in the initial discussion of the tax reform bill, Durwood Adams tried to establish some common ground for the committee.

"The weaknesses of the property tax have been observed and analyzed for years. All of us can agree to many of its limitations, but it also has some unique strengths. The incidence and impact of the tax, as well as the tax base, have changed. Recent research data show that it is much more elastic than critics have assumed. It has performed well for a long time and probably can continue to do so if we learn how to use it. Let's try to determine what its capabilities are and then build around them. Let's identify or design some supplementary techniques and new taxes to fill out our needs which the property tax cannot meet."

"Yes, Durwood," hastened Jess, "I think that is a positive direction for us to point the study team. I believe we have mentioned some considerations which should be included, at least implicitly, in a recommended charge to a study team.

"It seems to me we shouldn't circumscribe the activities of the study team, but instead give them the responsibility of finding the answers to general questions. During the discussion I tried to jot down the main ideas and the basic questions implicit in them. Let me try these with you for size.

"The major task of the study team should be to explore and answer the basic question, Should the state retain, modify, or abandon the present local property tax?

"The subquestions, which should be answered as a part of the exploration of the basic question, are:

1.   What local governmental functions are and should be financed by local taxes?

2.   What are the present and anticipated sources of wealth in the state?

3.   What are the local tax vehicles suited to tap this wealth?

4.   If the local property tax is to be retained:

    a.   What changes should be made in it?
    b.   What features are desirable in new and additional tax vehicles?
    c.   What features in existing tax vehicles should be retained?
    d.   What features should be deleted?"

Questions for Discussion

1.   Why did the local property tax seem to be appropriate in this state during its early years?

2.   What appeared to be the major changes in the state's economy which signaled the necessity to change the local tax pattern?

3.   Can you cite similar examples in other states or regions where changes in the economy required the modification of a tax program?

4.   In your opinion what were the most relevant arguments presented to retain the property tax in this case study? What were the most relevant arguments to modify it? To abandon it?

5.   To what other questions should the study team address itself? Why?

Case 44.   Local Taxation: Form Follows Function

Until recently, the residents of one of the nation's large industrial cities considered this community to be very stable. The population had remained about the same for the last decade and nothing new was happening. However, urbanologists saw many things happening to this Midwest industrial city of a million population. It was true that in some ways the city had matured. The heavy industry that character-ized it was still there, and the ring of suburbs around it prevented any geographic expansion. However, inside the city an active urban para-dox was in process. Many new migrants—especially from the rural South and Appalachia—were streaming into the city. But at the same time thousands of the white middle class were streaming to the suburbs. As a result, the core of the city was in a state of decay. This part of the community was characterized by high-density slums or ghettos with a patchwork of modest attempts at urban renewal. The demographic character of this part of the city could be summed up as poor, often transient, uneducated, and with much unemployment.

The city as a whole reflected a bygone era in its public facilities and services. Public buildings were generally old—several elementary schools were built before 1875. Some schools were acutely over-crowded, but a few in the central district were only partially filled because of changing neighborhoods. Twenty-one of the one hundred thirty-seven buildings were built within the last ten years. Six of these are within one square mile and serve almost exclusively the city's high-rise public housing units.

City government facilities are cramped and inefficient. The civic center was established in a two-square-block area adjacent to a park which in turn borders on the lake. This complex, laid out sixty years ago, is clearly inadequate and nearly every municipal department has an "annex" in another building—frequently a factory or warehouse vacated by an industry which also joined the flight to the suburbs.

The city-owned transportation system is unreliable and con-stantly in financial difficulty despite the fare increases in the past eight years.

Fifty years ago the municipal recreation program was a source of community pride. The city boasted four municipal gymnasia (only recently called "recreation centers"). The Western European character of the population at that time was reflected in the gymnastic apparatus and facilities for calisthenics, etc. Although basketball leagues are active, many parts of the buildings are not now in use. Reasons for low utilization include lack of interest, inadequate (in both quantitative and qualitative areas) personnel and supervision, and severe vandalism. The latter was given as a reason for closing all shower rooms in the buildings recently.

Freeways and other limited-access traffic arteries have been cut through the city. These have literally served as arteries carrying the flow of economic life blood from the city's heart to the visible, active, and mobile suburban appendages. Literally hundreds of thousands of commuters pour into the city from the suburbs in the morning, work their jobs and earn their living during the day, then return to their residential suburbs in the late afternoon.

Only after severe racial disorders in the city and the national visibility given to the crisis existing in metropolitan centers did the complacent and passive mood of this city change. In a "story book" campaign, Joe Cousino beat the establishment's political machine which had governed the city for decades. Cousino, because of his own upbringing in the city's slums and his own unique activity in the civil rights movement, received the support of the "ethnic," Negro, and white liberal voters. Joe campaigned on a program for change and renewal and won a 53 percent majority of the final vote.

Coincidental with the change in city administration was a change in the administration of the public school system. Cyril Howland assumed the superintendency following the twenty-two-year tenure of his predecessor. Howland's appointment reflected the new mood of the city. The board of education, buoyed up with new courage, resisted the pressure to name an insider, and sought out Howland who had achieved national prominence in establishing harmony in a prestigious Eastern suburb which of its own volition successfully integrated its schools.

After each had been in his respective position for a full year, both Mayor Cousino and Superintendent Howland realized that the problems they had observed before taking office were in actuality much larger than they had originally thought. It appeared that no matter what the approach, nothing significant could be done to really solve any of the problems without the expenditure of huge sums of money—and this would require substantial increases in tax revenues.

Cousino and Howland came from different backgrounds, had different specific interests, and employed very different methodologies in their work. However, they found they could work together on issues not amenable to handling by their subordinates. Both were direct, well informed, and insightful. Furthermore, both recognized each would have to be dependent on the other if either were to enjoy success. Consequently, when long-range financial planning was being conducted by both units of government, liaison sessions were held in order to assess and hopefully coordinate financial planning so as to increase the possibilities of success in both city and school government.

The two chief executives of the city's largest governmental units exchanged ideas as to the most pressing needs of their community. After considerable and spirited debate, they agreed to a common set of program needs. The Cousino-sponsored programs had their major thrust in upgrading the quantity and quality of programs in the ghetto. Among the high-priority programs were overhauling and expanding the public assistance and welfare programs; upgrading (in terms of both salary and qualifications) the police department; expanding facilities and programs for public recreation; developing, planning, and coordinating urban renewal projects; expanding sanitation and health services; reconceptualizing and expanding public housing facilities; and establishing centers for employment opportunity (including counseling, recruitment, placement, and training).

Howland, speaking for the needs of public education, identified school needs as: abandoning five obsolete and hazardous elementary schools and replacing them with two new elementary buildings and two middle schools to be initially used as elementary units; remodeling three junior high schools so as to update them for eventual use as four-year high schools; refurbishing eleven senior high school buildings and six junior high buildings to be used eventually as four-year high schools which will provide enrichment teachers in all inner-city schools and coordinate this program with an expanded version of a federal program already underway, develop a program of curricular enrichment to identify and enhance content relevancy in inner-city schools, establish a comprehensive teacher personnel program (which provides for systematic and comprehensive teacher need identification, recruitment, orientation, in-service education, and appraisal), and upgrade the teachers' salary schedule to equal and keep pace with suburban systems; and establishing a planning and research center to give direction to program change.

City and school system programs were priced out in terms of both adequate and minimal funding. Even after taking out the capital outlay for basic facilities and equipment, it was found that minimal operating costs would exceed a million dollars annually. Several options were available, however. Under state law, school districts were limited to the property tax for locally raised revenue. The city government could, and did, exercise the option of raising revenue from local property taxes, local sales taxes, and locally levied income taxes. Although it was possible for both city and school district to construct buildings by utilizing local property tax levies, neither had ever used this option. Instead both had always floated a serial bond issue. The debt so incurred was serviced by a local property tax levied at the rate required to satisfy the amount of principal and interest coming due each year.

Cousino and Howland agreed that all capital improvements and additions should be financed through a series of bond issues including both city and school projects in a given sequence. The master financing plan for other elements in the program was much more difficult to design. Clearly, the school district programs would have to be financed largely through additional local property tax levies. Probably, some of the additional cost would be borne through the state aid program, as it was primarily an equalization program based on local effort and local ability. However, it would be in a proportion much lower than that currently being contributed by the state.

The basic problem arose as to the best method to finance the city program innovations. Cousino observed that for years the school levies on the local property tax had always taken precedence over city levies because of the structure and the "emotional appeal of children and their educational needs." Thus, increased school taxes jeopardized the passage of city levies and bond issues. This form of de facto preemption had forced municipal government to look to local sales and income taxes. Howland agreed that the lack of any local tax option for school systems in the state had indeed contributed to the present state of affairs. At the same time he pointed out that large city school systems were also the victims of this legislation. He reminded Cousino that the proportionately higher municipal government costs in the urban centers had increased local property taxes going for municipal purposes some 15 to 20 percent over the same taxes in smaller cities and communities. This "municipal overburden" on property taxes in the metropolitan centers results in these city school districts getting a comparatively smaller proportion of the total property tax than school districts in the smaller cities and less densely populated areas. Both men agreed that the present tax system did not provide real equity in tax burden.

Because of this limitation of the property tax as a source of revenue for the new city programs, Cousino and Howland turned their attention to the two nonproperty tax options: the sales tax and the income tax. Mayor Cousino expressed some concern over increasing the local sales tax in the city. He observed that many retail enterprises had already left the city in the flight to the suburbs. Local business interests had been cooperating with city hall in protecting and improving the downtown shopping area in order to prevent the spread of further blight, maintain and expand the semiskilled job market, and stabilize the receding property tax base in the city. An increase in the municipal sales tax would accelerate the movement of much desirable economic activity to the suburbs. If this were done, residents of the city would be even more attracted to the mushrooming suburbs. This would work against Cousino's program to attract residents of the suburbs back to the large main stores in the downtown shopping area. The Mayor was of the opinion (which was subsequently shared by Howland) that an increase in the municipal sales tax would, in the long run, do more harm than good.

The other major option for a local tax source for the city's program innovations was that of the local income tax. The tax was currently set at ½ percent and levied on all wages, salaries, and profits of nonincorporated businesses and professional activities earned in the city. This tax was relatively new having been instituted in 1962. It had always been a good provider—it was quite elastic since it tapped the rapidly expanding personal income of the whole region because suburbanites paid it on that portion of wages and salaries they earned within the corporate limits of the city. No suburban cities had levied their own income tax—probably because of the built-in state provision for reciprocity. Many suburbanites feared that this would increase their overall rate as the city would certainly increase its rate if the suburbs siphoned off some of these monies. Since suburbs had attracted a considerable amount of "clean" industry, they preferred to retain the property tax for this primary source of local tax revenue.

Cousino and Howland were well aware of the suburban attitudes as well as the mechanics of the city income tax. Agreement was easily reached that an increase in the city income tax was probably the best source of revenue, but there was probably some point where suburban communities would establish their own income taxes and as a result force the city to reduce the rate applied to those nonresident taxpayers. This, in turn, would result in city residents again paying a higher proportion of taxes which support the city's services.

After considerable discussion, the Mayor and the school superintendent were able to articulate their agreements regarding an integrated municipal-school system financing plan. Basic features of the plan included:

1. A series of joint municipal-school system capital improvement bond issues should be proposed. "Packages" including predetermined municipal and school projects are to be agreed upon and neither unit of government is to proceed until both elements (municipal and school) in each package have been approved at the polls.

2. In order to finance the operational aspects of its improvement

program, the city government is to propose the expansion of the city personal income tax from $\frac{1}{2}$ to 1 percent on wages, salaries, and net profits of unincorporated businesses and professional activities earned in the city or by residents of the city. The city in turn is to reduce the local tax on property at least 10 percent per year for five years following initiation of the increase. The mandatory debt service levy required for capital improvements bond issues is not to be included in the reduction program.

3. The public school system is to finance the operational aspects of its improvement program through increasing the rate of local property taxes for public school purposes. These increases should not exceed a levy which is double that released by the city (the annual 10 percent reduction in its property tax levy for five years).

The two executives concluded that after five years both city and school district revenues would be substantially increased, that suburbanites who derive their living in the city would be sharing in the support of those city services which in turn supported their sources of livelihood, and that residents of the city would be investing their tax monies in services which were crucial to the resolution of their problems. The program thus not only provided for increased revenues and increased taxes but also provided for a reallocation of taxes between city and school government which is more appropriate for purposes to be served.

Questions for Discussion

1. What characteristics of the local property tax caused Cousino and Howland to deemphasize its use rather than abandon it?

2. If the Cousino-Howland financing plan is appropriate for the immediate, what actions should they consider for the long term?

3. What concept appeared to be the underlying rationale for their decision to not tamper with the local sales tax? How valid was the decision?

4. What might be the net effects of the Cousino-Howland plan in terms of the pattern and rates of the local taxes? What generalizations might be made regarding the amount of revenues to be obtained under this plan? What generalizations might be made regarding the incidence of this local tax program?

Suggested Readings

Concept P—Local Tax Systems

Advisory Commission in Intergovernmental Relations: *Measures of State and Local Fiscal Capacity and Tax Effort*, Washington, D.C.: The Commission, 1962.

Battelle Memorial Institute: *Local Government Tax Revision in Ohio*, Columbus, Ohio: The Institute, 1968.

Burkhead, Jesse: *State and Local Taxes for Public Education*, Syracuse, N.Y.: Syracuse University Press, 1963.

Committee for Economic Development: *Modernizing Local Government*, New York: The Committee, 1966.

Freeman, Roger: *Taxes for the Schools*, Washington, D.C.: The Institute for Social Science Research, 1961.

McConnell, Campbell R.: *Economics*, 4th ed., New York: McGraw-Hill, 1969, chap. 9, pp. 140–142.

National Education Association: *New Local Sources of Tax Revenues*, Washington, D.C.: The Association, 1959.

————: *Revenue Potentials of the States*, Washington, D.C.: The Association, 1964.

————: *Valuation of Property*, Washington, D.C.: The Association, 1959.

Ohio Tax Study Commission: *1967 Ohio Tax Study Commission Report*, Columbus, Ohio: The Commission, 1967.

Samuelson, Paul A.: *Economics*, 7th ed., New York: McGraw-Hill, 1967, chap. 9, pp. 157–162.

Thatcher, George W.: *Tax Revision Alternatives for the Tax System of Ohio*, Columbus, Ohio: Ohio Tax Study Committee, 1962.

concept q
Debt and Borrowing

the problem

In the past few years public education has been referred to as a growth and growing industry. If this is true, then it follows that it has some of the same characteristics as a growth and growing industry in the private sector. A key characteristic common to these industries appears to be the need to borrow and go into debt. If they are characterized by deferred profits, then it follows that capital will be needed to begin operations and expand them until such time that one needs only to maintain them.

The growth and growing industry label seems to fit contemporary education for many reasons. First, education is an investment—in many ways increases in economic productivity are deferred many years from the first educational investment.

This is a growing industry as the segment of the total population to be served is increasing. Some years ago basic education incorporated schooling in grades 1 through 8, then kindergarten through grade 12 was the standard. Now we are beginning to accept nursery school through grade 14, technical school, or college as the standard.

Other dimensions of the growth or growing industry are broadening programs, longer school days and school years, and continuing education for adults.

All the other features of contemporary educational programs suggest a greater demand for physical facilities or the fixed assets of the educational program. As such, these assets are often best financed through the long-term rather than the current budget. Thus, debt and borrowing becomes significant even beyond the financing of the growing day-to-day or current budget of the public school. Debt and borrowing departs from current operations. It introduces an additional set of variables into the complex process of providing the most effective means of financing the public education enterprise. Concept Q speaks to these variables and how they are considered in the total process.

the concept

Although widely used, debt is highly unpopular and very much discouraged. By definition, a debt is an obligation to pay something (usually money) at sometime in the future. It is therefore, a liability.

For the person who will receive the future payment, however, the obligation is an asset. The volume of credits and the volume of debits obviously balance and so do the increases in assets and liabilities caused by the debt transaction.

In spite of its unpopularity, the great benefits of debt should not be overlooked. An individual may borrow today to increase his consumption when that additional consumption has a high utility and then repay the debt at some future time when the dollars have less utility, either because his income is higher or because his needs have decreased. Or a business man may borrow today and with the increase in assets which he has available may increase his earnings by an amount which exceeds the interest charges which he must pay on the borrowed funds. The desirability or productivity gained from the increased assets must be compared with the loss of utility or productivity experienced when repaying the debt. In this respect, government debt is no different than private debt. The desirability of the government debt depends upon the utility gained from the assets acquired with the borrowed funds compared with the utility which must be given up at some future period in the form of taxes so that the debt can be repaid.

In measuring the utility of the government debt, it is necessary to consider the effects of the entire borrowing and spending transaction on the economy. As has been discussed in previous chapters, income is caused by spending, and if the government borrows funds which would have otherwise remained idle and in turn spends these funds, income will be increased.

There is a widespread belief that government debt is not like other debt and therefore need not be subjected to the same tests. Government debt, it is said, "we owe to ourselves" and when that debt is to be retired all that occurs is that we give up some assets to pay the taxes and receive other assets as payment of the debt obligation. This is a naïve explanation, and those who make such statements overlook several very fundamental facts. First, the persons who must pay the debt (the taxpayers) are not the same ones who will receive the debt retirement payments from the government. That is, each taxpayer does not own government debt in exact proportion to the taxes he pays.

A second error suggested by those who imply that we need not be concerned about how much the government borrows arises from the fact that there is a limit to our productive resources. We can produce only so many goods and services from our supply of labor, resources, and capital goods; and if our productive resources are already fully employed and if additional efforts are made to obtain the use of these productive resources (by the government, for instance, with funds obtained through borrowing), the result will be an increase in the price of the resources, or, as it is commonly called, "inflation."

The most common cause of inflation is a level of spending which increases more rapidly than the output of goods and services. An increase in spending is caused by either an increase in the money supply or an increase in the rapidity (or velocity) in which the existing supply of money is spent. The overwhelming source of money is debt held by the commercial banking system. Therefore, an increase of debt, public or private, which is acquired by the banking system will lead to an increase in the money supply. Also, borrowing money which already exists from nonbank sources will probably have the effect of increasing the velocity of that money. The borrower will certainly spend the money, whereas the lender might have held the money idle. The effects of government borrowing on the price level, then, will depend upon the amount of idle resources in the economy. If a considerable portion of our productive resources is idle, the government by borrowing and spending will, in all probability, cause an increase in production which is not accompanied by an increase in prices. If our productive resources, however, are to the largest extent fully employed, the government borrowing and spending process will require the "hiring away" of the productive resources from another use, and this hiring away can only be accomplished by paying higher prices.

It should be pointed out that private borrowing and spending has the same inflationary effects as does government borrowing and spending. And it should also be noted that government taxing and spending programs do not have the same inflationary effect as does borrowing and spending, although to the extent that the taxes are paid with funds which would not have otherwise been spent, there is an inflationary pressure.

In the overall inflationary effects of the government borrowing and spending, it is also necessary to consider what the banking system might have done if it had not purchased government debt. The purchase of government debt by the banks increases the money supply just as does the purchase of private debt. Furthermore, the purchase of government debt precludes lending to private borrowers, for there is a limit to the amount of reserves (and the money-creating ability) of the commercial banks. If the commercial banks would have increased their loans to private borrowers in the absence of purchasing government debt, then the money supply would have increased irrespective of the government borrowing decision.

It must be concluded then that government debt has the same effect upon the economy as does private debt and the desirability of both private and public borrowing must be determined by the same measuring stick; that is, the utility or the profit created by the increase in assets at the time the debt is created as compared with the utility or assets which must be given up when the debt is repaid.

These conclusions contain many important policy implications for government officials. In considering a proposal to finance a phase of operations from borrowing (a building program, for instance), officials must determine the state of employment in the economy. Are there productive resources including labor now idle which the building program would put to work, or are the preponderance of resources already employed so that price inflation would ensue? A relatively fully employed economy should not necessarily cause the proposed government program to be canceled, but great attention will have to be given to the relative desirability of the alternative uses, and the project certainly cannot be undertaken as a program to bolster the economy.

The federal government is usually credited with the role of maintaining full employment, for its operations are so much larger than those of any state or local government, and the federal government's ability to borrow is so much greater. State and local governments also have a greater responsibility to retire their debt, while the federal government apparently can keep on refunding its debt indefinitely. The effects of state and local government spending, of course, have the same effect on the economy as does federal spending, except insofar as the latter is greater. State and local activities, therefore, do affect the level of employment, and this effect must be considered in evaluating any spending or borrowing proposal.

References are made above to the relative desirability of public and private activities. This requires a subjective determination (for no empirical data are available) of the utility-producing abilities of the government proposal under consideration and the private activities which will be replaced. In some instances, the public use of the productive resources will yield a greater utility than will the private use of these resources, but this is not always the case. The utility yielded by the programs under consideration will depend upon the existing supply of the public and private facilities and the prevailing wealth and income of the economy. The latter factor is important, for as wealth and income increase, utility yielded by government programs will also increase. A poor economy will need to spend a much greater proportion of income for the production of goods, an activity which the private sector is much more qualified to carry out than the public sector. As wealth and income increase, however, certain services which government can best supply will begin to yield a relatively greater

utility than will the consumption of additional goods. This is a fundamental reason for wealthy economies producing a greater proportion
of their output through government than do the poorer economies.

Another consideration must be the anticipated future level of
prices. If it is anticipated that price inflation will prevail in the future
when the need will be more acute, the savings in construction costs
may be a significant amount. For the same reason, pay-as-you-go
programs are often more expensive than building with borrowed
funds. Saved interest charges may be more than offset by increases in
costs.

It should be pointed out that building in advance of established
need places an additional responsibility on the government decision
makers, for they must then estimate need, and this may be very difficult to do.

Borrowing by the public and by the private sectors may be very
beneficial to the economy and therefore highly desirable activities.
This desirability will depend upon the relative utility created through
the use of the borrowed funds as compared with the utility created
by the alternative use of the resources. Each borrowing proposal must
be examined individually to determine its relative merits.

Case 45. The Utility of Debt Incurred
for Teachers' Salaries

Since the federal aerospace complex was installed in a medium-sized
city in the Old South, new life was breathed into the community.
Changes were initiated by the first group of newcomers—the engineers, construction workers, and those in charge of building the
physical facilities. This phase of the development of the complex
stretched over a three-year period so many of these people became semi-
permanent residents of the community. Consequently, school facilities
and staff had to be expanded rapidly. As the construction phase
ended, these workers left. However, this signaled the beginning of a
new phase—the influx of personnel to operate the highly sophisticated
installation. This second wave of immigrants were scientists, technicians, career military personnel on special assignment, and management specialists.

The transition from the construction phase to the operational
phase was more traumatic for the school system than was the transition from "the old days" to the initial construction phase. When the
latter was in full swing, the school system recruited teachers from all
over the area, and any other place where teachers could be found.

By and large the search was successful. With federal government assistance, every youngster nearly always had a classroom and a full-time teacher. However, during the transition from construction to operation, the school administration faced a new staff personnel question with two sides. Immediately after construction was completed, fewer teachers were needed since most of the construction crews left the city for work on other projects. Teachers who were not tenured did not have their contracts renewed. Teachers of marginal quality were either dismissed or did not receive new contracts. At the same time, highly educated and educationally oriented groups of scientists, technicians and managers arrived in the city with their families. A more vigorous and cosmopolitan set of demands on the educational system was articulated. With almost no exception these parents had one or more college degrees and held high expectations for their children's achievement. They frequently insisted on school programs similar to those they were accustomed to in the many previous locations from which they came. The teachers, caught in the pincers of job insecurity and increased expectations, soon adopted a militant posture not unlike that reflected in the national scene.

A third force tended to augment this movement to collective action. The school administration in serving the new demands for highly qualified personnel literally scoured leading teacher training institutions for bright, able teacher recruits. These newcomers to the faculty brought with them the campus and teacher activism and the concomitant demands for recognition, participation, and welfare considerations.

As a result of these several factors, a very aggressive education association was formed. Despite the fact there were many opposing views expressed within the organization, agreement was reached on adopting a strategy of collective action to promote teacher security, teacher participation in educational policy formulation, and upgraded salaries and working conditions. In its first test, the educational association was highly successful as it was recognized by the board of education as the sole bargaining agent of the teachers.

The first community opposition to the association's proposals was based on the belief that the community could not support the association's proposed salary schedule. This initial action from the older segment of the city brought a secondary but sharp reaction from the "federally connected" personnel. This newer segment of the community expressed the idea that the proposed salary schedule was not unrealistic (it was still lower than those found in many other parts of the country), and it undoubtedly was necessary to attract well-qualified teachers. This ground swell of support which was initiated by the federally connected personnel in the city was increased by the support of a large number of the newest arrivals, the people of adjunct industries and businesses which serviced the aerospace installation and its personnel.

Both groups of recent arrivals tended to be change and future oriented. They believed in education as a basic means of social improvement, and were quite cosmopolitan in background and outlook. With large and increasing numbers, considerable visibility, indirect political influence, and a high degree of dedication, the newer groups promoted community-wide acceptance of the fact that salary increases were necessary and acceptable. The debate then shifted from whether or not salaries should be raised, to the question, How shall the necessary revenues be obtained?

The professional negotiation process involving the education association and the board of education began in earnest when the teachers sensed the emerging community support for their general program. The conservative point of view surfaced in both the board and the community when a proposal was made to increase salaries in steps over several years. This would provide for a small, if any, tax increase as the assessed value of real property in the school system continues to increase.

In both the board and community, the more liberal point of view was expressed also. Groups of this persuasion took the position that a gradual approach would not solve the problem satisfactorily. Instead, they suggested that since the community's ability to pay was rapidly rising and would do so for the next several years and since the value of local property subject to taxation was increasing at nearly the same pace, it would be appropriate to borrow against anticipated tax collections to provide adequate salaries immediately rather than waiting for several years until this could be achieved. The state taxation laws clearly provided for such a procedure, they agreed, and it should be used.

The issue was joined during the board-association negotiation on the last item on a list agreed upon by the board and the educational association. The association demanded a new salary schedule to begin the following school year while the board initially prepared an escalating across-the-board increase over a four-year period. When this was flatly refused by the association's negotiator, the board's negotiator requested a recess to caucus with the board members. It was apparent that as much negotiation would have to go on inside the board as would occur between the board and the association.

In the caucus the conservative faction argued that the schedule of salary increases should be maintained as presented, and only in case of impending impasse should it be reduced from four steps to three. The arguments to support this position included:

1. Principles of negotiation dictate that the board should not give in completely, instead, give only a little if necessary.

2. The alternative would involve borrowing money to support the association's proposal, and the costs of interest would add to the large burden of the taxpayers.

3. There is currently an inflationary condition in the nation; deficit financing by the board would contribute even more to it.

4. Teacher personnel resources are already fully employed, therefore, the local result will also be inflationary as no larger number of teachers will be employed as a result of borrowing the money.

5. The mere fact that the school system will borrow money through a bank (since banks buy tax anticipation notes) will increase the money supply and add even more to the inflationary spiral.

The arguments of the liberal faction were designed to counter some of the conservatives' points as well as to provide a different base for the decision. The liberal base was that of the high utility of the borrowed funds. They maintained that:

1. Granted, borrowing costs money; however, in this instance it is worth it. If the school system does not buy the highest quality instruction for a pupil this year, it won't have the same choice next year. A year of inadequate education cannot be replaced. Remediation always costs more than the original.

2. Teacher personnel resources are fully utilized now, but the additional income which will go to the teachers will find its way into the nonfully utilized segments of the local economy. The capacity of consumer good producers is not fully utilized locally.

3. The addition to the nation's inflationary trend will be negligible as the local and state economies are not operating at or near capacity. In fact, it will be a positive influence.

4. Education is one of the most productive of all investments. The greater amount of resources allocated to it, the greater return one will enjoy. This will, in turn, enable an easier funding of the debt. Thus, there will be an extremely high utility for the borrowed money.

The leaders of both the liberal and conservative factions within the board recognized the necessity of laying out the arguments on both sides of the issue. It was crucial that they reach a firm and viable decision on this question so a strong position could be taken by the board as it faced both the association's negotiator, as well as the public, when the agreement was signed.

Questions for Discussion

1. What are the problems attached to determining the utility of a debt incurred for public education?

2. What are some promising approaches currently being suggested for determining such utility?

3. What arguments might be posed for incurring debt to expand educational programs and facilities in a period of deflation and unemployment?

4. When debt is incurred to increase salaries but not increase the number of persons employed, what will be the likely effect on the total labor market in a period of relatively full employment?

5. What will be the likely effect on the total labor market in a period of relatively full employment when debt is incurred to increase the number of persons employed?

Case 46.   Developing a State Program to Finance Capital Outlay in Local Schools: Problems, Programs, and a Rationale

The dynamics of educational change have been felt throughout all the fifty states. However, one state in the southwestern quadrant of the nation has recently become aware of problems of growth, in terms of not only an increasing population but also a changing demographic character with countervailing demands on the schools.

A generation ago this state was rather sparsely populated. Ranching, mining, and a modest winter resort industry were the primary components in the economy. Now with the advent of large-scale water control and power, there is a booming agricultural industry. The new technology has stimulated mining and the related industries that spring up around a highly automated process. A sprinkling of varied exotic industries has also appeared.

The affluence of the nation as a whole has been a major contribution to a significant segment of the state's population. Increased personal earnings and savings have made it possible for people from all parts of the country to vacation in this state. The appeal of desert, high plains, timbered valleys, and snowy mountains have attracted increasing numbers of vacationers and retirees taking up permanent residence in the state.

The changing demographic character of the state has had a marked impact on it's school system. There has been a phenomenal increase in the school-age population. Consequently, it has been an uphill battle to provide enough adequate classrooms. The marked increase in the proportion of retirees, vacationers, and itinerants in the state has posed the problem of voter resistance to increased taxes for constructing new classrooms. This condition has become critical with the recognition of the necessity of providing adequate educational opportunity to many Indian youth and others who in the past have not had and demanded it.

A few fortunate school systems with a large real property tax base from mining operations, factories, and the like have done well in providing physical facilities. However, most school districts have found it extremely difficult to provide adequate school buildings under these circumstances. The problem is compounded by the state limitation on bonded indebtedness. This limitation is set at 6 percent of the assessed valuation of real property in the system. This limitation has stood for over fifty years despite periodic efforts to raise it.

The most recent efforts to modify the indebtedness ceiling and other state provisions for schoolhouse construction came about as a result of growing public concern with educational facilities throughout the state. A daily newspaper published in the state capital ran a series of articles on conditions of school facilities around the state. Photographs and terse comments generated public concern over schools employing double or split sessions, rented classrooms, interdistrict disparities, and low-cost "eggcrate" construction not suited to the climate.

With pressure from individual legislators, PTA and school groups, civil rights organizations and activists, and leadership from the state's commercial interests (and their "image makers"), a special commission was appointed by the Governor to investigate the conditions of public school facilities and make recommendations for their improvement. The School Facilities Commission included two state legislators, a professor from a private college, two housewives, a public school administrator, a leader in the largest and most active civil rights organization, an executive from the business community, and a public school teacher. The commission was chaired by the dean of the school of law of the state university.

After considerable travel around the state in small task forces, many interviews with school and community leaders in the commission's offices, review of much data supplied by the state agencies and local school districts, the commission reported its findings. Key points could be summarized as follows:

1. The conditions of education facilities in the state were reported to be sufficiently bad as to constitute a crisis. Many of the facts cited in the news stories on inadequate facilities were verified. Other data indicated that some conditions were even more shocking than those published prior to the commission's appointment. Specific instances were cited where children attend classes in condemned buildings and structures formerly used as sheep sheds. There was concrete evidence of unconscionable overcrowding—more than sixty children crowded into a room designed to accommodate thirty. Instances were cited where boards of education were paying exhorbitant rents for inadequate facilities. Graphic descriptions were drawn regarding facilities which posed—despite health hazards—children drinking water from wells contaminated by open privies.

2. A generalization of educational deficit incurred by such school facilities was developed by the commission: "The state is not providing its most precious resource, our youth, with adequate facilities. In many instances, we are providing them with a school environment that is often so bad it might be worse than none at all. Instead of an environment which develops a love of learning, the atmosphere in some classrooms mitigates against learning, health, and common human decency. Often youth are driven from the school because of its inhospitable facilities which results in an abortion of the learning process.

Survey data show that well-trained and dedicated teachers are forced to abandon modern teaching methods and never fully utilize their professional training in overcrowded, underequipped, and inadequate facilities."

3. The nature of the fiscal dimension of the problem was described. It was found that the state's economic potential was not ideal, but far from fully utilized. The state was only slightly below the national mean in terms of income per capita. It ranked at the top of the lower third of states in personal income per pupil in school attendance.

It was found there was considerable variation among local school systems in terms of taxable property per pupil. Among the larger school systems (5,000 pupils or more), the range exceeded twenty to one—$101,000 to $4,898. Among the smaller systems the range was even greater.

Nearly one quarter (24.6 percent) of all the state's school systems were at the bonded indebtedness ceiling (6 percent of the total tax valuation), and 58.6 percent of the systems had reached an indebtedness level between 5 percent and 6 percent.

Many systems had adopted a pay-as-you-go procedure to supplement the capital funds provided by bond issues. It was found that 32.1 percent of the school systems had employed this practice to some extent. Pay as you go was most prevalent among the the wealthier systems. The poorer systems which did provide capital outlay on this basis in turn reflected cutbacks in operational costs to accommodate expenditures for capital outlay.

Although the charge given to the commission did not require any specific steps to be taken in the resolution of any problems it was to unearth, individual members pushed hard for at least some approaches to the resolution of the problems identified. An analysis of proposals made in a New England finance study[1] provided a basis for general recommendations made by the commission:

1. An aid for construction component should be added to the state aid program to school systems. The aid should be paid to the system in a lump sum upon completion of a state-approved facility. No definite proportion of cost was specified by the commission.

2. The limitation on school system indebtedness should be raised from 6 to 10 percent of the total assessed valuation of real property in the system. State assistance should be provided in the system's debt service payments. State aid should be commensurate with the interest rate paid on the bonds. Thus more state assistance would be provided to the poorer systems which typically have to pay the highest interest rates.

---

[1] Charles S. Benson and G. Alan Hickrod, *Are School Debt Finance Costs Too High? An Investigation in New England*, New England School Development Council, Cambridge, Mass., 1962, pp. 7–12.

3. The state should provide an $80,000,000 bond fund which will be available to those school systems with severe problems of growth. This fund will afford an opportunity for those systems that need additional facilities even after the 10 percent ceiling is reached. The school system will be required to repay the principal and the interest on the state bonds by means of an additional local property tax levy.

Even after consensus was reached on the general recommendations, some uneasiness was apparent among commission members. The major concern centered around a justification of the recommendations. It was decided that some kind of a rationale for the recommendations must be worked into the document before it was submitted to the Governor. As individuals on the commission "warmed up" to the task, it was recognized that the development of a rationale for the recommended program was a crucial and rigorous exercise.

Questions for Discussion

1. How might the commission incorporate the concept of utility of debt in the rationale for its proposal?

2. What might be some undesirable effects of pay-as-you-go financing plans as used in this state, and how might the commission's proposals negate this effect?

3. What arguments favor the inclusion of a debt service component in a state aid plan?

4. How should the commission face the problem of increased debt causing increased income and this stimulating inflation?

5. In developing a rationale for its program, what other data should the commission gather?

6. How might additional data and a consideration of the rationale for the proposed program effect of the proposals? What parts of the proposed program might be changed because of this new thinking?

Suggested Readings

Concept Q—Debt and Borrowing

Benson, Charles S., and G. Allan Hickrod: *Are School Debt Finance Costs Too High?*, Cambridge, Mass.: New England School Development Council, 1962.

Castetter, William B.: *Public School Debt Administration*, Philadelphia: University of Pennsylvania Press, 1958.

Chamber of Commerce of the United States: *Debt: Public and Private*, Washington, D.C.: The Chamber, 1966.

Heilbroner, Robert L., and Peter L. Bernstein: *A Primer on Government Spending*, New York: Vintage Books, 1963.

McConnell, Campbell R.: *Economics*, 4th ed., New York: McGraw-Hill, 1969, chap. 15, pp. 271–274.

Samuelson, Paul A.: *Economics*, 7th ed., New York: McGraw-Hill, 1967, chap. 19, pp. 344–351.

Index

Index